DHAMMA

WESTERN ACADEMIC AND SINHALESE BUDDHIST INTERPRETATIONS A STUDY OF A RELIGIOUS CONCEPT

DHAMMA

WESTERN ACADEMIC AND SINHALESE BUDDHIST INTERPRETATIONS A STUDY OF A RELIGIOUS CONCEPT

by

John Ross Carter

Assistant Professor of Philosophy and Religion
Colgate University

1 9 7 8
THE HOKUSEIDO PRESS

First published in 1978

ISBN. 0-89346-014-1

PRINTED IN JAPAN

Published by The Hokuseido Press
3-12, Kanda-Nishikicho, Chiyoda-ku, Tokyo

TO

SANDRA

ACKNOWLEDGMENTS

This study was first submitted to the Committee on Higher Degrees in the Study of Religion, Harvard University, for the degree of Doctor of Philosophy, in April, 1972. The years of study leading to the completion of the program at Harvard enabled me to learn from a number of dedicated scholars and to them I now formally express my gratitude. Professors Hugo Culpepper, James Leo Garrett, Eric Rust, and Wayne Oates, of the Southern Baptist Theological Seminary in Louisville, Kentucky, (1960–1963) helped me to discern a pressing need for more Western young men and women to launch a study of mankind's religious traditions in a manner that is not dissociated from questions of Christian faith in a religiously plural world, of systematic theology, of philosophy of religion in a personalistic context.

Professors Geoffrey Parrinder and H. D. Lewis of King's College and Dr. David L. Friedman at the School of Oriental and African Studies, the University of London, (1963–1965) contributed significantly to my understanding of the major religious traditions of mankind, to my appreciation of the broad range and relevance of philosophical issues in this area of study, and to my attempts to fathom the impressive religious heritage of India.

It is particularly to Professor Wilfred Cantwell Smith, formerly Professor of World Religions and Director of the Center for the Study of World Religions at Harvard, now McCulloch Professor of Religion at Dalhousie University, and Professor Masatoshi Nagatomi, my advisors for this study at Harvard (1965–1972), that I express gratitude for their guidance and encouragement that helped to engender and to sustain this study. Fortunate, indeed, is a student who has had the exhilarating learning experience of studying under the simultaneous guidance of historians of religion and Indologists/Buddhologists such as Geoffrey Parrinder and David L. Friedman, Wilfred Cantwell Smith and Masatoshi Nagatomi.

There have been others with whom I have worked and from whom I have learned much. Professor M. Palihawadana, of the University of Sri Lanka, spent many hours with me and shared a great deal in discussing matters related to *dhamma*. Dr. G. D. Wijayawardhana and Dr. W. S. Karunatillake of the University of Sri Lanka were patient in introducing me to their mother tongue and in directing me as I learned to read the impressive Sinhalese Buddhist literature of the past and modern periods. To Professor David J. Kalupahana, of the University of Hawaii, formerly of the University of Sri Lanka, I wish to record my thanks for the time he shared in discussing some of the more intriguing passages in the Pāli commentaries. Professor O. H. de A. Wijesekera and Dr. Maurice Sri Rammandala gave many afternoons in conversation on matters of mutual interest related to Buddhist thought about life. To Dr. B. Sirisena, Dr. Jinadasa Perera, Dr. Labuduva Siridhamma Thera, Dr. Lily de Silva, and Dr. H. Ñāṇavasa Thera, I wish to express my appreciation for having had the opportunity to discuss aspects of Buddhist life and details of my reading.

Numerous have been the occasions when persons in Sri Lanka have extended the quality of thoughtfulness and kindness that secures the bonds of enduring friendship. Genuine friendship and receptive hospitality are expressions of *dhamma* which provided me with a remarkably wholesome setting for learning from and with others how to strive to live life well. To Mrs. A. Abrahams, Miss Beeta Hagoda, Miss Lili Hagodage, Mr. M. G. Dharmadasa, Mr. Godwin Samanaratna, Mr. Jinadasa Liyunaratna, Mr. Prasad Wijeweera, Mr. Lloyd Ranatunga, Professor David J. Kalupahana and his family, Professor M. Palihawadana and his family, Mr. Albert Edirisinghe and his family, I express my gratefulness for their contributing significantly to my being at home among dear friends while studying *dhamma* in Sri Lanka.

Working with these competent scholars and living among admirable people in Sri Lanka leads me to reaffirm a very old phrase "*Atthi loke sīlaguṇo saccaṃ socceyy' anuddayā,*" "There is in the world the quality of virtue, truth, purity, and caring."

Also I here acknowledge my gratefulness to the Fulbright-Hays Program, the staff of the United States Educational Foundation in Sri Lanka, the Teagle Foundation, Harvard's Frank Knox Traveling Fellowship, and The Fund for Theological Education for enabling my wife and me to spend three academic years in Sri Lanka (1968–1971) and a fourth (1971-1972) at Harvard undertaking research related to this study.

Professor Kenneth W. Morgan, Professor of Religion emeritus of Colgate University, my predecessor, kindly read the manuscript and made a number of helpful suggestions. Mrs. Elizabeth H. Davey,

Secretary to the Director of Chapel House, Colgate University, patiently assisted in typing portions of the manuscript and preparing it for publication. I express my thanks to Professor Hajime Nakamura, Professor emeritus of Tokyo University, who read the manuscript and provided several corrections. It is an honor to have this study on *dhamma* published in the series sponsored by The Eastern Institute under the able leadership of Professor Nakamura. That a study of *dhamma* in the Western Academic tradition and in the Sinhalese Theravāda Buddhist tradition undertaken by a Western student of mankind's religiousness is sponsored by The Eastern Institute and published by the Hokuseido Press in Tokyo, Japan, is demonstrative of the interrelatedness of man's emerging sense of global community.

One sees more when one shares a view with another, learns more through discussions with another, recognizes more when a pilgrimage is shared. To my wife Sandra I am continually grateful for the support that she has given and for sharing with me her perceptive insights into the religious life of men and women.

John Ross Carter

Chapel House
Colgate University
Hamilton, New York

TABLE OF CONTENTS

INTRODUCTION

This is a study of *dhamma*, a study that is developed from a historical perspective, not in a static sense that emphasizes one particular time or contextual setting in the past, ancient or rather recent, but in a sense fundamental to historical inquiry; that history is process and the history of a religious tradition is one of process. Consequently, this study presents interpretations of *dhamma* developed within the Theravāda Buddhist tradition and maintained within the Sinhalese Theravāda tradition for at least a millennium and a half. That these interpretations have been maintained in a religious tradition demonstrates a deliberate creative response on the part of countless unknown Buddhists who have chosen to sustain a continuity with a religious heritage that has provided perspective in process, meaning in one's life and in history.

This weighty term *dharma/dhamma*, long known in India, providing a profound notion within the Hindu tradition, transformed within the Buddhist tradition, translated into Tibetan, Chinese and Japanese, has now also had a history in the Western academic tradition. This study will document that history within the Western academic tradition over the course of nearly a century and a half. We have a case in which a profoundly significant religious concept has become addressed in different ways by many people living in various cultural contexts, under differing circumstances, at different times, in different centuries.

The Western academic tradition is merging with, developing within the Theravāda Buddhist tradition and the latter is finding a place within the former. Our study of *dhamma* will demonstrate this by presentation and representation; presenting how this has taken place in the West and representing itself an example of how this process is continuing.

The word *dhamma* has many meanings. The Sinhalese Theravāda Buddhist tradition has long been aware of this and, somewhat recently, Western scholars have also made this point. In order to remain manageable, a study of *dhamma* in the Sinhalese Theravāda Buddhist tradition would require some restriction in the scope of sustained investigation.

Of the many meanings of *dhamma*, a series of meanings has to do with a *dhamma* or *dhammas* (plural, *dhammā*) that can be grasped, known by the "mind-organ" (*manas*) because discernible characteristics are borne by them, that are themselves without substance but cooperate in a changing but orderly co-production in such a manner that they can be noted, thought out, and mastered, so to speak—internal psychic and external physical patterned processes, as "knowables." Closely akin to this notion is *dhammatā*, a feminine abstract noun meaning something like patterned process or regular recurrence, a process whose regularity is such that one can count on it, rely on it, anticipate it. One of its several usages is to describe the standard sequence of the coming of the Buddhas. A study of the concept *dhammakāya*, "*dhamma*-body," in the Pāli commentarial tradition and Sinhalese literature would yield considerable insights that might complement a parallel study of the concept in Sanskrit, in Chinese and in Tibetan Buddhist literature. These aspects of the term *dhamma* are highly significant but a thorough inquiry would necessitate either a greatly expanded or separate study.

The form of presentation of this study is not argumentative but, rather, is historical, synthetic, and cumulative. We will develop the history of *dhamma* in the Western academic tradition and its centrality within the Sinhalese Theravāda Buddhist tradition in order to maintain the thesis, not yet fully developed by scholars of the subject, that the central religious concept in the Theravāda tradition is *dhamma*, the presence of which provides doctrinal coherence in the entire Theravāda system of thought and soteriological continuity from this life to that which transcends.

CHAPTER I

DHAMMA IN THE WESTERN ACADEMIC TRADITION

Beginning this study of *dhamma* by presenting the history of that concept in the Western academic tradition does not represent a conviction that what Western scholars have said about *dhamma* is of foremost importance. *Dhamma* is not primarily important for students of the Buddhist tradition because of what Western scholars have written about it, but, rather, because Buddhists have held *dhamma* to be of utmost importance and consequently Western scholars have turned their attention to a serious consideration of the concept. Nor is it the intention in this study to list at the outset the interpretations suggested by Western scholars in order to criticize those interpretations in light of materials available to a researcher working on the subject today. It is hardly worthy of the subject of this study to develop an argumentative posture, to take to task the interpretations of former scholars on the bases of materials not readily available to them, to criticize their cross-cultural probes because one has been enabled to spend several years living with Buddhists through the generosity of funding agencies and in the hospitality of one's Buddhist friends.

Great scholars the Western academic tradition has produced and their greatness is to be measured, in major proportions, by the brilliance of their insights in the presence of resources now known to have been limited. As more materials become available, as more Western scholars spend more time living and working with Buddhists, more will become known, and known more adequately.

A number of Western scholars have discussed *dhamma*, each bringing to their scholarly inquiry their particular competence, interests, and methods. Philologists, philosophers, and historians have made their contributions at different times, in various settings and each, in turn, has participated in the history of *dhamma* in the Western academic tradition. In tracing the development of Western interpretations, one will note diachronic and synchronic patterns, a gradual increase in knowledge of the subject and deepening insight in thematic reflection.

Historical Survey

This study begins with a recognition that *dhamma* has had a history in the Western academic tradition and seeks to chart the course of that history.

In 1844, Eugène Burnouf, recognizing an orderliness and authoritativeness in *dharma*, translated it "la Loi" and this weighty Western concept has continued to be one of the most frequent renderings for the term in Western languages,[1] a rendering, however, rather early discerned to be not entirely adequate in itself. Six years after the publication of Burnouf's *Introduction*, R. Spence Hardy, alert to the numerous meanings of *dhamma*, wrote, "It is not unfrequently [*sic*] translated 'the law,' but this interpretation gives an idea contrary to the entire genius of Budhism [*sic*]. The Dharmma [following a form of Sinhalese orthography] is therefore emphatically, the truth."[2]

In 1875, Robert C. Childers defined *dhamma* as "Nature, condition, quality, property, characteristic; function, practice, duty; object, thing, idea, phenomenon; doctrine; law; virtue, piety; justice; the

---

[1] Eugène Burnouf, *Introduction à l'historie du buddhisme indien* (Paris: Imprimerie Royale, 1844), Tome premier, note 2, p. 80. See also *Ibid.*, p. 283. The Reverend Benjamin Clough in his work, *A Sinhalese-English Dictionary* (New and enlarged ed., Under the Patronage of the Government of Ceylon, Colombo: Wesleyan Mission Press, Kollupitiya, Ceylon, 1892 [the first ed. published in 2 vols.: vol. 1, 1821; vol. 2, 1830]), p. 268b, does not give "law" as a translation for *dharma/dharmma.*

[2] R. Spence Hardy, *Eastern Monachism: An Account of the Origin, Laws, Discipline, Sacred Writings, Mysterious Rites, Religious Ceremonies, and Present Circumstances of the Order of Mendicants founded by Gótama Budha* (London: Partridge and Oakey 1850), p. 167.

law or Truth of Buddha; the Buddhist scriptures; religion."[3] A little more than a century ago, Childers had provided the meanings of *dhamma* generally accepted in the West.

A third of a century after Burnouf's *Introduction* was published, and a few years after Childers' dictionary was made available, Thomas William Rhys Davids published, under the auspices of the Society for Promoting Christian Knowledge, a book on the life and teachings of Gautama the Buddha. The British barrister was restless with the translation "law" for *dhamma*. Having spent a decade in the Ceylon Civil Service, competent in Pāli, having a knowledge of Sinhalese, he argued:

> Dharma (Pāli Dhamma) is not law, but that which underlies and includes the law,—a word often most difficult to translate, and best rendered here [*i.e.*, in the compound *dhammacakka*] by truth or righteousness; whereas the word "law" suggests ceremonial observances, outward rules, which it was precisely the object of Gautama's teaching to do away with.[4]

Four years later, in 1881, a remarkable young man, Hermann Oldenberg, thought he saw a pattern within the many meanings of *dhamma*:

> Das Wort *Dhamma*... "Ordnung, Gesetz" pflegt in der buddhistischen Sprache "Wesen, Begriff" zu bedeuten, insofern das Wesen einer Sache gewissermassen ihr eignes immanentes Gesetz ist. So dient das Wort dann auch zur allgemeinsten Bezeichnung für die (von Buddha gepredigte) Lehre oder Wahrheit.[5]

---

[3] Robert Caesar Childers, *A Dictionary of the Pali Language* (London: Trübner & Co., 1875), p. 118b.

[4] T. W. Rhys Davids, *Buddhism: Being A Sketch of the Life and Teachings of Gautama, the Buddha* (Twentieth Thousand, a new and rev. ed. with map; London: Society for Promoting Christian Knowledge, 1903 [first published in 1877]), p. 45.

[5] Hermann Oldenberg, *Buddha: Sein Leben, seine Lehre, seine Gemeinde* (Berlin: Verlag von Wilhelm Hertz, 1881), n. 1, p. 256. William Hoey, who translated this work as *Buddha: His Life, His Doctrine, His Order* (London: Williams and Norgate, 1882), note, p. 250, translated "Ordnung" as "order," which indeed it could mean. However, since Oldenberg, *op. cit.*, p. 206, when he drew from the *Mahāparinibbāna Sutta*, translated *vinaya* as "Ordnung,"

Across the Atlantic, H. C. Warren, in 1896, noted that *dhamma* was a difficult term to translate. He got at what he considered the root of the issue and put before his readers the observation, "The two terms *dhamma* and *saṅkhāra* are very troublesome to render into English, both because they each of them mean so many things and because their ground meaning is not translatable into English, being expressive of a different philosophy."[6]

By the end of the nineteenth century, Western academics were well aware that *dhamma* posed a problem. The scope of meaning that the term had was baffling. The depth of meaning was intriguing.

Meanwhile, working steadily was an impressive group of Western philologists/Indologists who, under the energetic leadership of Professor Rhys Davids, coordinated their labor in producing, for the Pali Text Society, critical editions of the Pāli scriptures. In 1897, sixteen years after the society was founded, Professor E. Müller's edition of the *Atthasālinī* was published. That text, a commentary on the *Dhammasaṅganī*, which itself had been published in 1885, enabled Western scholars to note an old, brief, fourfold definition of *dhamma* current in Sri Lanka over fifteen hundred years ago.

In 1900, Mrs. Caroline Augusta Foley Rhys Davids translated from Pāli into English the *Dhammasaṅganī*.[7] In the introduction of her translation, she noted four meanings of *dhamma* drawn from the

---

perhaps "Ordnung," at p. 256, means "regulation." Hoey's translation was uneven when he rendered into English Oldenberg's German translation from the Pāli *Mahāparinibbāna Sutta*. Hoey, in his translation, *op. cit.*, p. 202, translated "Lehre" (Oldenberg's choice for "*dhamma*") "law."

[6] Henry Clarke Warren, *Buddhism in Translations*, Vol. III of "The Harvard Oriental Series" (Cambridge, Massachusetts: Harvard University Press, 1922 [first published in 1896]), p. 116. Warren proposed "Doctrine" for *dhamma* when it referred to Buddha's teachings. For the plural *dhammā*, as subjects for total concentration, he suggested "elements of being" and mentioned that this rendering was not quite satisfactory.

[7] *A Buddhist Manual of Psychological Ethics: of the Fourth Century B. C.*, trans. Caroline A. F. Rhys Davids, Vol. XII of The Oriental Translation Fund new series (London: The Royal Asiatic Society, 1900).

Atthasālinī and rendered them as follows: *pariyatti*, "doctrine"; *hetu*, "condition or cause"; *guṇa*, "virtue or good quality"; for *nissatta-nijjīvatā*, "absence of essence or of living soul."[8]

In 1912, Mrs. Rhys Davids wrote a little book of significance in the Home University Library series.[9] It represented the first attempt in the West to interpret the Theravāda movement in terms of *dhamma*. She placed *dhamma* in the center of her consideration and called it "Norm." The second chapter represented the turning point—turning away from what was generally known and moving ahead, with flashes of brilliance, into a remarkable study, no less so because of the period in which it was written. She noted her husband's interpretation of *dhamma* as "good form"[10] and went on to say, "As signifying then 'good form' raised, as mathematicians say, to a higher power, Dhamma implies that view or procedure which is, as we say, according to conscience, and constituting a more or less recognized standard, guiding rule, or norm."[11]

She seemed aware of a depth of meaning in *dhamma* especially when she considered the Buddha's relation to it. Indeed, the Buddha in preaching *dhamma* speaks not only of his attainment, but also of something

> that was, and had in the infinite past been, and would ever be, objectively and constantly valid and true for any and every human society, nay something that was cosmic law, eternal, necessary, omnipresent, whether discerned or not. And the function and hall-mark of a Buddha was not to devise, or create a new Dhamma, but to rediscover, recreate and revive that ancient norm.[12]

---

[8] *Ibid.*, "Introduction," p. xxxiii.

[9] Mrs. Rhys Davids, *Buddhism: A Study of the Buddhist Norm* ("Home University Library"; London: Williams and Norgate, n.d. [1912]).

[10] See T. W. Rhys Davids, *Buddhist India* (London: T. Fisher Unwin, 1903), p. 292.

[11] Mrs. Rhys Davids, *Buddhism*, pp. 32–33. The reader should note this passage carefully as Mrs. Rhys Davids continued to elaborate this idea throughout the then remaining thirty years of her life.

[12] *Ibid.*, p. 33.

Joining her husband in fathoming the depth of meaning in *dhamma*, she, in this regard, was "not concerned so much with the ethical aspect, as with that background of philosophical postulates which, uttered or unexpressed, lies at the back of our [*i.e.*, probably, mankind's] most solemn judgments about life and the whole of things."[13]

No deity did Mrs. Rhys Davids see *dhamma*.[14] Suggestive in separating "Dhamma, Tao, Anangkē (necessity), Agathon (Plato's 'Good')" only by commas, she reflected an evolutionary orientation by noting that they "represent as many utmost fetches of the early human intellect to conceive an impersonal principle, or order of things prior to, and more constant than, the administrative deity representing it."[15]

Again following the Pāli commentarial definition recorded in the *Atthasālinī* and in the *Dhammapadaṭṭhakathā* (Volume I, part 1, published in 1906), Mrs. Rhys Davids structured the remainder of her book. Beginning with the third chapter, she considered *nissatta-nijjīvatā* as "the Norm as Theory of No Soul";[16] *hetu* she made the basis of a chapter, "The Norm as the Law of Causation";[17] *guṇa* provided the starting point for her treatment, "The Norm as Moral Law."[18]

---

[13] Mrs. Rhys Davids, *Buddhism*, p. 35.

[14] *Ibid.*, pp. 35, 36.

[15] *Ibid.*, p. 36. It would seem reasonable to suggest that Professor and Mrs. Rhys Davids collaborated to some extent on the more general, comparativist line of inquiry. Five years after Mrs. Rhys Davids wrote the above passage, Professor Rhys Davids gave a lecture, "Cosmic Law in Ancient Thought," [Paper read in November, 1917] *Proceedings of the British Academy*, Vol. VIII (London), pp. 1–11, in which he proposed "Normalism," as a conceptual category complementary with Tylor's "Animism," as a means by which data drawn from his studies in comparative religion might be integrated and classified. In the same year, Mrs. Rhys Davids published what was to become chapter ten of *Buddhist Psychology, Supplementary Chapters* (London: Luzac & Co., 1924). In this work, p. 219, she speaks of *dhamma* as "cosmic law."

[16] The title of her third chapter, *Buddhism*, pp. 48–77.

[17] The title of her fourth chapter, *Ibid.*, pp. 78–106.

[18] The title of her fifth chapter, *Ibid.*, pp. 107–149.

In her consideration of *dhamma* in the sense of "The Norm as Idea,"[19] Mrs. Rhys Davids noted that it was with regard to *dhamma* that values were set and ideals structured.[20] It is of particular interest that in her seventh chapter she introduced the four paths and four fruits with a discussion of *nibbāna*.

Across the channel, in Germany, another scholar expressed his opinion about the word *dhamma*. H. Beckh, in about 1916, joined the growing number of Western academics who had noted the wealth of meaning of *dhamma* and the difficulty of concisely grasping its import. Beckh noted that *dhamma* as used by Buddhists had no corresponding term in Western languages. He wrote:

> Es [*dhamma*] bedeutet die von Buddha in ihrer universalen kosmischen Gesetzlichkeit erkannte Natur der Dinge, eine Gesetzlichkeit, in der unsere Begriffe von Naturgesetz einerseits, Moralgesetz andererseits durchaus in einen Begriff zusammenschliessen, dessen Nuance dem abendländischen Denken fremd ist. Der *dharma* ist die wahre, hinter den Dingen (von denen als etwas Wesenhaften im Buddhismus gar nicht gesprochen wird) verborgene geistige Realität, wie sie sich dem Geistesauge (*dharmacakṣus*) des Buddha oder Heiligen offenbart, die höchte geistige Wesenheit, wie Buddha sie geschaut hat, und zu deren Erfassung man im Wege der Meditation gelangt.[21]

Beckh was aware that the lack of a corresponding term in Western languages—and on this point he went beyond Warren who limited his comment to the case of the English language—was due to

---

[19] The title of her sixth and seventh chapters, *Ibid.*, pp. 150–172, 173–233. She was not explicit regarding the relation of these two chapters with the definitions of *dhamma* noted in the *Atthasālinī* and *Dhammapadaṭṭhakathā*. It seems, however, that she was developing her study in these chapters in terms of *pariyatti, desanā*.

[20] See *Ibid.*, p. 150.

[21] H. Beckh, *Buddhismus* (Berlin: G. Göschen'sche Verlagshandlung, 1919, 2nd ed. [copyright, 1916]), I, n. 1, p. 20. In 1918, a study by Otto Rosenberg was published in Russian. This work was translated into German in 1924, as *Die Probleme der buddhistischen Philosophie*. In the work, Rosenberg drew attention to what he thought most scholars had overlooked regarding *dharma*, namely what he called the *dharma*-theory. His suggestions will be noted below along with the observations on *dharma* given by Th. Stcherbatsky.

dhamma's (Skt. *dharma's*) reflecting a notion not prominent in Western thought. This German scholar suggested that in Buddhist meditation the two Western concepts of natural law and moral law converge.

By 1920, Western academics had noted the difficulty of translating *dhamma*, had become aware of the wide spectrum of meaning the term conveyed, had recognized in the notion a depth of meaning that was considerably important in Buddhist thought. From Munich that year came a monumental work on *dhamma* and it began with a familiar idea, "Von allen Ausdrücken, die uns im Pāli-Buddhismus begegnen, ist wohl keiner so vieldeutig wie das Wort *dhamma*."[22] Yet, Professor Wilhelm Geiger and his wife, Magdalene Geiger, had taken on a task of impressive proportions not before attempted. They sought the meaning of *dhamma* by concentrating on the Pāli canonical literature and said of their effort, "Unsere Arbeit ist, wie wir nachdrücklich betonen, rein philologisch."[23]

It remains an admirable trait in scholarship that an investigator be cognizant of the limits of his work. In spite of the massive amount of data the Geigers had collected, pondered, and classified, they maintained knowledgeable equipoise and noted in their preface, "Dazu kommt schliesslich noch, dass die verschiedenen Bedeutungen so unmerklich in einander übergehen, dass es immer wieder mehr oder weniger dem subjektiven Empfinden überlassen ist, welche Übersetzung als die passendste erscheint."[24]

Working with some of the commentarial sources available at the time of their research and basing their observations on the comments recorded at *DA*. I. 99.1 ff., *DhsA*. 38.24, and *DhA*. I. 22 (New Edition,

[22]Magdalene und Wilhelm Geiger, *Pāli Dhamma: vornehmlich in der kanonischen Literatur*, Abhandlungen der Bayerischen Akademie der Wissenschaften; Philosophisch—philologische und historische Klasse (München: Verlag der Bayerischen Akademie der Wissenschaften, 1920), Band 1, p. 3. It is a general consensus that Mrs. Geiger provided only clerical assistance for her husband in the course of their work. Whatever the case might be, I follow the illustrious German professor's lead in noting his wife as co-author of this work. Henceforth this work will be noted as *PD*.

[23]*Ibid*. [24]*Ibid*.

p. 18, on *Dh.* vs. 1), Professor and Mrs. Geiger noted five traditional meanings of the term *dhamma*:

(1) *guṇa* (*DA*, *DhsA.*, *DhA.*) "Eigenschaft, Fähigkeit, Tugend"
(2) *desanā* (*DA.*, *DhA.*) "Lehre, Predigt"
(3) *hetu* (*DhsA.*) "Ursache"
(4) *pariyatti* (*DA.*, *DhsA.*, *DhA.*) "heiliger, kanonischer Text"
(5) *nisatta* (*DA.*, *DhA.*) *nisatta-nijjīva* (*DhsA.*) "Unbelebtes, Ding, Sache"[25]

In the opinion of the Geigers these categories encompassed the principal meanings of *dhamma*. Alert to nuance, they did not overlook *ādīsu* (locative plural form of *ādi*, technically meaning "beginning with" as a lead term in an incomplete listing, and hence carrying the force of "such as" or "etcetera," "and so forth"), a highly significant part of interpretations of *dhamma* in traditional commentarial literature, and noted, "Aber die ganze Fülle der Entwicklung des Begriffes *dhamma*, namentlich in den feineren Nüancen, ist damit keineswegs erschöpft, wie dies auch durch das Wort [*ādi*] in Stelle 1 [*DA.* I. 99.1 ff] und 2 [*DhsA.* 38.23] vom Kommentator selber angedeutet wird."[26]

It would be, perhaps, more than tedious to summarize in a manner remotely approaching thoroughness the detailed presentation submitted by the Geigers. However, because their work represents what was then and remains the only study of *dhamma* of its kind, it deserves considerably more than a passing comment.

Beginning with the etymological meaning of *dhamma*, Professor and Mrs. Geiger presented a plausible process of the term's development of meaning.[27] They concisely stated what had previously been

[25] *Ibid.*, p. 4.

[26] *Ibid.*, p. 4. At page 121, of their work, Professor and Mrs. Geiger under "Register I Verzeichnis der Abkürzungen" list "MKo. Majjhima-Kommentar Papañcasūdanī. Ceylon, 1898 ff. (Unser Exemplar reicht bis S. 400. Sutta 27 des M.)." It is unfortunate that the study developed by the Geigers did not incorporate the more comprehensive classification given at *MA.* I. 17 (on *M.* I. 1.5). Apparently overlooked, this material might have led the Geigers to alter the structural procedure of their work.

[27] See Geiger, *Ibid.*, pp. 5–10, for a synoptic presentation of the more detailed study that followed in *PD.*, beginning with page 10.

suggested by H. Beckh and particularly, as the authors noted, by Mrs. Rhys Davids:

> Schliesslich wird *dhamma* Ausdruck für das grösste und umfassendste, was es gibt, für den *höchsten üpersinnlichen Begriff*, für das Absolute. Der *dhamma* wird Gegenstand der Verehrung, sogar für den Buddha; denn er steht noch über diesem, in dem er seine Verkörperung gefunden hat. Wir kommen damit zu dem wichtigsten Punkt unserer Untersuchung. *Dhamma* ist der eigentliche Zentralbegriff des buddhistischen Systems.[28]

Recognizing the perceptive observation made eight years earlier by Mrs. Rhys Davids regarding a similarity between *dhamma* for Buddhists, *tao* for the Chinese, ἀνάγκη and the Platonic ἀγαθόν for Greek thinkers, the Geigers decided to limit their observations to the Indian scene, noting that they saw in each of these concepts "der Ausdruck für das höchste unpersönliche Prinzip."[29]

The Geigers introduced into Western academic considerations of *dhamma* a new factor: *dhamma*, they noted, is homologous to *brahman*.

> Dem Buddhisten ist *dhamma* dasselbe, was dem brahmanischen Philosophen *brahman* ist. *Mit voller Absicht hat der Buddha den Begriff dhamma an die Stelle von brahman gesetzt*, an die Stelle der ewigen unveränderlichen Weltseele die Idee des ewigen Entstehens und Vergehens, an die Stelle der Vorstellung von der Substanz die von der Nichtsubstanz.[30]

There is much in the work of Professor and Mrs. Geiger that is

---

28 *Ibid.*, p. 7.

29 *Ibid.* The Geigers also noted the *Aggañña-sutta* (*D.* III. 80 ff.) as setting forth *dhamma* as "das höchste Prinzip, das allem zugrunde liegt. . . ." *Ibid.*, p. 79. Mrs. Rhys Davids, in her work, *Buddhism*, pp. 235 ff., chose this *sutta* to illustrate *dhamma* as "Norm." A discussion centering on this *sutta* forms the subject of her Chapter IX, "The Import of Dhamma," *Ibid.*, pp. 234–239.

30 *PD.*, p. 7. Since 1920, other Western scholars have touched upon this subject. Professor Geiger presented an article on this topic in 1921. A discussion of his opinions and those of others will be provided below. At *PD.*, p. 8, the Geigers mentioned that *attan* (Skt. *ātman*) appears, in a few passages, in close relation with *dhamma*, as in the Upaniṣads *ātman* is identified with *brahman*.

of interest in any consideration of *dhamma*. However, the authors informed their readers of what they thought was the most important part of their work, and this will provide the primary point of focus next in our consideration.

The Geigers suggested that there was a gradual and almost imperceptible transition in meaning of the term *dhamma* as "Lehre" through "wahre Lehre" to "Wahrheit."[31] "Truth," they proposed, was to be preferred as a translation of *dhamma* in those contexts where *dhamma* is mentioned as having been attained unto, realized, by the Buddha, or characterized as being hard to grasp, comprehend.[32] They realized that there was a considerable overlap in meaning where *dhamma* could mean either "Wahrheit" or "das Rechte, das Gute, die Tugend."[33] They continued to note that where passages speak of perception of *dhamma*, "Wir nähern uns da bereits dem Gebiet des Mystischen."[34]

Professor and Mrs. Geiger spoke of "Dhamma hypostasiert als höchster metaphysischer Begriff, als 'höchstes Sein', 'höchstes Wesen', als Ersatz der Begriffe ātman und brahman."[35] They mentioned passages in which *dhammo have rakkhati dhammacāriṃ* (*dhamma* indeed protects the one living *dhamma*) occurs, and suggested, "Hier ist *dh.* [*i.e.*, *dhamma*] schon fast wie ein persönliches Wesen gedacht, wie eine schützende Gottheit."[36] Further, they stressed passages at *S.* I. 138–40, *A.* II. 20–1, where the Buddha, having attained enlightenment, sought that which he was to venerate.[37]

Dhamma, the Geigers argued, came to occupy in the Buddhist system a place comparable to that held by the concept *brahman* in the older Vedānta doctrine.[38] This, they mentioned, is obvious because of the number of passages where *brahman* and *dhamma* are used as equivalents. They note, unfortunately only in passing, "Zwischen dem neutralen *brahman* und dem maskulinen *Brahman* wird anscheinend kein Unterschied gemacht. Dem letzteren entspricht eben der Tathāgata als Träger des *dhamma*."[39] A number of parallels

[31] *Ibid.*, p. 66. [32] *Ibid.*, pp. 66–67. [33] *Ibid.*, p. 68. [34] *Ibid.*, p. 71.
[35] *Ibid.*, p. 76. [36] *Ibid.* [37] *Ibid.* [38] *Ibid.*, p. 77. [39] *Ibid.*

were pointed out, such as the use of both *dhamma* and *brahman* as designations of *nibbāna; brahmacakka* and *dhammacakka; brahmayāna* and *dhammayāna;* and also *brahmabhūta, dhammabhūta.*[40]

The Geigers considered whether *attan* (Skt. *ātman*) like *brahman* occurs in the Pāli canon in the sense of *dhamma*:

> Es ist das viel seltener der Fall. Dies erklärt sich daraus, dass im Kanon immer wieder eifrigst polemisiert wird gegen das Vorhandensein eines *ātman=attan*. Die *anattatā* (Nett. 90) ist, neben *aniccatā* und *dukkhatā* Hauptlehrsatz des buddhistischen Systems. Das Wort *attan* bleibt also bei seiner Bedeutung 'Seele'. Indessen scheinen die Stellen, wo auch *attan*, wie *ātman* im Vedānta, Bezeichnung für das 'höchste Prinzip' ist und durch den *dhamma*-Begriff ersetzt wird, nicht völlig zu fehlen. Eine Anspielung auf die *ātman*-Lehre und die Gleichwertigkeit der Begriffe *ātman* und *brahman* in dieser Lehre scheint uns in *S.*V. 6 zu liegen: *etad attaniyaṃ bhūtaṃ brahmayānam anuttaraṃ* 'das ist die wahre Attan-Lehre, das höchste Brahmafahrzeug'.[41]

The Geigers were not saying that *dhamma* was the same as, was analogous to, the *ātman-brahman* notion of Vedānta. Their point was that the *ātman-brahman* notion of the earlier brahmanic system was replaced and surpassed in the Buddhist movement by the notion of *dhamma.*[42] They referred to *attadīpa-dhammadīpa* parallels in the *Dīgha* and *Saṃyutta-nikāyas*..[43]

---

[40] *Ibid.*, pp. 77–78. [41] *Ibid.*, p. 78. [42] *Ibid.*, p. 79.

[43] *Ibid.* Concerning their observations on *ātman-brahman/dhamma*, it is noteworthy that the Geigers were more explicit about the intention of the Buddha regarding *brahman/dhamma* than with regard to *ātman/dhamma*. They mentioned *dhamma's* occupying the place "im buddhistischen System" that *brahman* held in "Vedāntalehre." *Ibid.*, p. 77. Apparently, for the Geigers, the Buddhist tradition was consistent in maintaining this intention of the Buddha. The Geigers referred to passages in which *ātman/attan* was used in parallel expressions with *dhamma*. Moreover, these authors mentioned that *anattatā, aniccatā, dukkhatā* represented the major doctrinal statement "des buddhistischen Systems." *Ibid.*, p. 78. An explanation for a possible development from *ātman/attan*, used in parallel expressions with *dhamma*, to *anātman/anatta* in Buddhist thought is not provided by the Geigers.

It is conceivable that Mrs. Rhys Davids found in this work of the Geigers a stimulus for much of her later inquiries regarding *dhamma*. Her later opinions will be noted below.

In the course of their work, Professor and Mrs. Geiger suggested more than fifty German terms as translations of the one Pāli word *dhamma*. Later, there will be occasion to refer to some of the views held by the Geigers when a few leading ideas proffered by Western academics will be discussed topically.

In 1923, approximately three years after the Geigers' *Pāli Dhamma* had appeared, the fourth fascicle ("Cit—No") of the Pali Text Society's dictionary became available. In their entry under *dhamma*, T. W. Rhys Davids and William Stede referred the reader to the study by Professor and Mrs. Geiger and noted, "The exhaustive monograph . . . reached the editors too late to be made use of for the Dictionary."[44]

Immediately following their etymological entry for the term *dhamma*, Rhys Davids and Stede wrote, "A. *Definitions by Commentators*: . . . "[45] The entry on *dhamma* is the only place in their dictionary where such a format (that is, the reference to the commentators set off in italics at the outset) is presented.[46] They referred

---

[44] *The Pali Text Society's Pali-English Dictionary*, edited by T. W. Rhys Davids and William Stede (London: Published for the Pali Text Society by Luzac & Co., Ltd., 1966 [first published 1921–1925, reprinted in 1949, 1952, 1959, 1966]), p. 336a. Hencefourth this work will be noted as *PTSD*. Reference is to the 1966 "reprint." Unfortunately, the work by Professor and Mrs. Geiger on *dhamma* was not substantially utilized in the subsequent editions of the *PTSD*. It is a disappointment to learn that Professor Geiger had been compiling a glossary for the *PTSD* that was never utilized nor, unfortunately, ever subsequently published. This glossary, after Geiger enlarged it, is now said to contain three times as many entries as the *PTSD* with about six times as many references. See Heinz Bechert, "Editor's Introduction," in Wilhelm Geiger, *Culture of Ceylon in Mediaeval Times*, ed. Heinz Bechert (Wiesbaden: Otto Harrassowitz, 1960), p. xvi. With regard to a study of *dhamma*, Professor and Mrs. Geiger devoted 119 pages as compared to approximately nine columns in the *PTSD*. Incidently, in the *PTSD*, both *kamma* and *dhamma* have more space devoted to them than does *nibbāna*.

[45] *PTSD*, p. 335b.

[46] In many instances reference was made in *PTSD* to commentarial definitions, but not in an introductory manner that structured the consideration and not in italics. Often evaluations of commentarial explanations were made: "there was no fixed tradition on the point, and . . . he [Buddhaghosa]

to three passages in the commentaries—*DA*. I. 99, *DhA*. I. 22 (New Edition, p. 18), and *DhsA*. 38—as had already Mrs. Rhys Davids in *Buddhism* (1912) and the Geigers in *Pāli Dhamma*.[47]

In the *PTSD* one is presented with over fifty English terms, concepts, for the one Pāli term, *dhamma*. Rhys Davids and Stede attempted to integrate a fourfold definition—"doctrine, right or righteousness, condition, phenomenon"[48]—drawn from the three commentaries by presenting in two categories the applications and meanings: "Psychologically" and "Ratio-ethically," each category being subdivided into "subjective" and "objective."[49] They tried to fuse, under the second category, natural or cosmic law and moral law. Natural law they saw as the objective dimension of *dhamma* in its universal application; moral law, as the subjective dimension of *dhamma* in its social application coming under the category of ratio-ethical and stemming from the psychological category. The awkwardness of their suggested categories reflects what H. Beckh observed earlier,[50] namely, that *dhamma* holds together in one notion

himself was in doubt." (*s.v. Tathāgata*); "popular etymology" (*s.vv. jhāna, niraya, muni, yakkha*); "fanciful" (*s.vv. puñña, bhāgavant*); "fantastic expln. of native Commentators" (*s.v. puggala*). In some cases, references to commentarial explanations are entered early and apparently were of assistance to the editors (*e.g., s.vv. kāya, kula, dukkha, nibbāna, purisa*). It should be noted, however, that in these latter examples where reference is made to commentarial definitions, the presentations by the editors were not significantly structured in terms of the commentarial comments. Further, in the case of *nibbāna*, their opinion about the meaning of the term is presented first to be followed by reference to Buddhaghosa, *Vism*. 293 (PTS edition). Probably, Rhys Davids and Stede found the remarks regarding *dhamma* in the commentaries, if not immensely helpful, of more than casual interest.

[47] It should be noted that the more extended definition of *dhamma* at *MA*.I.17 was overlooked by the editors of *PTSD*. The *PTS* edition of *MA*.I was published in 1922, one year prior to the publication of the "Cit—No" fascicle.

[48] *PTSD*, p. 336a.

[49] *Ibid*., pp. 336a–337a.

[50] The *PTSD* makes no mention of a standard commentarial expression communicating the force of *dhamma*, namely, *dhāretīti dhammo*. Nowhere in their treatment of *dhamma* do the editors mention *navavidhalokuttara-dhamma*. The compound does occur in *PTSD* but it is to be found in the

what Western thought has tended to bifurcate as two concepts, those of natural law and moral law.

Through the work of Professor and Mrs. Rhys Davids, William Stede, and Professor and Mrs. Geiger, Western academics have placed before them a considerable amount of scholarly material to aid in translating the term *dhamma* as it occurs in the Pāli *suttas.* The early twenties of this century witnessed an impressive series of publications that kept *dhamma* a subject of interest among Western scholars. In 1922, Masson-Oursel, a French scholar, sought to integrate the many meanings that *dhamma* (Skt. *dharma*) communicated on the Indian scene in terms of a fundamental idea of order.[51] One year later, Paul Oltramare elaborated on what he regarded as the dual aspects of *dhamma* (Skt. *dharma*): "Le dharma positif: ce qui est," and "Le dharma normative: ce qui doit être."[52] In the same year A. Berriedale Keith repeated, for English readers, in a greatly condensed form, much of what the Geigers had presented in their *Pāli Dhamma.*[53]

In 1923, the Russian scholar Th. Stcherbatsky reminded Western scholars of a dimension of *dhamma* (Skt. *dharma*) that he thought they had, to some extent, not understood.[54] He began his work,

---

discussion on *lokiya.* It is there placed as a further elaboration of the term *lokuttara,* which, apparently, is so placed in order to facilitate its understanding in contrast to the term *lokiya.* The *PTSD* does not present a threefold aspect of *dhamma,* namely, *pariyatti, paṭipatti, paṭivedha.* These points will be discussed below. However, it must be noted, if the objective of the editors of the *PTSD* was for the work to be "a help to students and scholars of Pāli alike!" (W. Stede, "Afterword," *PTSD,* p. 738) they were remarkably successful.

[51] P. Masson-Oursel, "Note sur l'acception, à travers la civilisation indienne, du mot dharma," *Journal Asiatique,* Vol. XIX: No. 2 (1922), pp. 269–275.

[52] Paul Oltramare, *L'histoire des idées théosophiques dans l'Inde,* Tome II, *La théosophie bouddhique*; Pt. III, Chapitre premier, "Le Dharma bouddhique," (Tome 31, Annales du Musée Guimet: bibliothèque bouddhique d'études, Paris: Librairie orientaliste Paul Geuthner, 1923), pp. 462–478.

[53] See A. Berriedale Keith. *Buddhist Philosophy in India and Ceylon* (Oxford: The Clarendon Press, 1923), pp. 68 ff.

[54] Th. Stcherbatsky, *The Central Conception of Buddhism and the Meaning of the Word 'Dharma'* (London: The Royal Asiatic Society, 1923).

The Central Conception of Buddhism, by mentioning the attempt of the Geigers in their *Pāli Dhamma* "to solve the uncertainty which still prevails about the meaning of the term *dharma*."[55] Agreeing with the Geigers on the centrality of *dhamma* (Skt. *dharma*) in Buddhist thought, noting that their work was "purely philological," as they themselves had mentioned, Stcherbatsky submitted his work as an investigation of *dharma* from a philosophical standpoint.[56] From among the many meanings that the Geigers had noted for the word *dhamma*, Stcherbatsky suggested, "There is, indeed, only one that really matters, that is the specifically Buddhistic technical term *dharma*.[57] He continued, "The other significations which Buddhist literature shares with the Brahmanical do not present any serious difficulty."[58] Basing his study on the *Abhidharmakośa* of Vasubandhu, and following the lead of Otto Rosenberg,[59] Stcherbatsky presented a detailed study of what has come to be called, by Western scholars, the *dharma*-theory.

It is not of primary concern to present a discussion about the various opinions on this particular matter held by Western scholars, early Buddhist schools, and contemporary Sinhalese Buddhists. Such a study lies outside the scope of the present consideration. A few comments will be made later on the notion of *dhammā* (pl.) as coalescing to form and engender a new phenomenon. Let it be noted

[55] *Ibid.*, p. 1. [56] *Ibid.* [57] *Ibid.* [58] *Ibid.*

[59] The work by Rosenberg that served as precursor for the general orientation adopted by Stcherbatsky was first published in Russian in 1918. Stcherbatsky first made known to non-Russian-reading Western scholars Rosenberg's conclusions. Rosenberg's study appeared in a German translation by Frau E. Rosenberg in 1924 under the title, *Die Probleme der buddhistischen Philosophie*, Materialien zur Kunde des Buddhismus, Heft 7/8, herausgegeben von M. Walleser, Heidelberg (Leipzig: in Kommission bei O. Harrassowitz, 1924). This German translation is the source from which Rosenberg's opinions will here be drawn. It appears that although Stcherbatsky did not follow Rosenberg's procedure, he followed Rosenberg's conclusion rather closely. Rosenberg noted, *op. cit.*, p. 83, that *dharma* as "transzendenter Träger" was the most important meaning of the term. Stcherbatsky, *op. cit.*, p. 75, concluded his summary of what *dharma* in the sense of an "element of existence" meant: "It is transcendental!"

here, however, that with the work of Stcherbatsky, Western academics became more aware of an aspect of *dhamma*, particularly *dhammā* (pl.), and subsequently became more involved in studies related to the history of Buddhist thought as it could be extrapolated in terms of differing opinions expressed by several early Buddhist schools on the meaning of *dhammā*.

At the close of the first quarter of the twentieth century almost the entire Pāli canon had been edited in Latin letters and put at the disposal of interested scholars. The Rhys Davidses had noted the centrality of *dhamma* in the Pāli canon; the Geigers had provided an excellent lexicographical study of the term; and Stcherbatsky further elaborated *dhamma* (Skt. *dharma*) as it was structured in the *Abhidhamma* (Skt. *Abhidharma*) literature. The materials for further study were at hand and so, too, was Mrs. Rhys Davids. This energetic lady—to whom Stcherbatsky had expressed his gratitude noting that she was one "who was always ready to help with her vast knowledge of Pāli literature"[60] and to whom, eleven years later, he alluded when he referred to an amateur lady-scholar[61]—continued her study of the Pāli Buddhist tradition.

Stcherbatsky's remarks reflect a general change in attitude that was being developed by a few scholars toward the work of Mrs. Rhys Davids. Indeed, it has become almost the vogue to criticize this woman's method in her later research. Peripherally has her work been criticized, not head-on in a sustained manner. Perhaps this has been due to the realization by most scholars that Stcherbatsky was right when he spoke of her vast knowledge of Pāli literature.

In 1924, Mrs. Rhys Davids gave a short review of the Geigers'

---

[60] Stcherbatsky, *op. cit.*, "Preface."

[61] Th. Stcherbatsky, "The 'Dharmas' of the Buddhists and the 'Guṇas' of the Saṃkhyas," *The Indian Historical Quarterly*, Vol. X, No. 4 (Dec. 1934), p. 743. Actually, the wording Stcherbatsky used was "just as some amateur lady-scholars in Europe are astonished and unwilling to admit that Buddha preached no-Soul." In this context the allusion to Mrs. Rhys Davids is assured. Perhaps Stcherbatsky had also in mind Miss I. B. Horner.

Pāli Dhamma.[62] In her review she presented what she considered to have been the development that the meaning of *dhamma* underwent in the course of centuries. Regarding this development she wrote:

> Thus from Vedic culture came to it [*dhamma*] the legal meaning of "right" (*le droit*) and of order (*ṛta*) conceived as cosmic and prior to god-concepts. Far later, the analyses of Buddhist commentators realized a complexity in the term's meaning, and did their best to make this patent. A little later still, metaphysic, for which the commentators had no ability, but of which Vasubandu was capable, show *dhamma* to have superseded in importance (for his little world) the older *dhamma*, and to mean, for his Pluralism, a number of irreducible ultimates. In the Piṭakas of the Canon how interesting (if a little baffling) is it to see the meeting-ground of all this attracted matter, both of older and contemporary other-culture, as well as the germs of later developments, in that notable trinity of patchwork: Vinaya, Sutta, Abhidhamma! And all of it clustering onto the loadstone of the little, handy, current word *dhamma*, used probably without any more pregnant meaning than the *kērugmos* [*sic*] or 'preaching'. . . .[63]

She noted in the same review:

> We [Westerners?] have easily come to recognize the Buddhology in Buddhism, and the Sanghology was there very early. *We have not so clearly recognized the cult of Dhammology.* The Theravādins put a pregnant word in Gotama's mouth when he a-dying said the Dhamma was to be his successor.[64] (Italics mine)

This seems to represent the clarion call for Mrs. Rhys David's later process of interpretation of the meaning of *dhamma*.

The only exception that Mrs. Rhys Davids took to the work of

---

[62] C. A. F. Rhys Davids, a review of *Pāli Dhamma: Vornehmlich in der kanonischen Literatur*, in "Notices of Books," *The Journal of the Royal Asiatic Society* (October, 1924), pp. 673–675. It is not irrelevant perhaps to note that in 1923 she wrote *The Will to Peace* (London: T. Fisher Unwin Ltd., 1923), a moving plea that her readers, in particular those mothers whose sons were killed in World War I, would in future shape the world, positively, into a better world through will and determination. Mrs. Rhys Davids had lost a promising son and an eminent husband a few years prior to this work.

[63] C. A. F. Rhys Davids, *JRAS* (Oct. 1924), pp. 673–674.

[64] *Ibid.*, p. 674.

the Geigers concerns their assertion that "'The quintessence of the Buddha-teaching is: *ye dhammā hetuppabhavā tesaṃ hetuṃ*. . . .' (p. 85)."[65] She suggested that the *dhamma* of Gotama (as she preferred to call the Buddha) was a message of "the good way of life."[66]

Four years later, in 1928, Mrs. Rhys Davids reconstructed the message of the Buddha to have, as it were, that message presented to contemporary man. She had Gotama say, "For me the promise of a worthier conception [than had developed in India] of the Highest lay in the word DHAMMA, that is 'what should be.'"[67] She went on to say that "law" was inadequate as well as was "truth" to render the meaning of *dhamma*. "Norm" as a rendering she noted was better and yet not good enough. She had Gotama say, "Men of your world would now call dhamma 'conscience' in each man: a noteworthy word, for it means that awareness which long ago in India it was sought to name in such words as manas, viññāna, mind or consciousness."[68] She liked the French word "idéal," but had Gotama conclude, "It is better not to translate it."[69]

Mrs. Rhys Davids had touched on the idea "conscience" as coming near to what *dhamma* meant when the Buddha used it. She saw a volitive dimension in *dhamma* and began to see in the term, especially as she considered it to have been used in the beginning of the Buddha's teaching ministry, something similar to "will." She remarked that, in his first sermon, the Buddha

> relied. . . on men of good-will responding to his message by their having that in them which we call will. But he did not call upon them as willers. *He had not the word.* He used for it *dhamma*,

---

[65] As quoted by Mrs. Rhys Davids, *Ibid.*, p. 675. The full line in Pāli is "Ye dhammā hetuppabhavā tesaṃ hetuṃ tathāgato āha" (*Vin.* I. 40). "Those *dhammas* which proceed from a cause, of those the *Tathāgata* has told the cause."

[66] *Ibid.*

[67] Mrs. Rhys Davids, *Gotama The Man* (London: Luzac & Co., 1928), p. 56.

[68] *Ibid.*

[69] *Ibid.*

a word changed in much Buddhist usage to mean "doctrine," or religion.[70]

A strong volitive moral force of meaning Mrs. Rhys Davids sensed in *dhamma*: "Dhamma, I repeat, is the seeing in life the 'ought,' the 'should be,' 'may be,' the 'to be.'"[71]

Continuing her drive to get back to the original message of the Buddha, to the very early formative phase of the Buddhist movement, Mrs. Rhys Davids suggested a new term, for the West, to characterize what Westerners had called "Early Buddhism." It was *Sakya*. In a book by this title,[72] she again wrestled with what *dhamma* meant when the Buddha used it: "I have worded it in the restatement thus: 'It is not always quite clear, but a man usually knows'."[73] She related it to daimôn of Socrates and to the "'I find a law' of St. Paul, to the 'conscience' of our own day. In India the word was *dharma* (Pali: *dhamma*). In its truest sense it expresses this inward monitor."[74] She thus introduced a personalistic dimension into her understanding of *dhamma*. Adapting her language, perhaps, to her Hindu readers, she wrote that when a man lives according to *dhamma*, he is living according "to the hidden Divinity, Who, in virtue of his manhood, he was."[75] Moreover, referring to a passage that represents

[70] Mrs. Rhys Davids, *Kindred Sayings on Buddhism* (Calcutta: Published by the Univ. of Calcutta, 1930), p. 12. In her "Foresay" to this work, she noted, "So far as I can claim to have any knowledge of the forward-looking, cultured man of India, both past and present, I have striven to keep him before me, and to address myself to him rather than to readers of other lands and other traditions." *Ibid.*, p. vii. One might become restless about the accuracy of a study that elaborates concepts for which a language, or a religious tradition being studied, had no words. Mrs. Rhys Davids was not by this deterred. "Let her [*i.e.*, India] consider her worthy son who called to her with a new message," she said, "yet had not words wherewith to clothe it." *Ibid.*, p. 23. Mrs. Rhys Davids, *Ibid.*, p. 38, noted inadequate English renderings for *dhamma*—she listed duty, law, norm, ideal, truth, doctrine, and teaching. The plural usage, she mentioned, was also complicated.

[71] *Ibid.*, p. 91.

[72] Mrs. Rhys Davids, *Sakya or Buddhist Origins* (London: Kegan Paul, Trench, Trübner & Co., Ltd., 1931.

[73] *Ibid.*, p. 66. [74] *Ibid.* [75] *Ibid.*, p. 68.

the Buddha revering *dhamma*, Mrs. Rhys Davids noted *dhamma* there "as That under Whom he vowed to live."[76] Further, she urged her readers to take "*dhamma* as the working of the antarayāmin [*sic*], the inner controller. . . ."[77]

In 1932, one year after the publication of *Sakya*, Mrs. Rhys Davids was still struggling with the import of *dhamma*. Having referred to *dhamma* as "that hidden Divinity" and "That under Whom" and "*antarayāmin*" ("inner controller"), she expressed *dhamma* as "A Something." Focusing again on the Buddha's decision to revere *dhamma*, she remarked, "A Something it is he is placing where his country before his day and during his day, placed That Who is Highest: *Brahman, Ātman*."[78] Turning to a passage drawn from the *Theragāthā* (vss. 303–304), *dhammo have rakkhati dhammacāriṃ*, she said, "Here be it noted is *dhamma* conceived not as something the man guards; it is *dhamma* who guards the man, and guides him."[79]

Restless with her rendering "Norm" for *dhamma* two decades earlier,[80] having noted that *sīla*, "the moral code,"[81] was itself founded on *dhamma*, having characterized *anicca* as "a pitiful monk-wail" when compared to the "idea of man's becoming That Who he potentially is,"[82] she urged:

[76] *Ibid.* [77] *Ibid.*, p. 73.

[78] Mrs. Rhys Davids, *A Manual of Buddhism: For Advanced Students* (London: The Sheldon Press, 1932), p. 166. See also *Ibid.*, pp. 156–157, 172. With regard to *D.* II. 154, where the Buddha urges his followers to let *dhamma* be a refuge, Mrs. Rhys Drvids mitigates, to some extent, her personalistic interpretation. She, in *A Manual*, p. 167, said of the *Dīgha-nikāya* passage, "Anyway, it emerges that *dhamma* stood for something who, or which, was held to be efficient *as teacher and as guide*. . . ." On the term "*antarayāmin*," Mrs. Rhys Davids in *Sakya*, p. 73, wrote it as noted, *antarayāmin*, and so also in *A Manual*, p. 172. In 1941, in her "Preface to the Second Edition" of *Dialogues of the Buddha*, Part II, p. xi, she noted the term correctly, in its Sanskrit form, *antaryāmin*.

[79] Mrs. Rhys Davids, *A Manual*, p. 168. She oscillated between a personal and an impersonal interpretation. See also Geiger, *PD.*, p. 7.

[80] See Mrs. Rhys Davids, *A Manual*, p. 169. See also *Gotama The Man*, p. 56.

[81] Mrs. Rhys Davids, *A Manual*, p. 169. [82] *Ibid.*

> Man's best self was dynamic, was to be known as an urge to the better, as Dharma: That Who he should be, That Who was leading on, was guiding, was mothering, That Who was ever at hand, unfailing mighty Ally.[83]

Still grappling with the notion of *dhamma*, she mentioned that conscience in the sense of "'this Deity in my bosom'" was not distant from *dhamma*. Yet, this was not, for her, adequate.

> But neither is conscience a term really worthy of us. It is not enough to be *con-sciens*, aware inwardly. We may be silently aware that a fence of so many feet is before us. We need more to make the jump over it. When our great word 'will' brought into religion by Jesus, comes into its very own, then shall we find a better word than conscience.[84]

In 1932, the same year in which *A Manual of Buddhism* was published, Mrs. Rhys Davids made explicit her decision (and also that of F. L. Woodward) to drop "Norm" as a translation of *dhamma*.[85] "Norm" carried for Mrs. Rhys Davids a sense of "maintaining" that she sensed was inadequate for a central religious term. There had to be a sense of moral thrust in *dhamma* if it was vital in a great religious movement. She remarked that "the force of the Ought in this word" must be got in translation. "Duty" and "conscience" were recognized as available terms for this purpose but not quite precise enough to catch the "'oughtness' in dhamma."[86] She continued, "Deliberately, we are told, and told with utmost emphasis, he [Gotama] chose it [*dhamma*] to mean that immanent Godhead of his day: the Thou art That of the Upanishads, Whom alone he held

---

[83] *Ibid.*, p. 170.

[84] *Ibid.*, pp. 171–172.

[85] Mrs. Rhys Davids noted in her "Introduction" to *The Book of the Gradual Sayings* (*Anguttara-nikāya*), translated by F. L. Woodward (London: Published for the Pali Text Society by Luzac & Co., Ltd., 1960 [first published in 1932]), Vol. I, p. vii, that Mr. Woodward decided to drop the term "Norm" and that she agreed with his decision. The decision is strikingly noted in Woodward's translation. Under "Errata" one finds, "Page 69: *for* 'Norm' *read* 'Dhamma.'"

[86] *Ibid.*, p. viii.

meet that he should worship."[87]

Having decided to leave the term *dhamma* in the text of an English translation, reiterating that she had discarded "Norm" as a translation of *dhamma*,[88] Mrs. Rhys Davids continued to express herself on the meaning of *dhamma*. She wrote, in 1936:

> To this dual concept of the One, (Atman, Brahman) the first Sakyans brought their own new concept of a term it is hard for us to render exactly: their own concept of Deity as *dharma* (Pali *dhamma*). In this they sought to conceive Deity, as not only immanent, but as moving, urgent, ideal, as 'conscience,' as 'duty,' as 'the ought and ought not.'[89]

In the course of a few years, Mrs. Rhys Davids seemed to have seen less of *attā* (in the sense of Skt. *ātman*) in *dhamma* and more of something new—not only in the sense of a moral duty, "but of Mandator of duty."[90] And, in what was to be one of her last published comments on the term *dhamma*, Mrs. Rhys Davids noted that "Truth," "Law," and "Doctrine" were wrong translations if one were to grasp adequately what the import of *dhamma* was for the Buddha. The Pāli scriptures, in her opinion,

> show the Founder worshipping 'dhamma' before he had uttered a single word of his teaching. And he equated *dhamma* with *attā*: self or spirit, then worshipped as Deity. By *dhamma* was

[87] *Ibid.* Mrs. Rhys Davids referred to *S.* I. 139–140. In this passage the Buddha became involved in revering *dhamma*. Yet, nowhere in the Pāli canon, commentarial literature, or Sinhalese texts will a source be found to substantiate the meaning that she suggested. It appears that Mrs. Rhys Davids, perhaps, at this point stood in the shadow of that eminent German scholar, Wilhelm Geiger, who wrote in italics a similar observation—but with a difference. Mrs. Rhys Davids has taken as identity that which Geiger, *PD.*, p. 7, described as homologous, though he did not use this term. See also Wilhelm Geiger, "Dhamma und Brahman"; *Zeitschrift für Buddhismus* (1921), pp. 73–74.

[88] Mrs. Rhys Davids, *Buddhism: Its Birth and Dispersal*, in the series, "Home University of Modern Knowledge" (London: Thornton Butterworth Ltd., 1934, a rev. ed. of *Buddhism: A Study of the Buddhist Norm*, n.d. [1912]), p. 10.

[89] Mrs. Rhys Davids, *Buddhism: Its Birth and Dispersal*, p. 229.

[90] See Mrs. Rhys Davids, *What was the Original Gospel in "Buddhism"?* (London: The Epworth Press, 1938), p. 47.

> meant that 'ought' in conduct which we oppose to what 'normally is or is not done.' 'Duty,' still more 'conscience,' are better terms for *dhamma*: not a *static* Deity within us but a dynamic Urger to do or refrain from doing.
>
> Loosely translated perhaps 'religion' is the least objectionable term, religion being of course to be taken in the early Buddhist sense of, not ritual, nor creed, but the ideal of ever becoming a more in the long way towards the Most.[91]

During the course of her study of the Pāli canon and her writings about the Buddhist tradition a major theme that she stressed was that of doctrinal development. *Dhamma* has had a long history and for her this would mean a process of change in meaning.[92] Her objective was to cut through later doctrinal developments, later interpretations of *dhamma*, to determine what the Buddha taught, what he meant when he used the term. She, of course, did not say that *dhamma* in every occurrence of its singular form meant what she had, over several years, been arguing. She noted that there were passages where "teaching" or "doctrine" might be acceptable translations.[93] Generally, her opinion in her later writings was that a gradual process of externalization of *dhamma* soon got under way in the early Buddhist movement and hence the word came to mean a body of doctrine.[94] She made it clear that she was prepared to differ with both Buddhists and books dealing with "Buddhism" on the matter of *dhamma* meaning "an external code of doctrines" when the Buddha used the word.[95]

---

[91] Mrs. Rhys Davids, "Editor's Introduction," *The Minor Anthologies of the Pali Canon*, Part IV, ("Sacred Books of the Buddhists," Vol. XII; London: Luzac & Co., Ltd., 1942), pp. xi–xii.

[92] See Mrs. Rhys Davids, *Sakya*, pp. 66, 72–73.

[93] See Mrs. Rhys Davids, *A Manual*, p. 167.

[94] See Mrs. Rhys Davids, *What Was the Original Gospel in "Buddhism"?*, p. 193. See also her "Introduction," in *The Book of the Gradual Sayings*, Vol. I, vii–viii. See also her *Buddhism: Its Birth and Dispersal*, p. 10.

[95] Mrs. Rhys Davids, *What Was the Original Gospel in "Buddhism"?*, p. 51. In "Introduction" in *Gradual Sayings*, Vol. I, viii, Mrs. Rhys Davids noted, "A man of Ceylon will now say, if you ask: What is Dhamma? 'The Sutta-Piṭaka.'" And in *What Was the Original Gospel in "Buddhism"?*, p. 49, she said, "To the question put to pupils of Ceylon, 'What for you is *dhamma*?'

During the two decades in which Mrs. Rhys Davids continued to write, other Western scholars were not silent with regard to *dhamma.* E. J. Thomas discussed the term but said nothing that was new. He noted that *dhamma,* "as being the principle by which a man regulates his life, often corresponds with 'religion', but includes social and ritual activities. Hence it may sometimes be translated 'law'."[96] Six years later, Thomas altered his interpretation somewhat.

> In pre-Buddhistic use dharma is conceived as a prescribed course of action for anything in nature which may follow a natural or normal process. It may thus be translated 'law'. As applied to theories of human action it was much wider than morality, for it included all ritual, and was thus religion.[97]

Thomas chose "doctrine" as the translation of *dhamma* when the term meant "the Dhamma of Buddha."[98]

In 1934, one year after Thomas wrote *The History of Buddhist Thought,* Helena Willman-Grabowska presented a study of the term *dharma* in which she traced its semantic evolution from the Vedas to Mahāyāna Buddhist thought.[99] She suggested that in a semi-nomadic society, in the early Indian Vedic period, the notion "to support," like that "to bear" would have a definite, concrete meaning

---

the answer given me was 'The Sutta Piṭaka'." This answer is not incorrect. However, it would by no means represent a pass if this question were asked in an examination conducted in a Sinhaless Buddhist *pirivena.*

[96] Edward J. Thomas, *The Life of Buddha as Legend and History* (London: Routledge & Kegan Paul Ltd., 1960 [first published March, 1927, 2nd ed., with a few corrections, March 1931, 3rd ed., rev., 1949, reprinted 1952, 1956, and 1960]), n. 1, p. 174.

[97] Edward J. Thomas, *The History of Buddhist Thought* (London: Routledge & Kegan Paul Ltd., 1959 [first published, 1933, second ed., 1951, reprinted 1953 and 1959]), n. 2, p. 13. Apparently, Thomas found "religion" as cumbersome to handle as "*dhamma.*" He, further, relegates to a footnote in this work as well as in his *The Life of Buddha* comments regarding the term *dhamma.* Perhaps this scholar considered the meaning of *dhamma* a relatively closed matter.

[98] Thomas, *The Life of Buddha,* n. 1, p. 174, and *The History of Buddhist Thought,* n. 2, p. 13.

[99] Helena Willman-Grabowska, "Évolution sémantique du mot 'dharma'," *Rocznik Orjentalistyczny,* Tom X (1934), pp. 38–50.

where goods and families were frequently transported. Such notions would not have been very precise and at the same time could have expressed an everyday matter. Also, where society was mobile, fluid, there would be a concern for personal security. Willman-Grabowska proposed that the idea of support would have both a concrete and somewhat abstract meaning.[100] She maintained that these two nuances remained with the term *dharma* throughout its long history.[101]

Much less restless about the many dimensions of the term *dharma* than was Mrs. Rhys Davids, Willman-Grabowska remarked regarding *dharma* in general:

> Il n'est pas toujours nécessaire à la commodité du langage que les mots aient le sens précis. Le vague peut aussi rendre service. Il est comme un moule à moitié vide: chacun peut le remplir à son gré. Mais le premier contenu est toujours là en plus ou moins grande quantité; il communique sa saveur du mélange. La saveur du mot *dharma*, c'était la notion du devoir imposé par la religion ou par la nature, ce qui revenait au même; l'idée de stabilité ne dépendant de rein, fût-elle à son origine créée par l'homme. En dehors de cette notion générale, on prêtait à dharma des valeurs plus ou moins spéciales, selon le besoin. L'imprécision du sens permettait des emplois qui tantôt rétrécissaient, tantôt élargissaient le contenu du mot, mot malléable et souple grâce à la conjonction, dans son sens, de deux éléments contraires: concret et abstrait.[102]

She noted that the Buddha "était d'accord avec la conception generale en nommant sa doctrine *dhamma*."[103] Her discussion of *dhamma* in the Buddhist case quickly moved to a consideration of

---

[100] *Ibid.*, p. 38.

[101] See above, at n. 51, where it is noted that Masson-Oursel, in 1922, thought "order" was the underlying notion of *dharma*. See also above, at n. 52, where mention is made of the two aspects of *dharma* that Oltramare presented in 1923; "what is" and "what should be." Willman-Grabowska noted neither Masson-Oursel, nor Oltramare: nor, for that matter, the Geigers' *Pāli Dhamma*.

[102] *Ibid.*, p. 45. This remark represents a transitional comment between her discussion primarily based on Hindu sources and the beginning of her consideration of the Buddhist case. Her comment, "The idea of stability depending on nothing, would it, in its origin, have been created by man?" raises an old and provocative question.

[103] *Ibid.*, p. 46.

opinions proposed by Rosenberg, Stcherbatsky and others about *dhammā* in *Abhidhamma* (Skt. *dharmāḥ* in *Abhidharma*). Willman-Grabowska, for the period in which she wrote, was remarkably perceptive when she suggested that the indecisive comprehensiveness of *dharma* was in itself meaningful. Having noted the gradual rise in popularity of *dharma* as a religious term and the decline of *ṛta*, she mentioned:

> Il rivalise même avec d'autres termes religieux et abstraits, *vratá* et *satyá*, et ce n'est que le souvenir de sa notion cencrète qui lui fait encore occuper une position à part. Dans cette position, il perd ce qui lui restait de son ancien fond et devient mot symbole, mot emblème. Personne ne l'analyse, car tout le monde le comprend et chacun y met ce qu'il veut y trouver. La notion vague, indéterminée, d'ensemble de droits et de devoirs, contenant par conséquent un peu d'idée, ou d'impression d'une certaine stabilité: l'idée générale d'un conditionnement d'origine divine, ce qui voulait toujours dire d'origine inconnue ou 'sans origine'—le *dharma* se prête admirablement à ses nouveaux emplois, sous la plume des philosophes bouddhistes.[104]

Miss I. B. Horner, a student and colleague of Mrs. Rhys Davids, in 1936, gave to English readers interested in the early Buddhist movement as recorded in the Pāli canon a book discussing the *arahant*, or perfect man.[105] She adopted the position of Mrs. Rhys Davids in differentiating in the early Buddhist movement a period known as Sakya and a later phase known as monastic Buddhism. In the former, she noted *dhamma* as "his [the *arahant's*] inner guide" and in the latter, *dhamma* was "an externalized body of doctrines."[106] She followed Mrs. Rhys Davids' interpretation (in the latter's book, *Sakya*) very closely.[107] Miss Horner further noted, "Dhamma for Gotama was as absolutely real as was Brahma [*sic*] for the Upaniṣads."[108] One is uncertain of the import of her notion when she remarked that

---

[104] *Ibid.*, p. 49.

[105] I. B. Horner, *The Early Buddhist Theory of Man Perfected: A Study of the Arahan* (London: Williams & Norgate Ltd., 1936). Henceforth, this work will be noted as *EBTMP*.

[106] *Ibid.*, p. 40. [107] See *Ibid.*, pp. 47–48. [108] *Ibid.*, p. 146.

Gotama believed "that there is an order which transcended the personal, and one which each of his disciples should aspire towards, lit by the light of Self, of Dhamma within him."[109] Again, in the shadow of Mrs. Rhys Davids, Miss Horner spoke of "man with self [the Pāli of the passage alluded to has *attā* in compound] as refuge and lamp; man with conscience [the Pāli has *dhamma* in compound] as refuge and lamp. . . ."[110] For the next ten years, Miss Horner did not alter her course from the wake of Mrs. Rhys Davids.[111]

In 1948, Miss Horner submitted an article on the notion of *dhamma*.[112] In this work, she sought not to collect data drawn from every passage introduced by "I will teach you *dhamma*" and the like. Rather, she attempted "to consider the philosophical or doctrinal position and character of dhamma as found in the Pali canon."[113] She proposed a novel explanation of the breadth of meaning of *dhamma*. Beginning, "Primarily, dhamma means the natural state or condition of beings and things, the law of their being, what it is right for them to be. . . .", she remarked that if they, therefore, are right, they "are true to themselves. So dhamma also means truth, with the derived meaning of 'religious' truth, hence the Buddhist doctrine."[114] *Dhamma*, she noted "in addition may mean something

[109] *Ibid.* Twelve years later, in "Early Buddhist Dhamma," *Artibus Asiae*, Vol. XI, 1/2 (1948), p. 119, she spoke of this passage as "an apparent parallelism."

[110] *EBTMP.*, p. 317. However, she, at p. 146, mentioned, "Because man has conscience (the word was lacking in Pali). . . ."

[111] See I. B. Horner, "Translator's Introduction," *The Book of the Discipline* (London: Published for the Pali Text Society by Luzac & Co., Ltd., 1949 [first published in 1938 by the Oxford University Press; "Introduction" signed in 1938]), Vol. I, vi–vii, lvi. I. B. Horner, "Abhidhamma Abhivinaya," *The Indian Historical Quarterly*, Vol. XVII, No. 3 (Sept. 1941), p. 293. I. B. Horner, "Some Aspects of Movement in Early Buddhism," *Artibus Asiae*, Vol. XI, 1/2 (1947), pp. 139–140.

[112] I. B. Horner, "Early Buddhist Dhamma," pp. 115–123.

[113] *Ibid.*, p. 115.

[114] *Ibid.* Geiger at *PD.*, pp. 6–7, proposed "Wahrheit" as an extension of the Buddha's doctrine being the only true doctrine. Miss Horner repeated this paragraph almost *verbatim* in 1954 in "Translator's Introduction," *The Collection of the Middle Length Sayings* (London: Luzac & Co., Ltd., 1954), Vol. I, p. xix.

like our word 'conscience,' as does *attā*, self, the inner monitor, which in you knows what is right and what is wrong."[115]

In close agreement with Professor and Mrs. Geiger, Miss Horner, aware of the many meanings and nuances of *dhamma*, stated, "These often tend to slide into one another, so that it is not always possible to say that in any particular passage only one meaning is intended, and, if so, which one."[116] She decided not to translate the term *dhamma* and noted, "It must speak for itself. . . ."[117] She turned her attention to an old, standard description of *dhamma* and translated it as "Dhamma is well pointed out by the lord, it relates to present conditions, *sandiṭṭhika*, it is apart from time, *akālika*, it is a come-and-see thing, leading onwards, to be known for themselves by the wise."[118] She noted the same phrase's being used for *dhamma* and *nibbāna* (*A*. I. 156, 158) and suggested an apparent equation of the two.[119]

Miss Horner, having interpreted the Bodhi tree as the *Axis Mundi*, stressed that the Buddha as *Tathāgata* is one "dhamma-become, Brahma-become."[120] She was not explicit in whether she held *dhamma* to have been equivalent to *brahman*. She noted *dhammakāya* and *brahmakāya* as "literally the body of dhamma, the body of Brahman."[121]

---

[115] Horner, "Early Buddhist Dhamma," p. 115.

[116] *Ibid*. See Geiger, *PD*., p. 3. See also, Masson-Oursel, *op. cit*., p. 269.

[117] Horner, "Early Buddhist Dhamma," p. 115. Masson-Oursel, *loc. cit*., a quarter of a century earlier said, "Ceci dit, on choisit dans un cas tel sens, dans un autre tel, autre, ou l'on renonce a traduir. Nous craignons que cette affectation de scrupule atteste quelquefois un manque de courage."

[118] Horner, "Early Buddhist Dhamma," p. 116.

[119] *Ibid*. In the first passage, Gotama is asked, "Kittāvatā nu kho bho Gotama sandiṭṭhiko dhammo hoti akāliko ehipassiko. . . ." In the second passage, Gotama is asked, "Kittāvatā bho Gotamo sandiṭṭhikaṃ nibbānaṃ hoti akālikaṃ ehipassikaṃ. . . ." Brahmins are posing the question and hence "Gotama" is used for him whom Buddhists remember as the Buddha. The reply centers on abandonment of *rāga*, *dosa*, *moha*. These references are from the Pali Text Society editions of the *Anguttara-nikāya*, Vol. I, pp. 156, 158.

[120] Horner, "Early Buddhist Dhamma," p. 117. At *Ibid*., p. 118, she noted only Buddhas are "dhamma-become."

[121] *Ibid* , p. 117.

Further on she said, "So *dhamma* is to some extent to be identified with brahma [*sic*], the best and highest, if this is the meaning that brahma [*sic*] had under Early Buddhism and not merely in the commentaries on the Pali canon."[122]

Edward Conze, in 1962, devoted a chapter to a discussion of *dhamma* entitled "Dharma and Dharmas." He began, with some insight, "What others call 'Buddhism', the Buddhists themselves call 'Dharma'."[123] He immediately continued, with some lack of precision, "In its essentials the Dharma-theory is common to all schools, and provides the framework within which Buddhist wisdom operates."[124] Although he presented seven general meanings that he considered "philosophically important"[125] not all of the meanings are of major importance in this present study.[126] And, further, none of the meanings that he listed was unknown to Western scholarship.

---

[122] *Ibid.* She noted other parallel expressions that "also point to this identification."

[123] Edward Conze, *Buddhist Thought in India* (London: George Allen & Unwin Ltd., 1962), p. 92.

[124] *Ibid.*

[125] "(1) In an *ontological* sense Dharma is (1a) a transcendental reality which is real in absolute truth and in the ultimate sense. . . .(1b) Dharma is 'the order of law of the universe, immanent, eternal, uncreated' . . . .(1c) 'a truly real event', things as seen when Dharma is taken as the norm. . . . (1d) objective data whether dharmically true or untrue, mental objects or mental percepts. . . .(1e) characteristic, quality, property, attribute. . . .(2) As reflected in the conduct of life, *dharma* means the moral law, righteousness, virtue, right behaviour, duty and religious practice. . . .(3) The dharmic facts of 1 and 2 as interpreted in the Buddha's teaching. The word then means 'doctrine', 'scripture', 'truth' (cognitive and not ontological as at 1a), 'sacred text' or a 'doctrinal text'. . . ." *Ibid.*, pp. 92–94.

[126] Conze highlighted the philosophical aspect of Buddhist thought and noted that prior to the work of Th. Stcherbatsky "scholars had been so intent on making the Buddha appear as a moralist that the significance of the philosophical analysis of reality into its factors, or 'dharmas', was either overlooked or dismissed as a later scholastic elaboration." *Ibid.*, p. 92. Conze, perhaps, overstressed the philosophical aspect in order to underline his point. Étienne Lamotte, *The Spirit of Ancient Buddhism* (Venezia-Roma: Institute per la Collaborazione Culturale, 1961), p. 13, reminded his readers that "like all Indian systems of thought, the Buddhist *dharma* constitutes a moral doctrine rather than a metaphysical theory."

Thus far, in the present study, opinions expressed by some Western academics about the notion *dhamma* have been presented—opinions that reflect a history of the notion in the West.[127]

Heuristic Reflections

In the process of understanding the term *dhamma*, certain major themes have been developed by Western scholars. For some it has been important to consider what relationship there might have been between *dhamma* in early Buddhist thought—indeed, in the mind of the Buddha—and *brahman* in the Upaniṣads.

Professor and Mrs. Geiger, in the course of their study of *dhamma* in the Pāli canon, noted that *dhamma* was put in the place of *brahman* in the older brahmanic system. They suggested this was done by the Buddha "mit voller *Absicht*." Professor Geiger, on another occasion, said of this observation, "*Der Begriff dhamma von dem Begründer des buddhistischen Systems mit vollem Bewusstsein an die Stelle des älteren Begriffes brahman gesetzt wurde und diesen zu vor drängen und zu ersetzen bestimmt war.*"[128] In both statements, Geiger

[127] Others have written on *dhamma* who were themselves members of a spreading academic community structured in terms of Western modes of study, but who, themselves, were neither Westerners nor Sinhalese. Mention should be made of Bimala Churn Law, "Buddhist Conception of Dharma," *Journal of the Department of Letters*, Vol. XXVIII (1935), pp. 1–19, reprinted in the author's *Concepts of Buddhism* (Leiden: Published for the Kern Institute by H. J. Paris, 1937). P. T. Raju, "The Buddhistic Conception of Dharma," *Annals of the Bhandarkar Oriental Research Institute*, Vol. XXI, 1939–40 (Poona, 1941), pp. 192–302. This article was reprinted with only a few editorial corrections as section XVII, entitled "Metaphysical Significance of Dharma or Law in Buddhism," of Chapter V in the author's work, *Idealistic Thought of India* (Cambridge, Mass.: Harvard University Press, 1953), pp. 281–291. Govind Chandra Pande, *Studies in the Origins of Buddhism* (Allahabad, India: University of Allahabad, 1957), pp. 465–472. Special note should be made of an article by Hajime Nakamura, "The Indian and Buddhist Concept of Law," in *Religious Pluralism and World Community: Interfaith and Intercultural Communication*, edited by Edward J. Jurji (Leiden: E. J. Brill, 1969), pp. 131–174.

[128] Wilhelm Geiger, "Dhamma und Brahman," pp. 73–74.

was, through the use of italics, apparently, suggesting more than an hypothesis.

Geiger was again explicit in his article, "Dhamma und Brahman," about the *brahman/dhamma* relationship. He noted briefly several occurrences of *dharman/dharma* in the Vedas and repeated his examples drawn from the Upaniṣads.[129] The Buddha had, in the term *dharma*, an old notion with overtones of solemn sanctity. What the Buddha did, Geiger argued, was to take the term, fill it with new content and structure his world-view in such a manner that *dhamma*, for him and the Buddhists, took the place of *brahman* in contemporary brahmanic thought. An identity of *dhamma* and *brahman* or an analogous relation there was not. Geiger remarked:

> Welch ein Gegensatz! Das Brahman ist das ewige, unveränderliche Sein, gegenüber der Welt der Erscheinungen, die Realität schlechthin. Der Dhamma aber besagt: es gibt überhaupt kein Sein, es gibt nur ein Werden und Vergehen. Es ist nun aber echt buddhistisch, dass der ehrwürdige Begriff des Brahman keineswegs ohne weiteres beseitigt wird. Er erhält nur eine besondere Färbung, eine neue Beleuchtung. Die Vereinigung mit dem Brahman ist das höchste Ziel des Menschen. Also wird das Wort *brahman* dem Buddhisten zu einer Bezeichnung des Nirvana.[130]

The historical setting and the probability of an interchange of major terms were, for Geiger, reflected in the parallel expressions of *dhamma* and *brahman* in the Pāli canon.[131]

Geiger noted that in Bengal *dharma* was venerated as a god and was of the opinion that this was not a later development through brahmanic thought but Buddhist. He suggested that this also demon-

---

[129] *Ibid.*, pp. 75–76. See *PD.*, p. 8.

[130] Geiger, "Dhamma und Brahman," p. 76. Geiger noted *S.* III. 346, line 13, where *brahmapathe* is glossed in one manuscript by *amatapathe*. Further, *Ibid.*, p. 77, he mentioned *Chāndogya-Upaniṣad* 4. 15. 5 where the term, *brahmapatha*, occurs. He also pointed out that in several passages in the Pāli canon there is the phrase *brahmabhūtena attanā*.

[131] *Ibid.*, pp. 77–80. See also *PD.*, pp. 77–78. Geiger referred to *S.* V. 6 and suggested that this passage represented one of the very few places in the Pāli canon where *ātman-attan* and *brahman* are synonymous. "Dhamma und Brahman," pp. 78–79, *PD.*, p. 78.

strated the centrality of *dhamma* in Buddhist thought.[132] Regarding what he considered a more orthodox view of *dhamma*, Geiger said,

> Heir ist der Dhamma durchaus übersinnlich. Er wird 'geschaut', wie man Übersinnliches schaut. Es schaut ihn der, der das 'Dhamma-auge' besitzt. Aber er ist dabei doch etwas, dem man huldigt, das man hochhält und verehrt, wie man eine Gottheit verehrt.[133]

Geiger again referred to the phrase *dhammo have rakkhati dhammacāriṃ* and in words much the same as those he and his wife had used earlier, said, "So denkt man schon fast an ein persönliches Wesen, an eine schirmende Gottheit. . . ."[134]

Mrs. Rhys Davids seemed to have gone a step beyond Professor and Mrs. Geiger. One should keep in mind that the English lady, though covering much the same ground as the Geigers, began from another starting point. It was noted above that Mrs. Rhys Davids differed with the Geigers on what the "quintessence" of Buddha's teaching was. For her, *dhamma* had as its keystone not the idea that all component aspects of life are *anicca, dukkha, anatta/paṭicca-samuppāda*. *Dhamma* for the Buddha, she thought, had to be more than this.

When she wrote her little book, *Buddhism*, she made no mention of a relationship between *dhamma* and *brahman*. After that writing came the work of the Geigers. Subsequently, one notes Mrs. Rhys Davids giving considerable space to *dhamma/brahman-ātman*, stressing a special relationship.

Because Geiger was prepared to accept *paṭicca-samuppāda, anicca, dukkha, anatta* as central aspects of the Buddha's message, he could suggest an homologous relation between *brahman* and *dhamma* and at the same time say of their analogous relation, "Welch ein Gegen-

---

[132] Geiger, "Dhamma und Brahman," pp. 80–81. *PD.*, n. 1, p. 77.

[133] Geiger, "Dhamma und Brahman," p. 81.

[134] *Ibid.* See *PD.*, p. 76. Geiger concluded his article, "Dhamma und Brahman," by noting and translating *S.* I. 138–140, *A.* II. 20–21, where the Buddha revered *dhamma*.

satz!"[135] Mrs. Rhys Davids, however, finding it difficult to accept *paṭiccasamuppāda* and the *tilakkhaṇa* as central in the Buddha's message, appeared to have sensed a much closer relationship between *brahman* and *dhamma*. She remained less than explicit about that relationship. She mentioned that the Buddha meant by *dhamma* "that immanent Godhead of his day: the Thou art That of the Upanishads. . . ."[136] It appears that she would want *dhamma* to mean "immanent Godhead" and would let the matter there stand. She seemed to be of the opinion that *dhamma* in some way was a new way to conceive deity.[137] *Dhamma*, in Buddhist thought, also came to take the exalted place of "self" in brahmanic thought, she suggested.[138] One might suggest that, for Mrs. Rhys Davids, *dhamma* was both the Highest and the inner motivative force that urged one on to attain that Highest.

Miss Horner, following Mrs. Rhys Davids, suggested,

> Primitive Buddhism was an attempt to expand the *tat tvaṃ asi* of the Upaniṣads into *tat tvaṃ bhavasi*. Man was not to be regarded as being That Self Which was the Highest, but was potentially capable of becoming as That Self.[139]

Other scholars had not followed that train of thought. Professor

---

[135] Geiger, "Dhamma und Brahman," p. 76.

[136] Mrs. Rhys Davids, "Introduction," *The Book of the Gradual Sayings* (*Anguttara-nikāya*), Vol. I, p. viii.

[137] See Mrs. Rhys Davids, *Birth of Indian Psychology and Its Development in Buddhism* (London: Luzac & Co., 1936 [a rewritten and enlarged edition of *Buddhist Psychology* published in "The Quest" series, London, 1914, republished, 1924]), p. 229.

[138] See Mrs. Rhys Davids, *Outlines of Buddhism: A Historical Sketch* (London: Methuen & Co., Ltd., 1934), p. 21. See also *A Manual of Buddhism*, pp. 165–166, 192–193. Mrs. Rhys Davids was aware that the impersonal absolute of the Upaniṣads is not to be found in the Pāli canon. See her *Indian Religion and Survival* (London: George Allen and Unwin Ltd., 1934), p. 34.

[139] Horner, *EBTMP*., p. 103. She stressed a polarity between "man being that Highest Reality" in the Upaniṣads "which gave way to the Śakyan view that man can train himself to *become* as That." Horner, "An Aspect of Becoming in Early Buddhism," p. 283. Miss Horner, in "Early Buddhist Dhamma," oscillated between "Brahman" and "Brahma" without maintaining a precise distinction. See *Ibid*., pp. 117–118.

T. W. Rhys Davids had noted that the neuter *brahman* in Upaniṣadic thought, in the sense of the absolute, was not mentioned in the Pāli canon, that it was "quietly ignored."[140] Oldenberg had suggested that the impersonal *brahman* of the old Upaniṣads had been hypostatized by the early Buddhists into a personal God, Brahmā.[141] E. J. Thomas agreed with T. W. Rhys Davids and chose to differ with Oldenberg.[142] H. von Glassenapp also noted that the "*brahma* [*sic*]" that one finds in the Pāli canon does not represent a notion of the absolute, but the highest personal God.[143] The problem is focused when one notes, as did Professor and Mrs. Geiger and Mrs. Rhys Davids, that in the Pāli canon no distinction is maintained between the neuter *brahman* and the masculine *brahman* (*i. e.*, *Brahmā*) when forming a compound.[144]

Edward Conze, speaking of *nirvāṇa* as what is meant when one takes refuge in *dharma*, remarked, "Here 'dharma' has a position similar to that which *ātman* and *brahman* occupy in some Hindu systems."[145] Th. Stcherbatsky, in describing what he considered the positive side of Nāgārjuna's critique, noted an "almost absolute identity with Vedānta..." and phrased this as "the identity of *dhammakāya* and *brahma*. . . ."[146]

---

[140] T. W. Rhys Davids, "Introduction to the Tevigga Sutta," *Dialogues of the Buddha*, Part I ("Sacred Books of the Buddhists," ed. F. Max Müller, Vol. II; London: Luzac & Co., Ltd., 1956 [first published in 1899, reprinted in 1956]), p. 298.

[141] Hermann Oldenberg, *Die Lehre der Upanishaden und die Anfänge des Buddhismus* (Göttingen: Vandenhoeck & Ruprecht, 1915), p. 286.

[142] Thomas, *History of Buddhist Thought*, pp. 87, 90, 96.

[143] Helmuth von Glasenapp, "Zur Geschichte der buddhistischen Dharma-Theorie," *Zeitschrift der deutschen morgenländischen Gesellschaft*, Band 92, Heft 2/3 (schlussheft) Neue Folge Band 17 (Leipzig: 1938), n. 1, p. 407. See also Oldenberg, *Buddha*, n. 1, p. 65.

[144] See *PD.*, p. 77. Mrs. Rhys Davids, *Indian Religion and Survival*, p. 34.

[145] Conze, *Buddhist Thought in India*, p. 93. His source was the *Abhidharmakośa*. Apparently, his use of the present tense suggests that the idea in the *AK* "has a position similar to" the *ātman/brahman* notion among some contemporary Hindus. Conze, in a preceding note, referred to the Geigers' *PD.* and his choice of "position" looks like their "Stelle."

[146] Th. Stcherbatsky, *The Conception of Buddhist Nirvāṇa* (Leningrad: Academy of Sciences of the USSR, 1927), p. 52. See also *Ibid.*, p. 61.

Much ink was used by Western scholars in writing about the possible relationship between early Buddhist thought and Upaniṣadic thought as well as about later Buddhist developments on the Indian scene. And opinions have differed. To solve this issue—less adventuresome, to propose a line of inquiry that might shed light on the matter—is not the purpose of this study. Its rationale is to document what some Western academics have said about *dhamma*.

What is the relationship between the Buddha and *dhamma*? Opinions relevant to this question have been held by Western scholars. Oldenberg wrote, "Ueberall wird als Quelle der Wahrheit und des heiligen Lebens nicht eine unpersönliche Offenbarung, auch nicht das eigene Denken für sich allein, sondern die Person, das Wort des Meisters, des Erhabenen, des Buddha anerkannt."[147] He noted that in the early Buddhist movement there was little interest in recording a biography of the Buddha. Moreover, he said, "damals das Interesse am Leben des Meisters durchaus hinter dem auf seine Lehre gerichteten zurücktrat."[148] In speaking of the process by which a Buddhist is to seek release (Erlösung) from *dukkha* (Leiden), Oldenberg sug-

---

[147] Oldenberg, *Buddha*, p. 77. (*Eng. tr.*, p. 76.)

[148] Oldenberg, *Buddha*, p. 81. (*Eng. tr.*, p. 79.) Oldenberg's point will be misunderstood if one fails to see in "Leben des Meisters" an emphasis on a biographical dimension of the Buddha's life in the sense of recorded facts. Oldenberg would no doubt agree that the quality of that life was of profound influence on the early disciples. A Tibetan source, *Tibet's Great Yogī Milarepa: A Biography from the Tibetan being the Jetsün-Kahbum or Biographical History of Jetsün-Milarepa, according to the late Lama Kazi Dawa-Samdup's English Rendering*, edited with Introduction and annotations by W. Y. Evans-Wentz (London: Oxford University Press, 1928), pp. 232–233, reads, "Personal love and regard make ye think that I must be an Incarnation; but towards the *Dharma* ye commit the great sin of doubt and scepticism. This is because ye have not the power of earnest devotion. For it is by the great power of the Sacred *Dharma* alone that I have been able to attain such spiritual advancement as to be very near Perfect Buddhahood in the later portion of my years, although I had been guilty of such heinous sins in my youth and early manhood." Drawing from this passage, G. H. Mees noted that for men engaged in the path *dharma* is more important than the Buddha. Mees also referred to the *Mahāparinibbāna-sutta* (see *D.* II. 154). Gaultherus H. Mees, *Dharma and Society* (the Hague: N. V. Servier, 1935), pp. 38–39.

gested the doctrine of the Buddha remains in the background.[149] He remarked, "In der Glaubenformel der vier heiligen Wahrheiten kommt das Wort Buddha nicht vor."[150] The Buddha, in Oldenberg's opinion, was not a saviour. Persons "nehmen seine Verkündigung der Wahrheit an, nicht weil sie von ihm kommt, sondern weil, durch sein Wort geweckt, in ihrem Geiste selbsteigeness Erkennen dessen, wovon er zu ihnen redet, an das Licht tritt."[151] What makes the Buddha the Buddha, Oldenberg wrote, "ist, wie sein Name sagt, sein Erkennen."[152] T. W. Rhys Davids noted that the Buddha's discovery of and his showing the way whereby one can find release constituted his Buddhahood.[153] Rhys Davids noted that the Buddha was likened to a world monarch and that an ideal kingdom was "a kingdom of righteousness in the hearts of men."[154] Focusing on the enlightenment of the Buddha as viewed in the Buddhist tradition, he mentioned,

> The Buddhists regard Gautama's mental struggle under the Bo-tree as the most important event in his career, and the act by which he regained freedom for mankind. Hence the Buddhists look upon the Bo-tree as most Christians have looked upon the Cross.[155]

---

[149] Oldenberg, *Buddha*, pp. 329–330. (*Eng. tr.*, pp. 322–323.) He draws a contrast with the person of Christ in the Christian case.

[150] Oldenberg, *Buddha*, p. 330. (*Eng. tr.*, p. 323.) T. W. Rhys Davids made a similar observation. Regarding the *Dhammacakkappavattana-sutta* he said, "There is not a word about God or the soul, not a word about the Buddha or Buddhism." *Early Buddhism* (in the series, "Religions: Ancient and Modern," London: Archibald Constable and Co., Ltd., 1908), p. 53.

[151] Oldenberg, *Buddha*, p. 332. (*Eng. tr.*, p. 325.)

[152] Oldenberg, *Buddha*, p. 85. (*Eng. tr.*, p. 84.) Oldenberg, *Ibid.*, mentioned in this context Christ in the Christian case.

[153] T. W. Rhys Davids, *Buddhism: Its History and Literature, American Lectures on the History of Religions*, First Series, 1894–1895 (New York: G. P. Putnam's Sons, 1896), p. 145. He also remarked that the doubt about the Buddha does not refer to doubt about the Buddha as saviour. Rather, it is doubt about his Buddhahood. See *Ibid.*

[154] T. W. Rhys Davids, *Lectures on the Origin and Growth of Religion As Illustrated by Some Points in the History of Indian Buddhism*, The Hibbert Lectures, 1881 (London: Williams and Norgate, 1881), p. 136. He also spoke of the early Christian case in this context.

[155] T. W. Rhys Davids, *Buddhism: Being a Sketch*, n. 1, p. 39.

Mrs. Rhys Davids brought into clear perspective the idea that the Buddha rediscovered *dhamma* and therein lay his function.[156] She stressed the centrality of *dhamma* in Buddhist thought.

H. Beckh mentioned that in the early phase a doctrine of the Buddha was in the background. He considered, as a corrective to Oldenberg's suggestions, that Buddhist doctrine (buddhistiche Lehre) could not have given rise to what he called Buddhism had there been no Buddha.[157] Beckh noted that in the early period of the Buddhist movement the personality of the Buddha is not to be understood as equivalent to the personality of Jesus as viewed in the Christian tradition. He continued,

> Im Mittelpunkte des Buddhismus steht eine Lehre, die Lehre vom Leiden und vom Pfade der befreienden Erkenntnis. Im Mittelpunkte der christlichen Religion steht die Gestalt des Erlöser als des Vollbringers einer Tat, der Erlösungstat von Golgatha.[158]

James Bissett Pratt remarked, "In church theory the Buddhist truth is accepted because revealed by the Buddha."[159] He went on to mention that the Buddha urged each one to understand personally and not to accept a point merely because he, the Buddha, had made it.[160] "Something happened under the Bodhi Tree," Pratt noted, "and something has happened in every Buddhist's attainment of enlightenment, which cannot be set down wholly in terms of the intellect."[161]

Professor and Mrs. Geiger recorded most of the occasions in the Pāli canon in which *dhamma* stands in relation to the Buddha. It will not be necessary to demonstrate what they considered each oc-

---

[156] Mrs. Rhys Davids, *Buddhism*, p. 33.

[157] H. Beckh, *op. cit.*, pp. 21–22.

[158] *Ibid.*, p. 21.

[159] James Bissett Pratt, *The Pilgrimage of Buddhism and a Buddhist Pilgrimage* (London: MacMillan and Co., Ltd., 1928), p. 95.

[160] *Ibid.* Pratt's "church theory" is not clear. Probably his point was that one takes what the Buddha said as true because the Buddha said it, and that one is to go beyond this to come to *know* that what the Buddha said is true. Pratt referred to the *Mahāparinibbāna-sutta*, *D.* II. 100.

[161] *Ibid.*, p. 65.

currence to mean. They noted, for example, "*Dhamma* is 'Lehre, Lehrgebäude, Lehrsystem', wie ein Buddha sie ersonnen [*sic*] und der Welt verkündigt hat."[162] They noted, from the *Bu.*, that in previous lives the Buddha had heard the preaching of the Buddhas of each Buddha-aeon.[163] Further on they mentioned,

> Es ist klar, dass wir die Übersetzung 'Wahrheit' vorziehen müssen, wenn es sich um das Erkennen des *dhamma* durch den Buddha handelt. Denn der Buddha hat seine Lehre nicht erfunden oder ersonnen, sondern er hat nur, wie alle seine Vorgänger, die seit Ewigkeit und in Ewigkeit bestehende Wahrheit geistig erfasst. Dadurch ist er eben zum Buddha geworden, und aus der von ihm erkannten Wahrheit formt er seine Lehre.[164]

As a world monarch in the religious sense the Buddha, according to the Geigers, acts in the service of *dhamma*.[165] When, shortly after his enlightenment, the Buddha sought that which he might honor, he chose *dhamma*. The Geigers inferred from this passage, "Der *dh*. [*dhamma*] steht also über dem Buddha."[166] They, referring to *Miln.*, pp. 237–238, suggested that "im Buddha hat der *dh*. [*dhamma*] seine Verkörperung gefunden."[167]

Miss I. B. Horner noted that the Buddha took his place in the procession of Buddhas of the past as one who had rediscovered *dhamma* as will Metteyya (Maitreya) in the future. *Dhamma* "is discovered afresh by each Buddha at the moment of his Great Awakening as he sits under the Tree of Knowledge, which is the Axis Mundi, the Pillar of the World."[168] As a *Tathāgata*, the Buddha is spoken of as *dhammabhūta*, one who has become *dhamma*.[169]

The Buddha is recorded as having said to one Vakkali:

> Indeed, he who sees *dhamma* sees me. He who sees me sees *dhamma*. Indeed, Vakkali, the one seeing *dhamma* sees me; the one seeing me sees *dhamma*.[170]

---

[162] *PD.*, p. 33. [163] See *Ibid.*, p. 46. [164] *Ibid.*, p. 66.
[165] *Ibid.*, p. 73. [166] *Ibid.*, p. 76. [167] *Ibid.*
[168] I. B. Horner, "Early Buddhist Dhamma," p. 116.
[169] See *Ibid.*, p. 117.
[170] *S.* III. 120. See also *Itv.* 91, and *Miln.*, p. 7.

Western scholars have noted this passage. The Geigers mentioned that this called to mind the words of Christ, "I am the Truth."[171] Miss Horner implied in terms of this passage that when one sees *dhamma*, that is, "the moral, inner guide by which man recognized the divinity immanent within him, the will toward the highest, toward the right," one sees "the Highest in man."[172] Again she noted this passage to illustrate the meaning of the *Tathāgata's* having become *dhamma* (*dhammabhūta*).[173] Edward Conze referred to this passage and stated succinctly, "The Buddha has at all times been subordinated to the Dharma, and his significance lies in being a channel of its eternal Truth."[174]

Étienne Lamotte, on the question of the relation of the Buddha to *dharma*, said, "He was in essence a prophet."[175] Lamotte continued,

> Christ is not only the author of the Gospel teaching, but is Himself the life, the truth, the way: He is one with the truth and the life and is Himself salvation.
>
> Buddha, on the contrary, is clearly to be distinguished from the Good Law (*saddharma*), which exists independently of him. He did no more than discover and preach the Law, defining himself as "the sign which shows the path to follow".[176]

Again, on the same question, Lamotte wrote, "Le Buddha s'est volontairement effacé devant la Loi qu'il a découverte et prêchée. Il ne se donne pas pour dieu, mais pour voyant."[177] Not only did the Buddha (as did all the Buddhas) discover *dhamma*, he also taught it openly. *Paṭiccasamuppāda*, the process that he discovered, has been, is, and will be the case whether Buddhas arise or not. The Buddha decided to honor and revere the *dhamma* and approaching his *parinibbāna*

---

171 *PD.*, p. 70: "Ich bin die Wahrheit."

172 I. B. Horner, *EBTMP.*, p. 48.

173 I. B. Horner, "Early Buddhist Dhamma," p. 118.

174 Edward Conze, *Buddhist Thought in India*, p. 171.

175 Étienne Lamotte, *The Spirit of Ancient Buddhism*, p. 12.

176 *Ibid.*, p. 13.

177 Étienne Lamotte, *Histoire du bouddhisme indien: des origines à l'èra Śaka* (Bibliothèque du Muséon, Vol. 43, Louvain: Publications Universitaires, Institut orientaliste, 1958), p. 26. See also *Ibid.*, p. 222.

urged that *dhamma* be taken as refuge and guide.[178]

Wilfred Cantwell Smith in a recent essay attempted an interpretation of the force of *dhamma* in the early Buddhist movement. He mentioned, as have other Western scholars, that the Buddha and his followers stressed that *dhamma* was not something constructed by the Buddha. "He did not concoct this;" Smith noted, "he discovered it."[179] Moreover, Professor Smith interpreted the relationship between the Buddha and *dhamma* when he mentioned, "The Dharma that he taught does not owe its validity or authority to the fact that he was a wise and great man; on the contrary, he became a wise and great man because he awoke to its pre-existent truth."[180] Smith remarked that the Buddha's teaching was concerned with the way that arrives at *nibbāna*, the Other Shore, not with extrapolating the nature of *nibbāna*. And, further, he said, "His seeing that it would carry one across constituted his Vision, his Enlightenment, his Buddhahood."[181]

Nibbāna has had a place in occidental thought. Indeed, it has generated considerably more interest than has the notion *dhamma*. Over fifty years ago Louis de La Vallée Poussin cautioned, "For a Buddhist, the important thing is, not to know what Nirvāna is, but to reach Nirvāna; and inquiry concerning Nirvāna may prove disastrous."[182] Heeding his advice one might nevertheless cast a retro-

---

[178] See *Ibid.*, pp. 26–28.

[179] Wilfred Cantwell Smith, "Religious Atheism? Early Buddhist and Recent American," *Milla wa-Milla*, No. 6 (December, 1966), p. 10.

[180] *Ibid.*

[181] *Ibid.*, p. 9. The point of this statement seems to be that *dhamma*, which the Buddha realized, is salvific.

[182] Louis de la Vallée Poussin, *The Way to Nirvāna; Six Lectures on Ancient Buddhism as a Discipline of Salvation*, The Hibbert Lectures, February—April, 1916 (Cambridge: at the University Press, 1917), p. 112. See also Louis de la Vallée Poussin, *Nirvāna; Études sur l'histoire des religions* (Paris: Gabriel Beaucheone, 1925), p. 5, where this scholar remarked, "Le problème du Nirvāna, pour les bouddhistes de l'époque historique, est un problème d'order spéculatif, ou, pour parler sanscrit, d'Abhidharma, de 'théologie', plutôt que de Dharma ou de 'religion'." See Louis de la Vallée Poussin, "Nirvāṇa," *Encyclopaedia of Religion and Ethics*, ed. James Hastings (Edinburgh: T. & T.

spective glance at academic speculations on a possible relationship between *dhamma* and *nibbāna*.

Professor and Mrs. Geiger suggested that *dhamma* on occasions might stand for *nibbāna*,[183] and Miss Horner noted two passages where *dhamma*, in the first, and *nibbāna*, in the second, are used with the same adjectives.[184] Edward Conze commented that the ultimate reality, in what he called "The Old Wisdom School," was "also called Dharma by the Buddhists, or Nirvana. . . ."[185] Conze continued, "Nirvana is said to be *absolutely* good, and the Dharma *absolutely* true in the sense that they are good and true unquestionably, without any argument, and in all circumstances."[186]

Robert Lawson Slater made a perceptive study of the notion of *nibbāna*.[187] His book represents an attempt to integrate paradox as a form of expression dealing with religious ultimates, in the sense of ultimate notions. In the process of his work, Slater mentioned what he considered to be the relationship between the Buddha, *nibbāna*, and *dhamma*. He noted that Burmese Buddhists would reject a notion that the Buddha was divine.[188] Slater proceeded to say,

> It is not, then, to the conception of the Buddha that we must look for the religious ultimate of Southern Buddhism. Nor is it to the conception of the *Dhamma*, as some have suggested.[189] A

Clarke, 1917), Vol. IX, 376a–379b. On La Vallée Poussin's views on *nirvāṇa* see also Guy Richard Welbon, *The Buddhist Nirvāṇa and Its Western Interpreters* (Chicago: The University of Chicago Press, 1968), pp. 284–295.

[183] See *PD.*, p. 98.

[184] See Horner, "Early Buddhist Dhamma," p. 116. Her references are to *A.* I. 156, 157, 158.

[185] Edward Conze, *Buddhism: Its Essence and Development* (New York: Harper & Brothers, 1959 [reprinted by arrangement with Bruno Cassirer Ltd., Oxford, which published the original edition in 1951]), p. 110.

[186] *Ibid.*, p. 111.

[187] Robert Lawson Slater, *Paradox and Nirvana: A Study of Religious Ultimates With Special Reference to Burmese Buddhism* (Chicago: The University of Chicago Press, 1951).

[188] *Ibid.*, p. 31. It might be productive to inquire in what way one would express in Burmese the query, "Was the Buddha divine?"

[189] Professor Slater gave no reference for this statement. One might not

> highly sophisticated intellectual might conceivably worship the 'Law within' but the Burmese Buddhist is seldom highly sophisticated, nor does he think of the Dhamma as the Law within: It is the Law without, expounded by the *Saṃgha*.
>
> It is elsewhere we must look for the recognition of the divine.[190]

Noting the likelihood of a Burmese Buddhist village elder's entering a monastery in his last years, Slater said:

> A tardy beginning is better than none. It will not mean Nibbāna tomorrow, but it will mean a more definite step in the Way.
>
> Here, perhaps, we have a further significance of the concept, a reminder that Nibbāna imports a challenge as well as a promise —a challenge to that better, nobler, more sensible Way which a man may have disregarded for the greater part of his life. Since the Goal is never to be separated from the Way, Nibbāna is the reminder of Dhamma. While it holds the promise of deliverance and peace, it rebukes all that postpones that deliverance and denies that peace.
>
> Nibbana, then, is Mystery, but it is nevertheless the concept which completes faith and inspires conduct.[191]

Having quoted from Bimala Churn Law, a leading Indian expositor of Buddhist thought, that *nibbāna* (*nirvāṇa*) was the *summum bonum* of Buddhism, Slater mentioned:

> Nibbāna is the *gospel* of Buddhism, the term which signifies emancipation, salvation. The greatest assurance which can encourage the devout disciple is the assurance that he is indeed in the Path-of-the-Stream and will now, without doubt, attain Nibbāna. It is the term which turns pessimism into optimism and makes it absurd to describe Buddhism as a pessimistic religion. At the

---

be mistaken should one suspect that Slater was referring to Western interpreters and Western interpretations prior to 1951, as is implied (by alluding to Mrs. Rhys Davids?) in his next sentence quoted above.

[190] *Ibid.* A question should be raised at this point. The distinction, in this context, of Law within and Law without appears joltingly Western and probably reflects an opinion of Mrs. Rhys Davids. One would be surprised were one to meet this distinction in the Burmese lauguage.

[191] *Ibid.*, p. 47. There is considerable insight in Slater's words. "Way" could represent either *magga* or *dhamma*. In this context, it appears that Slater used it synonymously with *dhamma*. One might query whether a village elder in the closing years of his life would enter a monastery with *nibbāna* unassociated with *sagga/svarga*, "heaven," as his goal.

> same time, it is the term which makes it true to say that Buddhism *IS* a religion—not merely an ethic or a philosophy.[192]

At this point, Slater provided a footnote: "For this reason, *Nibbāna* rather than *Dhamma* is the consummating, central term of Buddhism —though much depends on the connotation assigned to *Dhamma*."[193]

Slater reminded his readers, "It [*Nibbāna*] is a religious aspiration —so definite that we have ventured to describe it as the religious ultimate of Southern Buddhism, in preference to *Dhamma*, and also to *Buddha*, who is indeed venerated, but is not regarded as divine: he is the Pathfinder but not the Goal."[194]

Winston L. King spoke of a relation between *dhamma* and *nibbāna* that, when taken together with *kamma* (Skt. *karma*) and the Buddha, provided what he called a "reality-complex or reality-structure."[195] He chose these four notions in order to determine "if, and in what way, they work together to provide a God-substitute or fulfill a God-function in [Theravāda] Buddhism."[196] About *dhamma*, King mentioned,

---

[192] *Ibid.*, p. 63. As a dramatist might note this particular passage quoted at the above place in this study as a "plant," a "pointer" here should be noted. One of the standard definitions of *dhamma* given by Buddhists is *dhāretiti dhammo*, *dhamma* in the sense that it supports.

[193] *Ibid.*, n. 76, p. 63. Slater seemed a bit restless on this matter, perhaps less so about the idea of *nibbāna* as the "consummating" term and more so about its being the "central term."

[194] *Ibid.*, p. 114.

[195] See Winston L. King, *Buddhism and Christianity; Some Bridges of Understanding* (London: George Allen and Unwin Ltd., 1963), p. 38. King was probing to find in Theravāda Buddhist doctrine that which led him to sense an inadequacy in the use of "atheism" to describe that doctrine.

[196] *Ibid.* King's title for this book demonstrates a difficulty engendered by conceptualizing "Buddhism" and "Christianity" as, in some manner, clearly differentiated entities. The use of the term "Bridges" makes this observation patent. That difficulty might be present should one infer from an assumption that there is an abyss between one doctrinal system and another that there is likewise an abyss between a man who is Buddhist and a man who is Christian. It is precisely our shared humanity that fills the gap, so to speak. King's proposal that the four concepts represented a "God-substitute," Slater considered plausible. See H. D. Lewis and Robert Slater, *The Study of Religions: Meeting Points and Major Issues* (Penguin Books Ltd., 1969 [first published as *World Religions*, 1966]), p. 75.

> Most narrowly interpreted, it means simply the teaching (law, norm, truth) of the Buddha. And there is something herein of the sheerly dogmatic Southern Buddhist assurance of the absolute truth of that teaching, that it is the account of all things, 'as they are,' which has been infallibly transmitted in the scriptures. But at its widest it also reaches out to include cosmic order.[197]

King suggested that of the four notions, *nibbāna* "in every way, is the most important of them all."[198] He mentioned, "In Nirvana is to be found the *essence* of the God-function of the fourfold reality-complex in Buddhism."[199] He noted what he termed "the Buddha's exemplification of nirvanic qualities in his life (comparable to the interpretation of Christ as God's son in the flesh or the incarnation of the Eternal Logos)."[200] For King, the fact that *nibbāna* exists enables one to have hope. *Nibbāna*, he said, "is a 'gift of grace,' for there *might* have been a world without Nirvana, hence a world without the hope of salvation."[201] King, it seems, in another work[202] mitigated the force of his comments about *nibbāna* in the concluding paragraph of his *Buddhism and Christianity*. Speaking of the Buddha as "Revealer of Truth," King wrote, *Without the teaching of a Buddha,*[203] *sentient beings can never come to the knowledge, let alone the attainment, of Nibbana.*"[204]

The opinions of Slater and King regarding *nibbāna* as the "central term of Buddhism" and "*essence* of the God-function of the fourfold reality-complex" have been challenged by Wilfred Cantwell Smith who wrote,

> though Nirvana was a distant reality, indescribable, not profitable

---

[197] *Ibid.*, pp. 38–39. [198] *Ibid.*, p. 45. [199] *Ibid.*, p. 57.

[200] *Ibid.*, p. 58. King immediately continued, "Yet one cannot exactly say that the Buddha was Nirvana-become-flesh. . . ." *Ibid.*

[201] *Ibid.*, p. 227.

[202] Winston L. King, *A Thousand Lives Away: Buddhism in Contemporary Burma* (Oxford: Bruno Cassirer, 1964).

[203] In Pāli, *dhamma.*

[204] King, *A Thousand Lives Away*, p. 171. See also, Smith, "Religious Atheism?" p. 13, where it is mentioned that *nibbāna* (*nirvāṇa*) is validated by the moral law.

of discussion, yet the Buddha saw and preached another absolute reality immediately available to every man. This is the moral law. To speak linguistically: while other scholars have argued that Nirvana is in some ways an equivalent or overlapping term to 'God', I would like to argue that Dharma is so also, and in fact first.[205]

Some Western scholars, beginning with Rosenberg, have used the term "*dharma*-theory"[206] more or less as a technical term to designate the aspect of Buddhist thought that became formally structured and classified in *Abhidharma*/*Abhidhamma* literature. There was considerable debate in the Occident about whether or not the Buddha taught such a doctrine.[207] H. von Glasenapp, in a study of the "*dharma*-theory" in the *Suttapiṭaka* noted that throughout this collection of the canon was a presupposition of a "*dharma*-theory" that played a role in conceptualizing a salvation process. That the "theory" is to be found so permeatingly therein makes it most

---

[205] W. C. Smith, "Religious Atheism?", p. 10. One might suggest that there are not two absolute realities but one, having a dimension that is immediately available and one that, for some people, might be more distant.

[206] See Rosenberg, *op. cit.*, pp. 78–79, 85. Th. Stcherbatsky, *Central Conception*, p. 49. Th. Stcherbatsky, "The 'Dharmas' of the Buddhists and the 'Guṇas' of the Saṃkhyas," p. 740. H. von Glasenapp, "Zur Geschichte der buddhistischen Dharma-Theorie," *ZDMG.*, Neue Folge Band 17 (1938), pp. 383–420. H. von Glasenapp, "Der Ursprung der buddhistischen Dharma-Theorie," *Wiener Zeitschrift für die Kunde des Morgenlandes*, XLVI Band, 1. und 2. Heft, (Wien, 1939), pp. 242–266. E. Conze continued the terminology. See his *Buddhist Thought in India* pp. 92, 96.

[207] A. Berriedale Keith, "The Doctrine of the Buddha," *Bulletin of the School of Oriental Studies*, Vol. VI, Part 2 (1931), p. 401, considered the classification of *dhammas* as a later development and not taught by the Buddha. This view was rigorously attacked by Th. Stcherbatsky, "The Doctrine of the Buddha," *Bulletin of the School of Oriental Studies*, Vol. VI, Part 4 (1932), pp. 867–896; especially pp. 886 ff. Keith continued to assert his earlier position. See A. B. Keith, "Pre-Canonical Buddhism," *The Indian Historical Quarterly*, Vol. XII, No. 1 (1936), pp. 1–20. Others had expressed a reluctance to accept the classification of *dharmas* as the teaching of the Buddha. See Stanislav Schayer, "Precanonical Buddhism," *Archiv Orientální*, Journal of the Czechoslovak Oriental Institute, Prague, Vol. VII (1935), pp. 121–132. Jean Przylusky suggested speculation about *dharmas* was later and of interest to an elite. See "Origin and Development of Buddhism," *The Journal of Theological Studies* (October, 1934), pp. 346–347.

probable that the Buddha taught it.[208]

To engage in a thorough discussion of the role of *dhammas* in Buddhist thought would be tangential to the course of this study.[209] A few general remarks might be sufficient to demonstrate that Western academics have been aware of a dimension of *dhamma* that pertained to *dhammas* and have sought to understand the use of one term to cover such an apparently wide spectrum of meaning. R. Otto Franke's proposal[210] was somewhat idealistic and stressed primarily a subjective, in the sense of Pāli *ajjhattika*, interpretation. H. Beckh noted that in Buddhist thought reality was seen not in substance but in the mental coherence of non-empirical phenomena—the *dhammas*.[211] Oldenberg mentioned that an order was to be discerned in the world of existence. Phenomena follow an established law that is denoted by the notion of flowing streams, that is *dhammā*, "Ordnungen." These unstable *dhammas*, being formed in dependence on other *dhammas*, stand under *paṭiccasamuppāda*, also called *dhamma*.[212]

---

[208] H. von Glasenapp, *ZDMG* (1938), pp. 416–417. Glasenapp was aware that the *Abhidharma* classifications represent an attempt to structure more precisely what was already present in the *Suttapiṭaka*.

[209] It would unduly prolong this study to entertain the various suggestions proffered by Western scholars about what *dhammas* represent. It is suggestive, at least, to note that there has probably been as wide a divergence on this matter among Occidentals as among the early Buddhist schools.

[210] "*Dhamma* (*dharma*) bedeutet auch 'Naturgesetz', 'Recht' und 'Lehre' (Buddha's), eben auch vom Grundgedanken 'das tragende, wesentliche Grundprinzip' aus, und selbst die Bedeutung 'empirisches Ding' und 'Sinnenerfahrung' ist damit zu vereinen, weil es sich da richtiger um unsere Begriffe handelt und weil auch Begriffe 'Normen' sind." *Dīghanikāya, Das Buch der langen Texte des buddhistischen Kanons,* übersetzt von R. Otto Franke (Gottingen: Vandenhoeck & Ruprecht, 1913), n. 3, p. 275.

[211] "Nicht in dem, was wir die 'Materie' nennen, sondern in den geistigen Zusammenhängen eines übersinnlichen Geschehens, den sog. 'Gesetzmässigkeiten' (*dhamma*), liegt für den Buddhismus das Reale." Hermann Beckh, *Buddhismus* (II, zweite Auflage; Berlin: Sammlung Göschen, 1920), II, 119.

[212] "Jede Bewegung jeder Welle im Meer des Geschehens gehorcht festem Gesetz. Auf ein solches Gesetz weist schon die Bezeichnung der einherfliessenden Ströme als Dhammā 'Ordnungen' hin. Ebenso, wenn man vom 'Unbeständigen, Gestalteten, in Abhängigkeit (von etwas anderm) Entstandenen' spricht: dem 'Unbeständigen' ist es also wesentlich, in solcher 'Abhängigkeit', wir würden sagen unter dem Kausalitätsgesetz zu stehen."

Professor and Mrs. Geiger sought to explain what appeared to them to be the major philological problem in their consideration of the term *dhamma*; namely, the development of meaning in the term *dhamma* to include "Ding, Sache."[213] Suggesting that when *dhamma* means "Ding" or "Dinge" it usually occurs in the plural; mentioning that so used, they, namely *dhammas*, come to represent the world of phenomena truly grasped by *manas*; the Geigers proposed,

> In diesen Dingen order 'Normen' offenbart sich aber eben der *dh.*, [*dhamma*] d.h. das Natur- und Weltgesetz von dem ewigen Werden und Vergehen, von der Flüchtigkeit und Nichtigkeit alles Seins. Sie sind die dem Beobachter sich bietenden Manifestationen dieses Gesetz [*paṭiccasamuppāda*], das Gesetz in seiner erkennbaren Vielheit und Vielgestaltigheit.[214]

O. Rosenberg stressed another point of view in determining the meaning of *dhamma* in the plural. He mentioned,

> Die grundlegende und wahrscheinlich auch die ursprüngliche Bedeutung des Terminus finden wir in philosophischen Werken und den sūtra, wo man unter dharma 'die Träger' versteht, oder die wahrhaftrealen, unerkennbaren Substrate der Elemente, in welche der Strom bewussten Lebens, d.h. das Subjekt und die von ihm erlebt äussere und innere Welt, in der Abstraktion zerlegt wird.[215]

Oldenberg, *Die Lehre der Upanishaden und die Anfänge des Buddhismus*, p. 300. See also his *Buddha*, n. 1, p. 265 (*Eng. tr.*, note, p. 250.) Oldenberg, in *Buddha*, p. 237 (*Eng. tr.*, pp. 231–232), referred to *dhammā* that stand in relation to *manas* as visible objects stand in relation to the eye.

[213] *PD.*, p. 8.

[214] *Ibid.*, pp. 8–9. The references to the opinions expressed by Franke, Beckh, and Oldenberg, in *LUAB*, were first noted briefly by Professor and and Mrs. Geiger in *PD.*, p. 8. A. B. Keith apparently following the Geigers' representation of these opinions rather closely passed off Franke's suggestion as "quite impossible to accept," discarded Beckh's opinion as "equally impossible" and sided with Oldenberg and the Geigers. He seems to have thought that the interpretation proffered by the Geigers was "too deliberately metaphysical a conception." *Buddhist Philosophy in India and Ceylon*, p. 73. Keith suggested *dhamma* as meaning the "fundamental or regular nature of a thing" looked more plausible as the source for the transition through which *dhamma* comes to mean "thing." *Ibid.*, pp. 73–74.

[215] Rosenberg, *op. cit.*, pp. 80–81. Rosenberg later on gave what might be taken as his formal definition: "*dharma heissen die wahrhaft-realen, trans-*

Stcherbatsky, following Rosenberg, argued that *dhammas* are not "things." They represent, he suggested, the negation of substance.[216]

One further dimension of *dhamma* about which Westerners have expresed opinions is *dhamma* as one of the three jewels (*tiratana*) or three refuges (*tisaraṇa*). Oldenberg remarked that the earliest form of a refuge statement was related to the Buddha and to the doctrine that he preached.[217] He argued that the *Saṅgha* would not have become one of the three refuges as long as the Buddha lived. "Sein Tod," Oldenberg stressed, "änderte Alles."[218] Further, the German scholar suggested,

---

zendenten, unerkennbaren Träger oder Substrate derjenigen Elemente, in welche der Bewusstseinsstrom mit seinem Inhalt zerlegt wird." *Ibid.*, p. 101. One might recognize in the opinions of Rosenberg, quoted above in the text, as well as his definition recorded in this note, aspects of the theories proposed by Franke, Beckh, Oldenberg and the Geigers. Rosenberg's contribution lay in his discerning the notion of "bearing," "supporting" as it pertains to *dhammas* (Skt. *dharmas*). Helena Willman-Grabowska, in her article, "Evolution sémantique du mot 'dharma'," subsequently noted that throughout the history of the *term*, these notions were present in its usage. H. von Glasenapp, "Zur Geschichte der buddhistischen Dharma-Theorie," *ZDMG.*, Neue Folge Band 17 (1938), p. 385, thought Rosenberg, unlike Oldenberg and the Geigers, failed to recognize the relationship between *dhamma* as the law (Gesetz) of all that is as well as all (*dhammas*) that participate in it. See also Glasenapp, "Der Ursprung der buddhistischen Dharma-Theorie." *WZKM*, XLVI Band, 1 (1939), pp. 253, 264.

216 See Stcherbatsky, "The 'Dharmas' of the Buddhists and the 'Guṇas' of the Saṃkhyas," p. 746.

217 Oldenberg, *Buddha*, pp. 345–346 (*Eng. tr.*, pp. 338–339). See also *Buddha*, p. 121 (*Eng. tr.*, p. 119), where Oldenberg noted Tapussa and Bhallika, the two merchants, who took refuge in the Buddha (*bhagavan*) and *dhamma*. Oldenberg suggested that the order of *bhikkhus* and *bhikkhunis* could not have continued had there not been a laity having faith in the Buddha and his teaching ("und Buddha's Wort," *buddhavācanam* [?]—probably, Oldenberg had in mind *dhamma*). *Buddha*, p. 390 (*Eng. tr.*, p. 382). T. W. Rhys Davids, in *Buddhism: Being a Sketch*, pp. 151–152, wrote, "It was his Society rather than his Doctrine—the Sangha rather than the Dharma, which first insured for his religion its great vitality and its rapid spread, and which afterwards excited the hostility of the Brahmans." One should note the perceptive remark of Mrs. Rhys Davids. "In the institution of an organized Fraternity and a loyal Laity—the Order giving, the Laity giving also, but believing it received yet more than it gave—the slow evolution of solidarity took the best shape practicable at the time." *Buddhism*, p. 50.

218 Oldenberg, *Buddha*, p. 346 (*Eng. tr.*, p. 338).

> Jetzt stand die Gemeinde als die einzige sichtbare Trägerin der vordem in Buddha verkörperten Idee da, als die einzige Besitzerin der elösenden Wahrheit; jetzt musste, wer dieser Wahrheit theilhaftig werden wollte, auch bei der Gemeinde seine Zuflucht nehmen.[219]

Generally, occidental scholars have taken *dhamma* in the three refuge statement to mean "Law,"[220] "'Law' or the Teaching,"[221] "the 'Doctrine,' the 'Word,' the Wisdom or Truth."[222] Some have noted that *dhamma* in this formula means the preaching of the Buddha now contained in the scriptures.[223] Rosenberg mentioned that, according to the *Abhidharmakośa*, *dhamma* (Skt. *dharma*), as that in which refuge is taken, is frequently not the teaching itself but the object of the teaching; namely, *nirvāṇa*.[224]

Within somewhat more than a century, Western academics have written a considerable number of paragraphs about *dhamma*. With each new opinion further speculation has arisen and in the process Western scholars have come to note that *dhamma* means considerably more than "la Loi." Several authors have noted the importance of *dhamma* in Buddhist thought whether they considered it philologically (linguistically, semantically) or philosophically or psychologically or

[219] *Ibid.* (*Eng.*, *tr.*, pp. 338–339). The implication of Oldenberg's comment is somewhat unclear. It is probable that "Idee," "erlösenden Wahrheit" and "Wahrheit" reflected in his mind the notion *dhamma*.

[220] See Burnouf, *op. cit.*, n. 2, p. 80.

[221] Slater, *op. cit.*, p. 132.

[222] *PTSD.*, p. 337b. *PD.*, p. 58, "die Lehre." T. O. Ling, "*Dhamma* (Pāli); *Dharma* (Skt.)—*Buddh.*," in *A Dictionary of Comparative Religion*, S. G. F. Brandon, General Editor (London: Weidenfeld & Nicolson, 1970), p. 235, noted, "In this usage, D. means the universal truth proclaimed by Buddha."

[223] Clough, *SED.* (*s.v. dharmaratnaya*), p. 269a. Hardy, *op. cit.*, pp. 166–167. Mrs. Rhys Davids, *Buddhism*, p. 235. A. B. Keith, *Buddhist Philosophy in India and Ceylon*, p. 133. See also Rosenberg, *op. cit.*, p. 82.

[224] Rosenberg, *op. cit.*, p. 82. E. Conze, *Buddhist Thought in India*, pp. 92–93, stated without further ado, "And it is in Nirvana that someone takes refuge when he takes refuge in the Dharma." His reference was to *AK.* iv. 78. See *L'Abhidharmakośa de Vasubandhu*, traduit et annoté par Louis de La Vallée Poussin, quatrième chapitre (Paris: Paul Geuthner, 1924), p. 78. La Vallée Poussin translates the passage, "Celui qui prend refuge dans le Nirvāṇa, c'est-à-dire dans le *pratisaṃkhyānirodha*."

doctrinally. From whatever starting point these scholars have begun, they have been aware that the notion of *dhamma* is profound, hard to grasp—to use adjectives over two millenia old—and that in every case, *dhamma* has to do in some way with a Buddhist's religious orientation to the world in which we find ourselves.

Western scholars have left us with an abundance of materials dealing with the notion of *dhamma*; lexical aids are at hand and interpretations, translations abound. The Geigers, in *PD*, provided more than fifty German words as translation for *dhamma*; T. W. Rhys Davids and William Stede, in *PTSD*, offered over fifty English terms. A reader of this study will have met, at this stage, approximately the same number proposed by more than twenty leading Western scholars of the Buddhist tradition in India and the Theravāda. Some of these scholars have worked with methods not entirely persuasive but have shared results that are remarkably suggestive.

Patterns have been discerned, primarily philologically; from true teaching, a truth, to the truth, from a causal patterned process to a manifestation or manifestations (*dhammā*, plural) of that patterned process (*paṭiccasamuppāda*). But one is more or less at a loss to discern in all these interpretations an integrating theme that the concept *dhamma* conveys, which allows simultaneously for levels of meaning of the term and soteriological continuity in and through life, for broad comprehensiveness devoid of theoretical, speculative patchwork; a theme that is central to the full spectrum of Theravāda Buddhist thought, riveting that spectrum with relevance for living life, supportive of efforts to live life well, providing quiet assurance that one is engaged in a soteriological process.

We make a move, now, to search afresh for that which provides coherence in the entire system of Theravāda thought, for that which also provides soteriological continuity from this life to that which transcends, for *dhamma* as Theravāda Buddhists have understood it and have remembered it.

CHAPTER II

DHAMMA IN THE PĀLI *SUTTAS* AND COMMENTARIES

We are told that about two millennia ago near Mātalē, Sri Lanka, the three *piṭakas*, and a commentary—perhaps the now extinct Sinhalese *Mahā-aṭṭhakathā*—on those canonical divisions, previously handed down orally were put into written form in order that *dhamma* might endure.[1] It appears plausible that the scriptures accepted as canonical by Sinhalese Theravāda Buddhists today represent what was written approximately five centuries after the Buddha's *parinibbāna*. To some extent this entire study represents a minor repercussion of that decision to write what previously had been spoken. I intend to circumvent a labyrinth of hypotheses and uncertainties that would, in the state of present scholarship, inevitably confront

[1] *Mhv.*, c. 33, vss. 100–111. *The Chronicle of the Island of Ceylon or the Dīpavaṃsa: A Historical Poem of the Fourth Century A. D.*, ed., Bimala Churn Law, *The Ceylon Historical Journal*, Vol. VII (July 1957 to April 1958, published as a monograph in 1959), c. 20, vss. 20–21. The writing of the three *piṭakas* and the *aṭṭhakathās* is said to have occurred during the reign of Vaṭṭagamaṇi in the last half-century B.C. See *Cūlavaṃsa: Being the More Recent Part of the Mahāvaṃsa*, Part II, trans. Wilhelm Geiger (Colombo: Ceylon Government Information Department, 1953), p. ix. See also Geiger, *Culture of Ceylon in Mediaeval Times*, p. 68. A leading Sinhalese Buddhist scholar writes, "The event decided the future not only of the Theravāda School of Buddhism but also the whole field of Pāli Literature." E. W. Adikaram, *Early History of Buddhism in Ceylon* (Colombo: M. D. Gunasena & Co., Ltd., 1953 [First Impression, 1946]), p. 79. See also G. P. Malalasekera, *The Pāli Literature of Ceylon* (Colombo: M. D. Gunasena & Co., Ltd., 1958 [First published, 1928]), p. 43. See as well Bimala Churn Law, *A History of Pāli Literature* (London: Kegan Paul, Trench, Trübner & Co., Ltd., 1933), Vol. I, pp. 26–27. It is probable that this event at Mātalē does not represent the first attempt by Buddhists to write that which had been heard. See E. Frauwallner, *The Earliest Vinaya and the Beginnings of Buddhist Literature* ("Serie Orientale Roma"; 1956), VIII, especially pp. 153–154.

the reader should an investigation of the scriptures be pursued in order to ascertain the earliest form and date of the *suttas* that comprise the Pāli canon.[2] Rather, I will attempt to trace a theme that is the basis for the Pāli canon, its content as well as its *raison d' être—dhamma.*

Attempts to understand *dhamma* did not originate in the West. By the time Western inquirers appeared on the scene, Buddhists had been probing the import of *dhamma* for centuries. The task at hand is to turn again to the Pāli *suttas* in an attempt to discern the way *dhamma* made a difference religiously for men and women who became Buddhists, who decided that they would live according to *dhamma.*

Although the primary source in this phase of the study is the *Sutta-piṭaka* of the Pāli canon, material from the Pāli commentaries on this portion of the *suttas* needs also to be included for the following three

---

[2] I leave it to others to go into what some have called "Precanonical Buddhism." Attempts have been made to establish a chronological spectrum into which one might peg certain portions of the scriptures. See B. C. Law, *A History of Pāli Literature*, Vol. I, pp. 1–24. Linguistic inquiries, in some cases, might be helpful in establishing the relative antiquity of strata in the Pāli canon. Heinz Bechert has drawn attention to a possible influence of Sinhalese on Pāli that might explain certain word forms that had, perhaps, previously suggested a relatively early date for passages under consideration. See "Über Singhalesisches im Pālikanon," *Wiener Zeitschrift für die Kunde Süd—und Ostasiens*, herausgegeben von E. Frauwallner (Das indologische Institut der Universität Wien, 1957), Band I, pp. 71–75. Other criteria such as style, in some cases meter, doctrinal statements and, to some extent, social conditions might form a method of analysis. More reliable but by no means certain, a relative date for some passages might be ascertained externally by finding the passages under consideration to be quoted or mentioned elsewhere. A leading Sinhalese Buddhist scholar has studied the *Sutta-nipāta* in the light of critical methods. See N. A. Jayawickrama, "The Sutta Nipāta: Its Title and Form," *University of Ceylon Review*, Vol. VI, No. 2 (April, 1948), pp. 78–86. This article is an extract from the author's "A Critical Analysis of Pali Sutta Nipāta, Illustrating Its Gradual Growth" (London University Ph. D. Thesis, 1947). Further extracts appeared in subsequent issues of the *UCR*. For references where the *SnA*. notes passages in *Sn*. as being added by reciters at one of the councils, see Jayawickrama, *UCR*, VI, No. 2 (April, 1948), 83. One should add to Jayawickrama's list *KhpA*. I. 165 and *SnA*. II. 477 where there is mentioned an uncertainty about whether or not two verses are to be considered as comprising the original *sutta*.

reasons: firstly, the Sinhalese Theravāda Buddhist tradition has taken the interpretations provided by the commentarial tradition quite seriously; secondly, the commentaries have provided a long established and mutually endorsed means by which Sinhalese Buddhists have tried to understand the teaching of the Buddha as it has been handed down, to grasp the intention of the Buddha and in process to move nearer, ideally, to the *bodhi* tree in their increasing awareness of *dhamma* that he rediscovered; and thirdly, because Western scholars, in an apparently concerted effort to get at the origin of the Buddhist tradition, to what an idea was to have meant originally, have tended to "leap frog" nearly two-thousand years of a religious tradition and to by-pass commentarial discussions about the occurrence of *dhamma* in the Pāli canon.

In discussing Sinhalese Buddhists' perspectives on *dhamma* as seen through the Pāli sources, the initial consideration will be of commentarial definitions of the term. Having dispensed with that, we will move on in an attempt to grasp the manner in which *dhamma* provided a theme in terms of which the unfolding and continuation of the Buddhist movement can be understood. In this regard *dhamma* will first be considered in terms of the noble quest of the *Bodhisatta*, the future Buddha. Following this, the setting in motion of the *dhammacakka* will be considered and subsequently, passages that depict the Buddha's reverence for *dhamma* and the preaching of *dhamma* by all Buddhas. From this discussion of the Buddha and his quest for, attainment of, and preaching about *dhamma* that he revered, attention will be turned to the purpose for which *dhamma* was taught and the participation on the part of the hearers as they heard and penetrated *dhamma*. Lastly, some consideration will be given to the manner in which faith was involved in an orientation to *dhamma* and to life by persons.

Commentarial Definitions of Dhamma

In providing traditional definitions of *dhamma*,[3] the commentarial sources follow a procedure of citing canonical passages that serve as examples and source of authority. Western scholars have been aware of the definitions provided in the commentary on the *Dīgha-nikāya*, in the *Atthasālinī*, and in the commentary on the *Dhammapada*, but there remain others; one, the commentary on the *Majjhima-nikāya*, provides the most comprehensive list.

From the *Sumaṅgala-vilāsinī* (*DA*. I. 99), the commentary on the *Dīgha-nikāya* (*D*. I. 12), one notes,

> The word *dhamma* occurs with regard to *guṇa*, *desanā*, *pariyatti*, *nissatta*, etc.

and the following examples:

guṇa, "quality, in the sense of virtuous, moral quality,"
"'By no means are *dhamma* and *adhamma* of equal recompense. *Adhamma* leads to hell; *dhamma* causes the attainment of a good bourne.'"[4]

desanā, "teaching"
"'O bhikkhus, I will teach you *dhamma*, which is admirable in its beginning' etc."

pariyatti, "authoritative teaching, texts"
"'Now then, a *bhikkhu* masters *dhamma*, that is, *sutta* [the discourses viewed as having been heard from the mouth of the Buddha and passed down orally], *geyya* [sections to be chanted],' etc."

---

[3] I have noted the commentarial definitions of *dhamma*, including Sinhalese materials in "Traditional definitions of the term *dhamma*," *Philosophy East and West*, 26, no. 3, (July 1976), pp. 329–337.

[4] *Thag*. vs. 304. *ThagA*. II. 128 on this verse renders *dhamma* as "*dhamma* that is good conduct, that is characterized as pertaining to this world and as transcending this world"—"Tattha *dhammo* ti, lokiya-lokuttaro sucarita-dhammo." *Loka* taken as "this world" might be misleading to English readers. It means "this world" but also includes other realms of existence in the whirl of *saṃsāra*. The force of the compound *lokiyalokuttara* in this *gāthā* is, I think, caught in the English translation.

nissatta, "that without a living being"
"'In this connection there are *dhammas*, there are aggregates [*khandhas*],' etc."

In the *Atthasālinī* (*DhsA*., p. 38), a commentary on the *Dhamma-saṅgaṇī* (*Dhs*), *hetu*, "cause," appears in the list of definitions and added is the term *nijjīvatā*, "lifelessness," to *nissatta*, forming *nissatta-nijjīvatā*, "that without a living being—lifelessness." For the writer of the *Atthasālinī*, *dhamma* is said to mean *hetu* in such passages as "analysis of *dhamma* is knowledge with regard to cause [*hetu*]."

The third commentary previously noted, the *Dhammapadaṭṭha-kathā*, the commentary on the *Dhammapada*, follows the list in the *Sumaṅgalavilāsiṇi* (*DA*. I. 99) and uses *nijjīva*, "lifeless" as a synonym for *nissatta*.[5]

In the *Papañcasūdanī* (*MA*.), the commentary on the *Majjhima-nikāya*, one meets a more comprehensive definition of *dhamma* than that noted in the commentarial sources by the Geigers and the *PTSD*.

> "Now this word *dhamma* appears as authoritative teaching [*pariyatti*], truth(s) [*sacca*], rapt concentration [*samādhi*], wisdom [*paññā*], natural condition [*pakati*], inherent nature [*sabhāva*], voidness [*suññatā*], merit [*puñña*], *vinaya* violation, that is, an offense committed within the *sangha* [*āpatti*], that to be known [*ñeyya*] and so forth [*ādi*]."[6]

The *Papañcasūdanī* (*MA*.), in keeping with an established procedure provides quotations from the canon to illustrate particular interpretations of *dhamma*. For those meanings not presented in the three commentaries previously noted, the *Papañcasūdanī* provides the following:

---

[5] *DhA*. I. (1). 18 (on *Dhp*. vs. 1). An old Sinhalese glossary on *DhA*., the *Dahampiyā Aṭuva Gätapadaya* (*DAG*), p. 15, in elaborating the *DhpA*. presentation regarding *nissatta*, *nijjīva* says, "'There are *dhammas*' means there are only *dhammas* because they are void in nature of self and that belonging to a self"—"Dhammā honti, ātmātmiya bhāvayen śūnya bävin dhamhu matuveti."

[6] Carter, "Traditional definitions of the term *dhamma*," *op. cit*., p. 331; *MA*. I. 17 (on M. I. 1).

saccāni, "truths"
"*diṭṭhadhammo, viditadhammo*," "one who has seen *dhamma*, who has known *dhamma*."

samādhi, "rapt contemplation"
"They [the *Bhagavans*] were of such names, such lineages, such morals [*evaṃ-sīlā*], such *dhammas* [*evaṃ-dhammā*], such wisdom [*evaṃ-paññā*]. . . ."[7]

At first blush one might think this attempt, in the canonical literature, to interpret *dhamma* as *samādhi* in the well-established and familiar triad of *sīla* (moral precepts, virtue), *samādhi* (rapt concentration), and *paññā* (wisdom) is forced, hardly consistent with the tradition. However, there are examples in the canonical literature, known in the commentarial tradition, where *sīla* and *paññā* are joined with both the singular and plural forms of *dhamma*,[8] and the commentarial tradition appears both cognizant of and consistent on this point.[9]

paññā, "wisdom"
For whom there are these four *dhammas*,
O Lord of monkeys, as in your case,
Truth, *dhamma* [i.e., *paññā*, "wisdom"], courage, liberality
He overcomes the visible [world]."[10]

---

[7] *Ibid.*, *MA.* I. 17 is quoting *D.* II. 8, 54.

[8] See, for example, *M.* I. 38, 465; *M.* III. 118; *D.* II. 8, 54, 81, 82; *S.* III. 209.

[9] See, for example, *MA.* I. 174; *MA.* III. 182; *MA.* IV. 167–168; *DA.* II. 426; *SA.* III. 209; *Pm.* 10. An elaboration is provided at *MA.* IV. 167–168; "*Evaṃ-dhammā* is understood here [i.e., *M.* III. 118. 18] as *dhammas* that are constituent parts of *samādhi*. The meaning is 'One is characterized as a *samādhin* by *samādhi* with regard to this world and that which transcends this world.'" Conceivably, *dhamma*/*samādhi* appears in this grouping to suggest an integrative coherence between *sīla* and *paññā*. *DA.* II. 426 gives an echo of a standard definition of *dhamma* having to do with the paths and fruits (to be discussed later) by extending an elaboration; "*Evaṃ-dhammā* is understood here [i.e., *D.* II. 8] as *dhammas* that are constituent parts of *samādhi*. The meaning is 'One is characterized as a *samādhin* by *samādhi* with regard to the paths and fruits, by *samādhi* with regard to this world and that which transcends this world.'" *SA.* III. 209 follows verbatim. These references have been noted in Carter, "Traditional definitions. . . ." *op. cit.*, p. 336, note 16.

[10] *MA.* I. 17. The quote is from *Jā.* I. 280.

Yass' ete caturo dhammā vānarinda yathā tava
Saccaṃ dhammo dhiti cāgo diṭṭhaṃ so ativattatī ti.

pakati, "natural condition, natural state"
jātidhamma, "that having as *dhamma* [i.e., *pakati*, "natural condition"] birth."

The *Papañcasūdanī* (*MA*.I.17) is here quoting *M*.I.161–162, but turning in this same commentary (*MA*.II.170) to the interpretation of that canonical passage, one notes, "*jātidhammo ti jāyana-sabhāvo*," "that having as *dhamma* birth means that having as inherent nature arising." Apparently, subtle distinctions between *pakati* ("natural condition, natural state," Sanskrit *prakṛti*) and *sabhāva* ("inherent nature," Sanskrit *svabhāva*) are subsumed in the use of *dhamma* as the second member of a *bahubbīhi* compound. This becomes evident upon consulting a passage in the *Sārattha-ppakāsinī* (*SA*.) where both *pakati* and *sabhāva* are utilized in the commentarial gloss.[11]

sabhāva, "inherent nature"
As in such places where *kusalā dhammā*, "wholesome dhammas," appears.

suññatā, "voidness"
"'Now in this case there are *dhammas*'"[12]

Jā.I.280 glosses *caturo dhammā* with *cattāro guṇā*. *Guṇa* is not in the list noted in *MA*.I.17, although it does occur as a definition in *DA*.I.99, *DhsA*. 48, and *DhpA*.I.(i).18. *JāA*.I.280 glosses *dhamma* with "investigative wisdom" (*vicāraṇapaññā*). *CpA*.230 comments on this *gāthā* and follows *JaA*.I.280 verbatim. In both cases, *saccam*, "truth," is understood as "truth speaking." This *gāthā* is quoted in the Sinhalese text *Pūjāvaliya*, p. 85. A glossary on this text, *Pūjāvali gäṭapada vivaraṇaya*, p. 22, glosses *dhammo*, "investigation and intelligence." In the Pāli commentaries, *dhamma* is elsewhere glossed by *paññā*. See *AA*.IV.4. *ItvA*.I.151 renders *dhamma-mayam* at *Itv*., p. 38, as *paññāmayaṃ*.

[11] *SA*.I.159 (on *S*.I.88): "*Jāti-dhammā* ti, jāti-sabhāva jāti-pakaṭika."

[12] This is a very suggestive gloss, one a thorough, sustained investigation of which would take us too far afield. It appears that the import of the gloss is a recognition that a statement "there are *dhammas*" does not represent a bare ontological assertion but, rather, a delicate demonstration that *dhammas*, when understood, not only bear (from the root *dhṛ*/*dharma*, *dhamma*) their own characteristics but are themselves empty (*suñña*) of inherent nature, or "own-being" (*sabhāva*). This remains inconclusive, however, since we have noted no hesitation, in the commentarial tradition, to use the term *sabhāva*.

puñña, "merit, meritorious behavior"
"'*Dhamma* well lived brings ease.'"[13]

āpatti, "*vinaya* violation or an offense committed within the *saṅgha*"
"'Two undetermined *dhammas*'"[14]

ñeyya, "that to be known"
"'All *dhammas* come into focus by every means in the face of the knowledge of the Buddha, the *Bhagavan*.'"[15]

In keeping with this gloss, one would have reason to translate *dhammā* (in the plural form) as "knowables."

The *Madhuratthavilāsinī* (*BuA.*), the commentary on the *Buddhavaṃsa* (*Bu.*), stands in the wake of the *Papañcasūdanī* (*MA.*) making an elaboration on the interpretation given there of *dhamma* as *saccāni*, "truths;" *catusaccadhamma*, "*dhamma* that pertains to [the] four [noble] truths."[16]

---

[13] See Carter, "Traditional definitions of the term *dhamma*," *op. cit.*, p. 336, note 19. I repeat the information for completeness: *MA.*I.17. This last quote is taken from *Sn.*182. *SnA.*I.232 (on *Sn.* vs. 182) says, "'*Dhamma*' means *dhamma* that is the ten modes of wholesome conduct or *dhamma* that is comprised of giving, morality, and meditation; *well lived* means well done, well practiced; *brings ease* means it brings ease among men as in the cases of Sonaseṭṭhiputta, Raṭṭhapala and others, heavenly ease as in the case of Sakka and others, and in the end, the ease of *nibbāna* as in the case of Mahāpaduma and others. . . ."

[14] *Vin.*III.187 quoted at *MA.*I.17.

[15] *Pṭs.*II.194 quoted at *MA.*I.17. The *Saddhammappakāsinī*, III.647 (on *Pṭs.* II.194) notes, "'All *Dhammas*,' means taking all together all *dhammas* that are conditioned and unconditioned." In *Sn.* vs. 471, regarding one who is "*tathāgata*," the phrase "he knew *dhamma* by highest vision" (*dhammañ ca ñāsi* [alternate reading, *aññāsi*] *paramāya diṭṭhiya*) occurs. *SnA.* II.409 notes, "*Dhammañ ca aññāsī ti sabbañ ca ñeyyadhammaṃ aññāsi; paramāya diṭṭhiyā ti sabbaññutañāṇena*." The Geigers, *PD.*, p. 67, note this *Sn.* passage and prefer the translation "Wahrheit" rather than "Lehre."

[16] *BuA.*13 (on *Bu.*, p. 1). See further *ThagA.*I.55 (on *Thag.* vs. 9) where, in speaking of *dhammas* that are classified or proportioned, the commentary mentions "*dhammas* that are to be known [*ñeyyadhammā*—the commentary notes this compound in the locative plural, °*esu*], or *dhammas* that pertain to tranquility [*samatha-dhammesu*]." The commentary mentions an interesting differentiation between *dhammas* that are classified by several other religious leaders (*nānā-titthiyehi*) as "natural condition, etcetera [*pakati-ādi*]," and those classified by the Fully Enlightened Ones (*sammāsambuddhehi*) as

Summarizing the definitions mentioned in the Pāli commentaries one finds the following:[17]

guṇa "quality, in the sense of virtuous, moral quality," (*DA.*, *DhsA.*, *DhA.*)

desanā "teaching" (*DA.*, *DhA.*)

pariyatti "authoritative teaching, texts" (*DA.*, *DhsA.*, *DhA.*, *MA.*, *BuA.*)

nissatta "that without a living being" (*DA.*, *DhA.*)

nissatta-nijjīvatā "that without a living being—lifelessness" (*DhsA.*)

suññatā "emptiness, voidness" (*MA.*, *BuA.*)

hetu "cause" (*DhsA.*)

"*dukkha* etcetera." The commentary continues to paraphrase *Thag.* vs. 9, "Or, among the *dhammas* that pertain to inherent nature [*sabhāva*], that have been classified according to actuality [*yathā-sabhāvato*] by the Fully Enlightened Ones alone [*eva*] in the sense of wholesome *dhammas* etcetera [*kusalādi*], aggregates etcetera [*khandhādi*], I have reached [*upāgamiṃ*] the *dhamma* comprised of paths, fruits, and *nibbāna* [*taṃ magga-phala-nibbāna-dhammaṃ*], which is the best [*seṭṭham*] highest [*uttamaṃ*], noblest [*pavaraṃ*]."

F. L. Woodward, who edited *ThagA.*, notes variant readings on this passage. Source A, in Sinhalese script, reads *magga-nibbānaṃ-dhamma* while source C, the printed Hewavitarne edition in Sinhalese script, Woodward notes, omits *nibbāna*. The reading of source A is acceptable. By omitting *nibbāna* from the compound, source C would apparently read *magga-phala-dhamma*, which is also acceptable. Perhaps the Theras who edited source C were reluctant to allow the term "*nibbāna*" to be a part of a compound that could be construed syntactically in a locative relation with *kusalā* and *khandhā*. However, I follow Woodward because the entire compound as translated is a more comprehensive interpretation of *dhamma* and occurs throughout the commentarial literature.

[17] This list is a partial listing of traditional definitions drawn from Pāli and Sinhalese sources and previously noted in my "Traditional definitions of the term *dhamma*," *op. cit.*, p. 333. I place in parentheses the commentaries in which the terms are listed and note here the particular references: *DA.* I. 99; *DhsA.*, p. 38; *DhpA.* I. (i). 18; *MA.* I. 17; *BuA.* 13. One should not be misled to think that such a list of definitions makes it easy to determine in just what sense *dhamma* is used in the canon. About 1,500 years ago three interpretations were given for *dhammesu* (locative plural) appearing at one place in the canon. One Thera took it to mean *catusaccadhamma*; another proposed, "the state of an arahant [*arahatta*]"; and a third suggested it referred to the virtuous qualities (*guṇa*) of the Buddha. See *DA.* III. 882–883 (on *D.* III. 102). Often the commentaries will offer several interpretations, all of which would be acceptable, the slight dissociation being noted only by the particle *vā*.

saccāni "truths" (*MA.*)

catusaccadhamma "*dhamma* that pertains to [the] four [noble] truths" (*BuA.*)

samādhi "rapt concentration" (*MA., BuA.*)

paññā "wisdom" (*MA., BuA.*)

pakati "natural condition" (*MA., BuA.*)

sabhāva "inherent nature" (*MA., BuA.*)

puñña "merit, meritorious behavior" (*MA., BuA.*)

āpatti "an offense committed within the *saṅgha* (*MA., BuA.*)

ñeyya "that to be known" (*MA., BuA.*)

ādi "*etcetera* [that is, the scope of meaning of the term is not exhausted by the definitions listed]" (*DA., DhsA., MA., BuA.*)

What inferences about *dhamma* might be drawn from these definitions? One might suggest that because one term, *dhamma*, was used in many different contexts in the canon its usage in this way presupposed a ready understanding of its import by the early hearers. Further, one might suggest, had *dhamma* meant *puñña* (meritorious behavior) in this passage and *paññā* (wisdom) in that, surely the latter two terms could have been used by the Buddha or other spokesmen and with much less apparent ambiguity. These suggestions and the presence of commentarial definitions might lead one to surmise that the commentators did not know the original meaning of the term *dhamma*.

This line of inquiry, though of interest and of value in lexicographical or philological studies of the term, is perhaps inadequate for gaining an understanding of the remarkably significant role *dhamma* has played in the course of the development of the religious cumulative tradition of Theravāda Buddhists. To define a term is, by definition, to limit it. Defining the term *dhamma*—how it is used, what it means—is an interesting undertaking. Discerning a perspective for life—how it is to be lived, what it means—is of far greater import, more momentous, of cosmic consequence. Buddhists have been and are concerned with the meaning of *dhamma* not primarily as a means to facilitate textual translation but as a means to transform life.

For the commentators, Pāli, on the one hand, was not their mother tongue and, on the other hand, it was, at one and the same time, a canonical language and a monastic *lingua franca* analogous with Latin among many in the Christian community for centuries. In this case, Pāli was a second, third or fourth language for Buddhists—conceivably for the first disciples of the Buddha, possibly in several geographical locales during the Buddha's lifetime, probably shortly after his *parinibbāna* and certainly by the time of the third or fourth generation of followers and subsequently. Pāli represents a language studied and held in high regard. To some degree the presence of definitions in the commentaries reflects this development. When definitions are noted, there is an attempt on the part of commentators to be precise and complete because the canon represented the means by which one could learn the intention of the Buddha. It should come as no surprise that the one definition that is common in all the commentaries noted above is *pariyatti*, that which is to be mastered, the authoritative teaching.

The force of *pariyatti* would be missed should one translate it as "text" and even, perhaps, as "scripture." The term seems to have undergone a development in meaning.[18] *Pariyatti* means in some *sutta* passages "accomplishment, competency, that with which one is to familiarize oneself." In the commentaries *pariyatti* is a gloss for *dhamma* when *dhamma* is used to refer to the *suttas* and the like. Substituting *pariyatti* for *dhamma*, the *sutta* passage mentioned at *DA*.I.99 would read, "Now then, a *bhikkhu* masters [*pariyāpuṇāti*] *pariyatti*, that is, *sutta*. . . ." *Pariyatti* refers to something with which one is to familiarize oneself, to learn by heart, to keep in mind.

[18] The feminine noun, *pariyatti*, is derived from $\sqrt{\bar{a}p}$ meaning "to obtain" and the prefix *pari*, having the force of "round about, around." *Pariyatti*, when used with *dhamma*, reflects the mnemonic manner in which *dhamma* was handed down from teacher to pupil.

Moreover, the commentaries reflect an awareness that there is a particular body of teaching that is called *pariyatti*. When *pariyatti* is joined in a compound with *dhamma*, as *pariyattidhamma*, it means *dhamma* that is to be thoroughly learned, memorized, remembered. *Pariyatti*, when used in association with *dhamma*, whether as a gloss or in a compound, refers to the words of the Buddha that are to be learned by heart and, through extension, it is the authoritative teaching.

Another aspect of the term *dhamma* noted by the five commentaries pertains to the fleeting conditionally related patterned processes of the life setting. This setting being pluralistically considered, the term *dhamma*, when designating these processes, is found more often in the plural. In this sense, *dhammas* are viewed as *nissatta*, "without a living being," or *nijjīvatā*, "lifelessness," or *suññatā*, "voidness." This aspect of the term *dhamma* becomes more readily understandable when it is related with the more familiar notion of *anatta*, "that not soul." Though lifeless, without something inside it, so to speak, a *dhamma* is not static; it is a cause, *hetu*. A *dhamma* does not only function causally but also can be known (*ñeyya*) and hence psychic and physical processes are neither random nor chaotic.

Frequently, what a man says is not the most important part of his communication but rather what he assumes, what he takes for granted, the frame of reference that he might consider unnecessary to explicate and in terms of which he takes his own statements seriously. The commentaries noted above do not communicate all the meanings that the word *dhamma* might convey and four of the commentaries note this fact with the term *ādi*, "and so forth, etcetera."

We now turn to an examination of the *Sutta-piṭaka*, of the Pāli canon, and the related Pāli commentaries, to demonstrate how *dhamma* provides an integrative structure for the entire spectrum of Theravāda Buddhist thought. Much of what will be considered does not appear explicitly in the formal list of definitions provided in the commentarial literature; it tends to fall implicitly in the use of *ādi*, "and so forth, etcetera;" providing a thematic structure left unspoken in the commentarial definitions, but well known to the commentators, and because of which there *are* commentaries and there *were* commentators.

The Noble Quest

Where does one begin a study of *dhamma*? The answer to this question—the decision to begin at this time in history rather than that, with one *sutta* rather than another, with any method established in the academic disciplines—would enable the reader to note assumptions that might be decisive for the adequacy of the undertaking. An outsider might begin with Mohenjodaro and Harappa; a Sinhalese Buddhist might remember having begun with what his parents told him about being kind. A Western academic might begin with the life of the Buddha, but one might ask, "Which account of that life?"

One might propose to avoid all this and begin with the Pāli canon. Perhaps one outside the Buddhist community might choose to begin with the last two *vaggas* of the *Sutta-nipāta*, generally agreed to be a portion of a very old stratum of the canon. A Sinhalese Buddhist, on the other hand, might recall having begun with the story of Paṭācārā.[19]

The discussion that follows is a study of *dhamma*, and it will begin with a study of a noble quest undertaken and carried through to completion by the Buddha and held out before Buddhists for centuries as that with which one should become engaged. The *Ariyapariyesanā*

[19] See G. P. Malalasekera, *Dictionary of Pāli Proper Names* (London: Luzac & Co., Ltd., 1960 [reprinted from the work first published in 1938]), II, 112–114. Following the suggestion of Sinhalese academics representing both the *sangha* and the lay strands of the Buddhist community in Sri Lanka, I began my studies with the *Ariyapariyesanā Sutta*. Their suggestion represents a point of departure somewhere between the somewhat polarized positions mentioned above.

Sutta—literally, "The *Sutta* Concerning [the] Noble Quest"[20]—tells of the quest for, the discovery of, and the decision to preach *dhamma*. Immediately one is confronted with the inadequacy of the terms "doctrine" and "teaching" to catch the depth of meaning of *dhamma* in this context for Buddhists.

This composite *sutta*, after giving the introductory setting, continues with a consideration of the torsion of living—the processes of birth, ageing, disease, death, grief, defilement—and presents Siddhattha Gotama, "the future Buddha [*bodhisatta*],"[21] becoming aware that he should seek that which is unborn, unageing, without disease, without death, without grief, undefiled, incomparable, a security from bonds, *nibbāna*.[22] The next segment of this *sutta*[23] speaks of the

[20] *M.* I. 160–175. *MA.* refers to this *sutta* as *Pāsarāsisutta*, "The *Sutta* Concerning a Heap of Snares," without providing a reason for the choice of this title. The word *pāsarāsim* occurs at *M.* I. 174 where it is said that a deer might lie down on a heap of snares and not be trapped. The concluding comments in *MA.* II. 193 note the alternate name of the *sutta*, *Ariyapariyesanā*. B. C. Law in *A History of Pāli Literature* (London: Kegan Paul, Trench, Trubner & Co., Ltd., 1933). I, 129, provides, disappointingly, only one sentence to describe this *sutta*. He notes that the *sutta* "furnishes us with one of the earliest examples of legends of the early days of Buddhahood, and as such it forms the historical basis of later legendary accounts in the Jātakas and Avadānas."

[21] *SnA.* II. 486 (on *Sn.* 683) interprets "*bodhisatta*" as "a being characterized by awakening, a being worthy to go to full enlightenment"—"*Bodhisatto* ti bujjhanakasatto sammāsambodhiṃ gantuṃ arahọ satto." Note the force of the infinitive *gantum* from √*gam* and compare the discussion below on *adhigata*. *SA.* II. 21 says regarding "*bodhisatta*," "Here *bodhi* means knowledge. A *Bodhisatta* is a being [*satta*] for the purpose of *bodhi* [*bodhiyā*]. One possessing knowledge, possessing wisdom, one learned is what is meant. This being, learned from the time of his resolution [*abhinīhāra* (see also *BHSD.*, p. 52b)], not a blind fool, is a *bodhisatta*. Or, just as a lotus that having gone up from water, firm, that has attained fullness will naturally be awakened [*bujjhissati*] by the warmth of the sun's rays and is called an 'awakened lotus' [*bujjhanaka-paduma*], so because of the gaining of the prediction in the presence of the Buddhas, having naturally fulfilled the perfections without interruption, he will awaken [*bujjhissati*]; and so a *bodhisatta* is a being characterized by awakening [*bujjhanaka-satto*]. He proceeds wishing for that *bodhi*, which is reckoned as the knowledge of the four paths and so 'a being attached to *bodhi*' is a *bodhisatta*." See *SnA.* I. 52 where *paccekabodhisattabhūmi* is mentioned.

[22] *M.* I. 161–163.

Bodhisatta who went forth from home searching for whatever was wholesome, seeking the incomparable, excellent path to peace.[24] He sought to live the higher life in the *dhamma* and *vinaya* of one Ālāra Kālāma[25] and soon thereafter mastered that *dhamma*.[26] Finding that a realization of the "sphere without anything" was not

---

[23] I speak of a segment because *M.* I. 163. 27 ff., is repeated elsewhere in the canon with minor variations. See *M.* I. 240; *M.* II. 93, 212.

[24] *MA.* II. 171 says, "The meaning is 'One seeking *nibbāna*.'"

[25] In this context *Ālāra Kālāma* is considered as a teacher having a *dhammavinaya*—the compound is unglossed in the commentary. I have taken it as a *dvanda* compound. It is reasonable to suggest that in the early period of the Buddha's ministry this compound was probably a *tappurisa* in locative relation meaning "training in *dhamma*" and that later, as the training became more thoroughly formulated, the compound might have lent itself to being interpreted as *dhamma* and discipline.

[26] *MA.* I. 171 comments, "'*That dhamma*' means that sacred text [*tanti*] of their community"—"*Taṃ dhamman* ti taṃ nesaṃ samayatantiṃ." This appears to be an anachronism. It is significant, however, that the commentator gives no more force to the term *dhamma* than *tanti*. Further, he seeks to differentiate that *dhamma* from the *dhamma* which he, apparently, followed and communicates no restlessness with the *sutta* noting that other religious figures had their *dhamma*. See *M.* II. 4, *S.* IV. 317, and *D.* III. 117 where Nigaṇṭha Nāthaputta is noted as teaching *dhamma*. *DA.* III. 905 notes the phrase in which the compound *dhamma-vinaya* is used but provides neither a gloss for its meaning nor an explanation of its presence. This, of course, is quite in keeping with passages elsewhere in the canon. See *M.* I. 170–171 where Upaka, an Ājivika, asks the Buddha, "Who is your teacher, or in whose *dhamma* do you find delight?" The Buddha, in *M.* III. 238. 17 ff., uses this phrase to question Pukkusāti. The same phrase occurs also in *Vin.* I. 8, 40, 41. Pūraṇa Kassapa is also noted as one teaching *dhamma*, *M.* II. 3. The Buddha prior to his enlightenment followed Uddaka Rāmaputta's *dhamma*, *M.* I. 165–166. In *D.* I. 230 ff., three kinds of teacher are said to teach *dhamma* to hearers but are themselves considered worthy of reproach. The criteria for judgement are certainty of the attainment of which the teacher speaks and the subsequent achievements of the hearers. Moreover in *M.* I. 168 and *Vin.* I. 5 it is noted by Brahmā Sahampati that in the region of Magadha, prior to the Buddha's going forth to preach, "*dhamma* that was not pure, devised by those with stains" had appeared. *MA.* II. 178, *VinA.* V. 962, *SA.* I. 199 explain this as "thought out by the six teachers who have stains." Brahmā urged the Buddha to preach "*dhamma* awakened unto by one without stains." See also *PD.*, p. 38.

These references demonstrate that *dhamma* was not used solely to designate *dhamma* preached by the Buddha. When *dhamma* is used in contexts relative to other teachers one might take it as meaning *desanā*, "teaching," or, following *Nd. 1.* I. 73 and *SnA.* II. 521 commenting on *Sn.* vs. 784 where *dhamma* is used in the plural, "opinions," *diṭṭhiyo*.

conducive to *nibbāna*, the *Bodhisatta* approached one Uddaka Rāmaputta to undertake the higher life in his *dhamma*. Having soon realized the "sphere of neither perception nor non-perception," the *Bodhisatta* again noted this did not conduce to *nibbāna*.

Seated in a peaceful grove seeking that which is unborn the *Bodhisatta* attained (*ajjhagamaṃ*) *nibbāna*. "Knowledge and vision arose in me: unquivering is my release; this is the last birth, now there is no successive becoming."[27]

The next part of the *Ariyapariyesanā Sutta*[28] deals with a momentous event in the history of the Buddhist community, and for that matter, mankind—namely, the Buddha's decision to preach *dhamma*. The Buddha ponders, "Attained indeed by me is this *dhamma* that is profound, hard to see, difficult to understand, peaceful, delectable, beyond speculation, subtle, to be known by the learned."[29] The text, in this context, speaks of *idappaccayatā paṭiccasamuppāda*, "conditioned co-production," the "calming of all impulses or clustering forces [*sabbasaṅkhārasamatha*]," the "renunciation of all substrata [*sabbūpadhipaṭinissagga*]," the "destruction of cravings [*taṇhakkhaya*]," the "absence of passion [*virāga*]," "cessation [*nirodha*]," and *nibbāna*.[30] The Buddha is represented as pondering whether or not to preach *dhamma* and perceiving this consideration, Brahmā says, "Lost indeed, Sir, is the world; indeed destroyed, Sir, is the world since, alas, the mind of the *Tathāgata*,[31] Worthy One,

---

27 *M.* I. 167.

28 *M.* I. 167. 30 ff. This segment is also in *Vin.* I. 4.32–10.9. See I. B. Horner's notes in her translation of the *Vinaya* passage in *BD.* IV. 6 ff. The narrative in *M.* is in the first person singular and in the third person singular in the *Vin.* account. This suggests that the narrative in *M.* might represent an older form. There are other minor variations. Occasionally clauses appear to be inserted in *Vin.* See *Vin.* I. 5.21, 6.5, 7.3 and 9.8. See also *S.* I. 136 ff.

29 *M.* I. 167. 30 ff. *MA.* II. 174 takes *dhamma* in this passage to mean the *dhamma* that is the four truths (realities?), "*Dhammo* ti catusaccadhammo," as does *SA.* I. 195 and *DA.* II. 464. *VinA.* V. 961 provides no gloss.

30 *M.* I. 167. 35 ff. This passage occurs also in *D.* II. 36.

31 For commentarial definitions of *Tathāgata* see *DA.* I. 59–68; *MA.* I. 45–52; *SA.* II. 287 (where eight definitions are listed and reference is made to the full discussions in the two previously mentioned commentaries); *AA.* I. 103–

Perfectly Enlightened One inclines to inactivity and not to the teaching of *dhamma*." Further, Brahmā makes a request, "Let the

---

112; *KhpA.*, pp. 195–196; *Sdpj.* I. 177 (on *Nd. 1.* 58 [on *Sn.* vs. 779]); *BuA.*, pp. 15–18; *PugA.*, p. 234. *UdA.*, pp. 128–155, provides the most comprehensive discussion of the term, interpreted, as is the custom in the commentaries, through the person of the *Tathāgata*. Having repeated the eight definitions as noted in *MA.* and *SA.*, the author of *UdA.*, reputedly Dhammapāla, adds eight more definitions. See *UdA.*, pp. 133 ff. An interesting gloss occurs in *PvA.*, p. 64, on a passage in the *Pv.* that depicts the Buddha consoling an *upāsaka* who had lost his dear son. "'*Yathāgata*' means 'by the mode *akāra* he has come, not summoned by us, so he has come.' '*Tathāgata*' means by just that mode he has gone. Just as by his own *kamma* he had come, so [*tathā*] by his own *kamma* he has gone [*gato*]. With this he shows that done on the part of *kamma*"—"Yathāgato ti yenākārena āgato amhehi na abbhito evaṃ āgato ti attho. Tathāgato ti ten' evākārena gato. Yathā saken' eva kammunā āgato tathā saken' eva kammunā gato ti etena kammassa kataṃ dasseti." See also Robert Chalmers, "Tathāgata," *The Journal of the Royal Asiatic Society* (January, 1898), pp. 103–115; Émile Senart, "Tathāgata," in "Correspondence," *JRAS* (October, 1898), pp. 865–868; F. B. Shawe, "Tathāgata," in "Correspondence," *JRAS* (April, 1898), pp. 385–386; C. de Harlez, "Tathāgata," in "Correspondence," *JRAS* (January, 1899), p. 131; M. Anesaki, "Tathāgata," *Encyclopaedia of Religion and Ethics*, ed. James Hastings (Edinburgh: T & T Clark, 1954 [first impression, 1921]), XII, 202b–204b. One might suggest a possible early meaning of the term that in no way contradicts the interpretations given in the commentaries. Perhaps "*tathāgata*" at the very early period of the Buddhist movement—conceivably a term known by religious wanderers on the Indian scene at large—meant "One who has gone [*gata*: from √*gam*, in the sense of 'gone all the way,' 'attained'] thusly [*tathā*]." As a term used by a religious leader it would designate one who has gone (*gata*) the way (*tathā*) of which he teaches. See below where √*gam* is used with the prefix *adhi* with regard to attaining *dhamma*/*nibbāna*. The precise, original meaning of the term "*tathāgata*" mattered little to the commentators; rather, it was what the *Tathāgata* did that was of cosmic significance—how it was that he came and went, what it was that he rediscovered and attained.

The term "*tathāgata*" is used to designate not only the Buddha but also *dhamma* and *saṅgha* in *Sn.*, vss. 236–238, in the *Ratanasutta*. This *sutta* occurs in the *Khp.* and the commentarial interpretations are in the *KhpA.*, pp. 195–196. Regarding *dhamma*, the discussion in *KhpA.*, p. 196, speaks of *dhamma* as *magga* and *dhamma* as *nibbāna*. *UdA.*, p. 153, incorporates this discussion, relating to *Sn.*, vs. 237, into its discussion of *tathāgata* and speaks of *dhamma* as *ariyamagga*, *dhamma* as *phala*, *dhamma* as *nibbāna*, and also *dhamma* as *pariyatti* (authoritative teaching). In terms of *dhamma* that is attained thusly (*tathā gato*) *KhpA.*, p. 196, speaks firstly of *dhamma* as *magga* and says, "Just as that which is to be gone to by the power of calm and insight that are correlated, it is gone unto thusly by one cutting away the realm of defilments. *Dhamma* as *nibbāna* is called *tathāgata* in the sense that as it is gone unto thusly by Buddhas and others [*buddhādīhi tathāga(ta)to*

Bhagavan preach *dhamma*; let the *Sugata* preach *dhamma*. Beings there are who have little dust in their eyes; who, from not hearing *dhamma*, deteriorate; who might become knowers of *dhamma*."[32] Moreover, Brahmā requests, "Open this door of the deathless; let them hear *dhamma* awakened unto by the Spotless One."[33] To this the Buddha responds:

> Opened for them are the doors of the deathless. They who have ears to hear let them disclose faith.[34]

The *Ariyapariyesanā Sutta*, thus, puts before the reader two levels of the term *dhamma*: *dhamma* as taught by religious teachers in general and *dhamma* as perceived, realized and taught by the Buddha. The former remains of interest to historians; the latter has enabled men, by becoming Buddhists, at one and the same time to shape what Westerners have known as history and to live meaningfully in, to transcend, what Buddhists have understood as the whirl of becoming (*vaṭṭa*, *saṃsāra*).

It was mentioned earlier that the *Ariyapariyesanā Sutta* represents the noble quest for, the discovery of, and the decision to preach *dhamma*. When the Buddha relates his attaining *nibbāna* as a result of his quest, *pariyesanā*, the term *ajjhagamam* is used[35] and when

—the parenthetical insertion was made by the *PTS* editors—*tathāgato ti vuccati*]." *UdA*., p. 153, reads, "*Buddhādīhi tathāgato sacchikato ti Tathāgato*." "*Sacchikato*" means "realized," "made manifest."

[32] *M*. I. 168. See also *Bu*. 1.

[33] *M*.I.168. *MA*.II.178, *VinA*.V.962, *SA*.I.199 explain this passage as follows: "'The door of the deathless' means the noble path that is the door of *nibbāna*, which is deathless. 'Let them hear *dhamma* awakened unto by the Spotless One' means he asks 'O Bhagavan, let these beings listen to *dhamma* with regard to the four truths that were awakened unto by the spotless Perfectly Enlightened One because he is without stains such as passion, etc.'" *Amatassa dvāra* or *amatadvāra* is explained as *ariyamagga* at *SA*. II. 59 (on *S*. II. 43), *MA*. II. 267. 21 (on *M*. I. 227. 11), *DA*. II. 471 (on *D*. II. 39).

[34] *M*. I. 169.

[35] *Ajjhagamam* is aorist tense, first person singular, formed with the prefix *adhi* and the aorist augment *a* from √*gam*, "to go." See Wilhelm Geiger, *Pāli Literature and Language*, trans. Batakrishna Ghosh (Delhi: Oriental Books Reprint Corporation, 1968 [first published in 1943 by Calcutta University]), p. 191.

the Buddha speaks of his attaining *dhamma* that is profound, hard to see, the term *adhigata* occurs.[36] *MA*.II.174 interprets *ajjhagamam* as meaning "attained," *paṭilabhim*, and *adhigata* as meaning "penetrated," *paṭividdha*,[37] in the sense of discovery and thorough mastering. *MA*. notes a subtle distinction, held in one word in the *sutta*, between what was penetrated by the Buddha and what was attained by him. When the commentaries interpret *dhamma* that was attained or penetrated by the Buddha as "*dhamma* that is the four truths," *catusaccadhamma*,[38] one, on first glance, might think "the doctrine of the four truths" mundane, might think that one has here a doctrine comprised of four statements that may or may not, upon analysis, prove true. However, the Buddha did not penetrate the *doctrine* of the four truths; rather, he is seen as having penetrated *dhamma* that is the four truths (realities?). The four truths, familiar to readers of Buddhist literature, represent the way things are and, as concepts, they function to hold together all aspects of Buddhist thought that have to do with salvation. They form the aperture of an hourglass, so to speak, and focus soteriological concepts in an upward centripetal movement onto a level at which a centrifugal movement of awareness begins. In this function one might speak of the four truths as religious symbols. To understand *dhamma* in this context as Truth is close to the mark if by that notion is meant "saving or liberating Truth." To say that the Buddha discovered, penetrated (*paṭi* + √*vyadh*) attained (*adhi* + √*gam*) *dhamma* in this sense is a way of saying he attained (*paṭi* + √*labh*, *adhi* + √*gam*) *nibbāna*.

The *Ariyapariyesanā Sutta* mentions the request of Brahmā that the Buddha open the "door of the deathless" and the commentaries interpret *dvāra*, "door," as *ariyamagga*, "noble path." "Noble path" is another comprehensive notion that represents the way of salvation.

---

[36] *Adhigata* is a past passive participle formed with the prefix *adhi* from √*gam*, "to go."

[37] For *adhigata* meaning *paṭividdha* see also *SA*.I.195, *DA*.II.464.

[38] *MA*.II.174; *SA*.I.195; *DA*.II.36. *VinA*.V.961 provides no gloss on this passage also occurring at *M*.I.167. 30 ff.

Ariyamagga is interpreted as the "path or way that transcends the world [of *saṃsāra*]."[39] When one takes refuge in *dhamma*, one takes refuge in the *ariyamagga* and *nibbāna*.[40]

Returning to the narrative developed in the *Ariyapariyesanā Sutta*, one reads that the Buddha, having decided to preach *dhamma*, pondered to whom he would first preach it. Having entertained the thought of preaching firstly to Ālāra Kālāma, the Buddha became aware that the man had died seven days previously. Next, the Buddha considered preaching *dhamma* to Udaka Rāmaputta, only to become aware that he too had died just the previous evening. Subsequently, the Buddha decided to preach *dhamma* to a group of five *bhikkhus* living in the environs of Banaras in the Deer Park at Isipatana.

En route the Buddha met Upaka, an Ājīvika,[41] and in response to the latter's question regarding under whom he went forth and in whose *dhamma* he found delight, the Buddha replied, "Conqueror of all, knower of all am I. . . ."[42] Further, the Buddha said, "I go to the city Kāsi to cause the *dhamma*-wheel to roll forth."[43]

Setting in Motion the Dhammacakka

In the famous *sutta* that came to be entitled *Dhammacakkappavattanasutta*, the term *dhammacakka*[44] occurs and from the immediate

---

[39] *SA*.I.36: "*Ariya-maggo* ti lokuttara-maggo."

[40] See, for example, *AA*.II.107. Also, the definition of *bodhi* given in *SA*.II.153 is of interest. "'Bodhi' means the tree, also path, also knowledge of omniscience, also *nibbāna*"—"*Bodhī* ti, rukkho pi maggo pi sabbaññuta-ñāṇam pi nibbānam pi."

[41] On the Ājīvikas see Basham, *op. cit.* [42] *M*.I.171. [43] *Ibid.*

[44] The *sutta* entitled by the commentary, *Dhammacakkappavattanasutta*, is in *Vin*.I.10 ff., and *S*.V.420 ff. This *sutta* is considered the first sermon preached by the Buddha. The symbol of the wheel incorporated in the compound, *dhammacakka*, reflects a sense of conquering authority. The precise derivation of the wheel motif remains uncertain. The wheel might reflect the wheel of a conquering chariot or, perhaps, a discoid weapon. It could represent the sun, conceivably that for which the sun is a symbol. See O. H. de A. Wijesekera, "The Symbolism of the Wheel," *S. K. Belvalkar*

context one infers that the *dhammacakka* was launched with the preaching of the "four noble truths." Elsewhere in the *Sutta-piṭaka*

Felicitation Volume (Banaras: Motilal Banarasi Dass, 1957), pp. 262–267; O. H. de A. Wijesekera, "Discoid Weapons in Ancient India: A Study of Vedic *Cakra, Pavi* and *Kṣurapavi*," *The Adyar Library Bulletin*, XXV, Parts 1–4, 250–267. See also Raffaele Pettazzoni, *Essays on the History of Religions*, trans. H. J. Rose (Leiden: E. J. Brill, 1954), c. IX, "The Wheel in the Ritual Symbolism of Some Indo-European Peoples," pp. 95–109. Horner, in "Early Buddhist Dhamma," pp. 120–121, interprets *cakka* in terms of solar symbolism and writes, "At the back of the Sun is the Other World, guarded by the revolving wheel, through whose rays or spokes you . . . must hasten with all speed on the quest for immortality, the object being to find the waters of life, the Cosmic Ocean of Hinduism, the 'still waters' of the Psalms, the sea of nibbāna of Early Buddhism." *Ibid.*, p. 120. "It is no wonder," Horner continues, "that the Buddha, before he became represented in sculpture in a human form . . . was indicated or symbolised by a wheel. It was the wheel through whose spokes the Kinsman of the Sun passed, thereby crowning his quest, which was for the Unborn, the Unageing and the Undying. And it was the wheel that he subsequently set rolling, so that not only he but others could pass through its spokes to the Other World, the Further Shore beyond." *Ibid.*, p. 121.

The *cakka* was at first a symbol not for the Buddha but for *dhamma*. Because he had thoroughly penetrated *dhamma*, the Buddha was able to set it rolling forth. See also A. Foucher, *The Life of the Buddha: According to the Ancient Texts and Monuments of India*, abridged translation by Simone Brangier Boas (Middletown, Conn.: Wesleyan University Press, 1963 [French edition, *La Vie du Bouddha*, copyright, 1949 by Editions Payot]), pp. 151–152.

Childers interpreted the force of the compound, *dhammacakka*, with the verb *pavatteti* as "'to inaugurate the reign of Religion,' or 'to set on foot the domain of the Law.' It is most important to bear in mind that this famous phrase is used not of the whole period of Buddha's ministry, but *only of his first sermon*, in which he 'began' or 'set on foot' his religion by imparting the knowledge of it to the five brahmins." *DPL.*, p. 116. T. W. Rhys Davids interpreted *dhammacakkappavattana* to mean, "'To found a kingdom of righteousness'." *Buddhism: Being a Sketch*, p. 43. In *Ibid.*, p. 45, he translates the compound in an attempt to get at its force, "'To set rolling the royal chariot-wheel of a universal empire of truth and righteousness'." It should be noted that the Pāli commentaries note the use of *cakka* in canonical passages and demonstrate that in different contexts it is interpreted differently. Five meanings of *cakka* are given in *DA*.III.1058 and ten are noted in *MA*.II.27 and *AA*.III.9: (1) *sampatti* [*DA*.], (2) *lakkhaṇa*, (3) *rathaṅga* [*DA*., *daru°*], (4) *iriyāpatha* [*DA*.], (5) *dāna*, (6) *ratanacakka* [*DA*.], (7) *dhammacakka* [*DA*.], (8) *uracakka*, (9) *paharaṇacakka*, (10) *asanimaṇḍala*. In the latter two commentaries the entry regarding *cakka* is occasioned by "*brahmacakka*" at *M*.I.69.33 and *A*.II.9.1, respectively. *MA*.II.27 notes, "Here brahman means best, highest, pure." The variance is to be noted in the use of *visiṭṭham* in the former commentary and *visuddhaṃ* in the latter. See also *AA*.I.120.

this is explicit.[45]

The commentarial tradition interprets *dhammacakka* as twofold[46] in the sense of "knowledge of penetration and knowledge of teaching."[47] This knowledge of penetration is a more personal realization whereby the fruit of the noble ones is realized personally, for oneself. This process is illumined by wisdom (*paññā*). The second dimension, that of "knowledge of teaching," is oriented to others and, being illumined by compassion (*karuṇā*), brings the fruit of the noble ones to those who hear.[48] Both aspects of knowledge reflected in the notion of *dhammacakka* are themselves twofold: firstly, knowledge of penetration being both "in process of arising and arisen," and secondly, knowledge of the teaching being "in process of rolling forth and rolled forth."[49]

The "knowledge of penetration" was in process of arising from the time of the Buddha's departure from his family life up to the path of arahantship.[50] At the fructifying instant (*phalakkhaṇa*) the knowledge of penetration "has arisen." The commentarial tradition seeking comprehensiveness proposes alternative interpretations. This process of arising could also be seen as being in force from the time that the *Bodhisatta* was in Tusita heaven up to the path of arahantship at the base of the Bodhi tree or from the time of making the vow to attain Enlightenment standing before Dīpaṅkara, a former Buddha, up to the path of arahantship. In all these cases at the fructifying instant, knowledge of penetration "has arisen."

---

[45] *M.*III.248: "Bhagavā etad avoca:—Tathāgatena . . . Isipatane migadāye anuttaraṃ dhammacakkaṃ pavattitaṃ . . . yadidaṃ catunnaṃ ariyasaccānaṃ ācikkhanā desanā. . . ."

[46] See *AA.*III.10, 12; *SA.*II.46–47; *MA.*II.28. See also *SA.*II.288 and *AA.*III.73.

[47] Paṭivedhañāṇañ ca desanāñāṇañ ca. *MA.*II.28 (on *M.*I.69.33).

[48] *PṭsA.*III.616 (on *Pṭs.*II.159) notes, "Paṭivedha-dhammacakkaṃ bodhipallaṅke, desanādhammacakkaṃ Isipatane."

[49] "Uppajjamānam, uppannan ti duvidhaṃ. . . . Pavattamānaṃ, pavattan ti duvidhaṃ." *MA.*II.28.

[50] *MA.*II.28, line 9, has *arattamaggā* which should be corrected to read *arahattamagga* as in line 11.

The knowledge of the teaching is also twofold in the sense of being both "in process of rolling forth and rolled forth." This "knowledge of the teaching" was in process of arising up to the moment of stream-attainment on the part of Aññā-Koṇḍañña, one of the five who heard the Buddha's first sermon. At the fructifying instant, it "is rolled."

The commentaries make the concluding remarks: "Of these, knowledge of penetration is transcendent [*lokuttara*], knowledge of the teaching is mundane [*lokiya*]; both [these forms of] knowledge are natural only among Buddhas and are not shared with others."[51]

The force of this discussion might be caught should one see in the comments about the "knowledge of penetration" a gradual dawning and subsequently a full illumination. In this sense *cakka*, "wheel," might be understood, perhaps, in terms of solar symbolism. With regard to "knowledge of the teaching," one might interpret the discussion in terms of a wheel formerly rolling and subsequently launched. Translating the compound *dhammacakkappavattana* as "setting in motion the wheel of the Law or Teaching" misses, on the one hand, the twofold dimension of the one who inaugurates and the others who participate and, on the other hand, a differentiation of process and fulfillment. Once the *dhammacakka* is arisen, or rolled, it remains so and no force in *saṃsāra* can roll it back.[52]

Another interpretation of *dhammacakka* proffered in the commentary to the *Paṭisambhidāmagga* sees in *cakka* a reference to *pahāraṇacakka*, a discoid weapon, and likens it to *dhamma* because it moves forward for destruction of attachment to defilements.[53] In the *Paṭisambhidāmagga*, *dhamma* in the compound *dhammacakka* is

[51] "Tesu paṭivedhañāṇaṃ lokuttaraṃ, desanāñāṇaṃ lokiyaṃ. Ubhayam pi pan' etaṃ aññehi asādhāraṇaṃ, Buddhānaṃ yeva orasaṃ ñāṇaṃ." *AA.* III.10, *SA.* II.47, *MA.* II.28.

[52] *M.* III.248, *Vin.* I.11–12, *S.* V.423. *M.* III.248 reads, "Tathāgatena . . . anuttaraṃ dhammacakkaṃ pavattitaṃ appativattiyaṃ samaṇena vā brāhmaṇena vā devena vā Mārena va [*read* vā] Brahmunā vā kenaci vā lokasmiṃ. . . ."

[53] *PṭsA.* III.616 (on *Pṭs.* II.159).

interpreted as meaning the entirety of the process of salvation including *nibbāna*.[54]

Dhamma Worthy of Reverence

Thus far we have noted the passages that deal with the Buddha's decision to preach *dhamma*, to roll forth the *dhammacakka*. One *sutta* that appears to have played a significant part in the shaping of Buddhists' attitudes toward *dhamma* mentions the Buddha's awareness that *dhamma* is worthy of reverence.[55] Having become fully enlightened the Buddha noticed that in the plane of *saṃsāra*[56] there was no one who was as complete as he in moral behavior, rapt concentration, wisdom, release, knowledge and vision of release and hence deserving of his reverence. The Buddha thought, "Now, this *dhamma* is fully awakened unto by me. What if I were to live, having honored, having revered, having relied on just that *dhamma*?"[57] The passage continues with Brahmā Sahampati's mentioning to the Buddha that, in effect, should he so live he would be participating

---

[54] *Pṭs.* II. 159–165. There is no Pāli equivalent in the *Pṭs.* for the English sentence used above. The *Pṭs.* takes the major tenets and practices recorded in the *suttas* and notes that he, the *Bhagavan*, the one established in *dhamma* etc., causes them to roll forth. When these tenets and practices become endorsed, when one becomes engaged, so to speak, with them, a process of salvation is undertaken. The *suttas* mention that Sāriputta rolled along the *dhammacakka* that was rolled forth by the *Tathāgata*. See *M.* III. 29; *S.* I. 191; *A.* I. 23; *Sn.* 557.

[55] *S.* I. 138; *A.* II. 20–21.

[56] The term *saṃsāra* is not in the Pāli passage. When the passage reads, "Na kho panāhaṃ passāmi sadevake loke samārake sabrahmake sassamaṇabrāhmaṇiyā pajāya sadevamanussāya. . . ." it stresses the human realm and those realms of gods including the forces of Māra. Of course other realms of existence, namely the animal realm and that of *petas*, would not contain any who are deserving of reverence. Hence, to use the term *saṃsāra* catches the force of the passage.

[57] *S.* I. 139; *A.* II. 20. "Yannūnāhaṃ yo pāyaṃ dhammo mayā abhisambuddho tam eva dhammaṃ sakkatvā garukatvā upanissāya vihareyyan ti." *SA.* I. 204 and *AA.* III. 25 interpret the phrase as follows: ". . . mayā paṭividdhaṃ navalokuttaradhammam eva sakkatvā upanissāya viharissāmī' ti cinteti. . . ."

in a patterned process in which the Buddhas in the past had participated.[58]

In the commentary on the *Majjhima-nikāya*, reference is made to the passage in *S.*I.138–140 and *A.*II.20–21. The *sutta* under consideration is the *Rathavinīta Sutta*, and the *MA.* understands the setting to have been in the area of the Buddha's birthplace. Why did the Buddha not inquire of the health of his relatives such as Suddhodana, Mahāpajāpatī and others, but rather speak only in terms of *bhikkhus*? Raising this question, the commentary continues,

> Because of their being dear. For *bhikkhus*, *bhikkhunis*, *upāsakas* and *upāsikas* who are pursuing the course are dear, pleasing to the Buddhas. For what reason? Because of their reverence for *dhamma*. For reverers of *dhamma* are the *Tathāgatas*. This fact of their being reverers of *dhamma* is to be understood in the sense of the intention that arose at the foot of the Ajapālaṇigrodha tree with this consideration, "Restless indeed dwells one without reverence, masterless."[59]

---

[58] *S.*I.139–140; *A.*II.21. I therefore take the Pāli, esā buddhāna dhammatā, as "this is the patterned process of [all] Buddhas." The passage in *S.* ends with Brahmā's concluding his point with a *gāthā*. However, the *A.* passage continues with the Buddha's stating that he did that of which Brahmā spoke and about which the Buddha earlier in the passage pondered himself. Furthermore, the *A.* passage concludes with the Buddha's saying, "There is keen reverence on my part for the *saṅgha*." *AA.*III.26 asks rhetorically, "But when was reverence shown [*kato*] for the *saṅgha* by the *Bhagavan*?" and continues, "At the time of a giving of robes by Mahāpajāpatī. Then the *Bhagavan* offered his own robe saying, 'Give to the *saṅgha*, O Gotamī [Mahāpajāpatī]. When they are given to the *saṅgha*, I and also the *saṅgha* are worshipped [*pūjito*].' And thus did he show reverence for the *saṅgha*." This account is drawn from *M.*III.253. The absence of this last paragraph from the *S.* account, the setting in which the *S.* and *A.* accounts place this *sutta*—namely, on the banks of the Nerañjara beneath the Ajapāla-nigrodha tree—and the temporal setting's being the fifth week after the Enlightenment, according to *SA.*I.203 and *AA.*III.24, seem to suggest that the last paragraph in *A.* represents a later addition.

Regarding the phrase, *esā buddhāna dhammatā*, the *Milindapañha*, p. 234, considered non-canonical by Sinhalese Buddhists, says, "This is the patterned process of all *Tathāgatas* that they preach *dhamma* at the request of Brahmā" —"...sabbesaṃ tathāgatānaṃ dhammatā esā yaṃ Brahmunā āyācitā dhammaṃ desenti." *BuA.*, pp. 5, 83, 133, 154, 161, mentions several Buddhas who in former times preached *dhamma* at the request of Brahmā.

[59] *MA.*II.136. The quote in *MA.* from *S.*I.139 and *A.*II.20 is "dukkhaṃ

Elsewhere the *MA*. speaks of the Buddhas as being those who revere *dhamma*.[60] The commentary raises the question of why the Buddha came to a certain place to preach *dhamma* to three young men. Firstly, he did so in order to befriend them; secondly, he did so because of compassion for lowly people;[61] and thirdly, because of revering *dhamma*.[62]

In another commentarial passage is written:

> Among Buddhas this thought does not arise, "This one is a *Khattiya*, this one a *Brahman*, this one wealthy, this one poor. Having made it [*dhamma*] superb for this one I will preach; not so for that one." Preaching *dhamma* on whatever subject, having placed at the forefront reverence for *dhamma*, they [the Buddhas] preach as if bringing down the celestial river from the sky.[63]

Dhammapāla, an eminent commentator who flourished in the sixth century A.D.,[64] began his commentaries with praise to the Buddha,

---

kho agāravo viharati appatisso." The etymology of *appatisso* is uncertain. See Edgerton, *BHSD*, p. 48b, *s.v. apratiśa*. The *BJTS* of *Anguttaranikāya*, Part II, p. 43, translates *appatisso* into Sinhalese as *pratiśraya nätiye*, "one not having a [place of] refuge." The *BJTS* of *Saṃyuttanikāya*, Part I, p. 253, provides a much freer Sinhalese translation: "kisivaku deṭu tanhi no tabā" —"not having made anyone as his senior [*deṭu* is an *Elu* form equivalent to the more 'sanskritic' *jyesṭha*]." Both Sinhalese translations follow very closely the Pāli commentaries *SA*. and *AA*., which render identical readings on the following phrase: "Appatisso ti patissayarahito, kañci jeṭṭhakaṭṭhāne aṭṭhapetvā ti attho." One might note the story in the Christian New Testament, Luke 8:19–21 (Matthew 12:46–50, Mark 3:31–35) where Jesus while teaching was informed that his mother and brothers were at some distance desiring to see or to speak with him. The passage in Luke records that Jesus responded, "*μήτηρ μου καὶ ἀδελφοί μου οὗτοί εἰσιν οἱ τὸν λόγον τοῦ θεοῦ ἀκούοντες καὶ ποιοῦντες*." "My mother and my brothers are those who are hearing and doing the word of God." Matthew and Mark speak of those who do "the will [*θέλημα*] of God" (Mark) or "the will of my Father in heaven" (Matthew) as being "my brother and sister [*ἀδελφὴ*] and mother."

[60] *MA*.II.236: "Buddhā ca nāma dhammagaruno honti." See also *UdA*.182 (on *Ud*.25) where it is mentioned, "Only those revering *dhamma*, Buddhas, *Bhagavans*, who are of right behavior are to be worshipped"—"dhammagaruno Buddhā Bhagavanto sammā-paṭipattiyā 'va pūjetabbā."

[61] *MA*.II.236: "Pacchimaṃ janataṃ anukampanato."

[62] *Ibid*.: "dhammagarubhāvato."

[63] *DhpA*.III.360. See *SdhRv*., p. 913. See also *M*.I.249 and *MA*.II.291.

[64] See A.P. Buddhadatta, "The Second Great Commentator, Ācariya-Dhammapāla," *UCR*., III, No. 2 (November, 1945), 49–57.

dhamma and *saṅgha.* With regard to *dhamma* he writes, "Homage to that highest *dhamma* worshipped by the Fully Enlightened Ones by which those endowed with knowledge and proper conduct are led on from the world [of *saṃsāra*]."[65]

The canonical passages in *S.*I.138-140 and *A.*II.20-21 make it clear that the Buddha revered *dhamma* as, indeed, is the case with all Buddhas, and the commentarial tradition is consistent on this point. A noteworthy comparison is drawn between a *cakkavattin* king, who honors and reveres *dhamma*, on the one hand, and the *Tathāgata*, who honors and reveres *dhamma*, on the other. A certain monk asked of the Buddha, "'Who, Sir, is king of a king who is a *cakkavattin*, characterized by *dhamma*, a *dhamma*-king?' '*Dhamma*, O *bhikkhu*.'" The *Bhagavan* said further,

> Now, *bhikkhu*, a king who is a *cakkavattin*, characterized by *dhamma*, a *dhamma*-king, having relied on *dhamma* alone, honoring *dhamma*, revering *dhamma*, respecting *dhamma*, having *dhamma* as banner, *dhamma* as standard, *dhamma* as master, provides a protection, ward, and guard that is characterized by *dhamma* for all people.[66]

---

[65] *ItvA.*, p. 1: "Vijjācaraṇasampannā yena niyyanti lokato vande tamuttamaṃ dhammaṃ sammāsambuddhapūjitaṃ." This verse occurs also in *PvA.*, p. 1; *ThagA.*, p. 1; *CpA.*, p. 1; *VvA.*, p. 1.

[66] *A.*I.109. The passage regarding the *cakkavattin* king goes on to mention that he provides protection for *khattiyas*, *brāhmans*, householders, those in outlying areas, *samaṇas* and *brāhmans*, beasts and birds. *Ibid.*, pp. 109–110. *Dhamma* as presented in the case of a *cakkavattin* king represents admirable qualities for a monarch. One should note that *dhamma* is considered *dhammikassa dhammarañño rājā*, *i.e.*, "*Dhamma* is sovereign [*rājā*] for a *dhamma*-king [*rājā*] who is characterized by *dhamma*." Assuming that this passage antedates Aśoka, or, perhaps, assuming that this passage reflects ideas current prior to Aśoka or even ideas endorsed during his reign, one might be somewhat reluctant to say, "We are of the opinion that *Dhamma* was Aśoka's own invention." Romila Thapar, *Aśoka and the Decline of the Mauryas* (Oxford: Oxford University Press, 1963 [reprinted lithographically from corrected sheets of the first impression, 1961]), p. 149. The relation of *dhamma* as probably viewed by Aśoka and Buddhist ethics is treated more thoroughly by É. Lamotte in the section, "Le Dharma d'Aśoka," *Histoire du bouddhisme indien*, pp. 249–261. It is regrettable that Thapar did not include in her chapter, "The Policy of *Dhamma*," *op. cit.*, pp. 137–181, the observations of Lamotte based on his many references to Buddhist

A little further on the same *sutta* draws the parallel,

> Indeed, just so, O *bhikkhu*, the *Tathāgata*, *Arahant*, Fully Enlightened One, is characterized by *dhamma*, a *dhamma*-king, having relied on *dhamma* alone, honoring *dhamma*, revering *dhamma*, respecting *dhamma*, having *dhamma* as banner, *dhamma* as standard, *dhamma* as master, provides a protection, ward, and guard that is characterized by *dhamma* with regard to bodily action—"such bodily action should be undertaken; such bodily action should not be undertaken."[67]

Of the *cakkavattin* king it is said, "He rolls forth the wheel only by means of *dhamma*. That is the wheel that cannot be reversed by any human being, by any living foe."[68] Of the Buddha it is said, "He rolls forth the wheel only by means of *dhamma*. That is the incomparable *dhamma*-wheel that cannot be reversed by a *samaṇa*[69] or a *brahman*, or a god, or Māra, or Brahmā, or anyone in the world."[70]

Comparing these parallel expressions, one notes that the *cakkavattin*, who is characterized by *dhamma* with regard to his subjects and who has *dhamma* as his own *rājā*, will find that *dhamma* will not be reversed by human agents. Including this and going beyond is *dhamma* honored by the Buddha that will not suffer reverse by any force in the entire realm of *saṃsāra*. There is no discontinuity between these aspects of *dhamma*. The commentary on this passage interprets *dhamma* in the context of the *cakkavattin* as *dhamma*

---

canonical passages, although neither Lamotte nor Thapar makes mention of *A*.I.109–110 in their considerations of *dhamma* as probably understood by Aśoka.

[67] *A*., p. 110. The Buddha also provides a protection for action related to speech and thought.

[68] *Ibid*., p. 110, lines 6–8.

[69] The meaning of *samaṇa* is difficult to grasp in one English word. The Pāli form merges two possible Sanskrit roots—√*sram*, "to exert," and √*sam*, "be calm." The force of the term as used in the Pāli canon might be caught if *samaṇa* were to be interpreted as "one striving for inner calm." The Sanskritic derivation, *śramaṇa* from √*śram*, is certain. It means "one exerting" and through extension, "one undertaking ascetic exertion religiously."

[70] *Ibid*., p. 110, lines 28–30.

which is "ten wholesome modes of conduct."[71]

The commentarial remarks regarding *dhamma* in the case of the Buddha enable the reader to note the interpretation of *dhamma* that was considered most comprehensive and most central over 1,500 years ago.

> "Characterized by *dhamma* [*dhammika*]"—The *cakkavattin* is characterized by *dhamma* in the sense of the ten wholesome modes of conduct, but the *Tathāgata* is so in the sense of the nine [-fold] *dhamma* that transcends the world [*navalokuttaradhamma*]. "*Dhamma*-king [*rājā*]" means "he rules the multitude with the nine *dhammas* that transcend the world [*navahi lokuttaradhammehi*]" and so [he is] *dhamma*-king. "On *dhamma* alone [*dhammaṃ yeva*]" means having relied only on the nine [-fold] *dhamma* that transcends the world, honoring only that [*tam eva sakkaronto*], revering that, respecting that. This *dhamma* is his banner in the sense that it is raised up and so he is "one having *dhamma* as banner"; it is his standard and so he is "one having *dhamma* as standard." Having made that alone master, supreme [*tam eva adhipatiṃ jeṭṭhakaṃ katvā*], he dwells, and so he is "one having *dhamma* as master." "A protection, a ward, a guard that is characterized by *dhamma*" means that *dhamma* that pertains to the world and transcends the world is a benefactor and a protection [*lokiyalokuttaradhammadāyikarakkhañ ca*] and a ward and a guard.[72]

---

[71] *AA*.II.178: "Tattha dhammo ti dasakusalakammapathadhammo." At *A*.V.266–268, the ten are noted: three relating to body—one abandons (1) killing, (2) taking that not given, (3) misconduct regarding desires; four regarding speech—one abandons (4) false speech, (5) sinister speech, (6) harsh speech, (7) idle speech; and three regarding mind—(8) one is not covetous, (9) one is without malevolent thought, (10) one has right perspective. *Dhamma* as ten wholesome modes of conduct, mentioned at *A*.V.266–268, is not such that it is restricted to Buddhist doctrinal thought alone. It will be noted below that by practicing *dhamma* in this sense one might attain heaven (*sagga*). See Thapar, *op. cit.*, p. 149, where her observations regarding *dhamma* and *sagga* as they have a bearing on possible motivation for Aśoka's humane outlook, are severely hindered by her overlooking the broad spectrum of meaning that *dhamma* has had and the role that *sagga* has had in the religious life of people who are characterized as living *dhamma*. Lamotte, *Histoire du bouddhisme indien*, pp. 249–256, in his consideration of "Le Dharma d'Aśoka," does not refer to *A*.V.226–228.

[72] *AA*.II.180 (on *A*.I.110). There will be occasion to consider the *nava (vidha) lokuttaradhamma* below.

All Buddhas Preach Dhamma

The Buddha, having become enlightened, devoted the remainder of his life, in what has come to be called India, to preaching *dhamma*. In doing so, he continued a process that was undertaken by the Buddhas of the past and will be continued by the Buddhas of the future; he illustrated the preaching of *dhamma* (*dhammadesanā*). A frequent phrase reads, "He [the Buddha] illustrated to him [a hearer] the very eminent [*sāmukkhaṃsikā*] preaching of *dhamma* of the Buddhas—*dukkha*, [its] origin, [its] cessation, and path [leading to that cessation]."[73] These are, of course, the four truths (*catusacca-dhamma*) and they are one of the most important interpretations of *dhamma*.[74]

---

[73] *Vin.* I. 16, 18, 19, 23, 37, 181, II. 156; D. I. 110, II. 41, 43, 44 (in the case of Vipassin, a former Buddha); *M.* I. 379–380, II. 145; *A.* IV. 186, 209–210, 213. See Geiger, *PD.*, pp. 39, 65. Also at *Ud.*, p. 49, "Yā buddhānaṃ sāmukkaṃsikā dhammadesanā taṃ pakāsesi: dukkhaṃ samudayaṃ nirodhaṃ maggaṃ." See *DA.*I.277; *AA.*IV.101–102; *UdA.*, p. 283. Interpreting *dukkha*, Mrs. Rhys Davids remarked regarding the Buddha, "He had found 'the world is out of joint.'" *A Manual of Buddhism*, p. 60. W. C. Smith has written, "This [*dukkha*] is usually translated 'suffering', which up to a point is valid though I personally also like to translate it as meaning all life is awry; . . ." "Religious Atheism?" p. 9. *Dukkha*, theoretically even in the sense of a poorly aligned axle setting, reflects a meaning of disarrangement, disorientation, disorder, being disjointed, and through extension, discontent, discord, and "dis-ease," concerning the physical (*kāyikadukkha*) and mental (*mānasadukkha*) dimensions of life, individually and socially considered. *Dukkha* means much of all of these English concepts held together and sensed as causing oppression (*paṭipiḷana*). See *MA.* II. 113 (on *M.* I. 138); *Sdpj.* I. 74 (on *Nd.1.* I. 17); and *SnA.* I. 151 (on *Sn.*, vs. 80). "Health is the highest gain; *nibbāna*, the highest ease" appears to have been an expression on the scene at the time of the Buddha. The Buddha, on hearing that statement, recognized its incomplete rendering and said, "This verse, Māgandiya, was spoken by former *Arahants*, Fully Enlightened Ones—Health is the highest gain; *nibbāna*, the highest ease. And of paths, the one eight-fold leads to rest, to that without death.'"

[74] See *AA.* II. 250, 302–303, III. 91, 217, 230, 266, IV.1, 116, 200; *SA.* I. 64, 190. *ThagA.* I. 166, II. 11, 71, III. 201 (on the term *ariyadhamma* in *Thag.*, vs. 1273, appearing also in *Sn.*, vs. 353, and glossed verbatim by *SnA.* II. 350); *UdA.*, p. 44 (where *catu-ariya-sacca-dhamma* is given along with other interpretations); *Sdpj.* I. 222 (on *Nd.1.* I. 92, being itself a comment on *Sn.*, vs. 792); *SnA.* I. 292 (on *Sn.*, vs. 250), 350, 364–366, II. 507 (on *Sn.*, vs. 749); *DhpA.* III. 386 (on *Dhp.*, vs. 259).

The fourth truth, the way, *magga*, represents what the Buddhist movement is all about. (Indeed, that one speaks of the Buddhist movement in the twentieth century A.D. assumes the movement of Buddhists along the way for approximately twenty-five centuries.) On the question of what one must do to be saved, what one must do to put an end to the torsion of living, perhaps no religious tradition has had as much to say as the Buddhist, and, in one way or another, all that has been said on the matter coheres in the notion of *dhamma* as *magga*. *Magga* has many aspects not all of which can be easily differentiated chronologically by an historian concerned with a quest for "the original." And yet many aspects, if not all, were readily assimilated by the writer of the *PṭsA.*,[75] who was, one might assume, engaged in a process more futuristic in perspective than that reflected in the writings of some more recent historians. That commentator speaks of *magga* as "way, in the sense that it ends in the plunge into that without death, *nibbāna*."[76]

> O *bhikkhus*, I viewed an ancient way, an ancient straight way followed by former Fully Enlightened Ones. And what is this ancient way . . . ? Just this noble eightfold way.[77]

Having enumerated the eight constituents of the way, the Buddha said, "I traveled that."[78] And that which he traveled is elsewhere

---

[75] See *PṭsA.*II.82–85 where the four paths, which will be discussed below, provide the structure and the eightfold path provides the theme for a discussion with other features of Buddhist doctrine providing variations.

[76] *PṭsA.* II. 85: "Amatogadhaṃ nibbānaṃ pariyosānatthena maggo ti." *SnA.*I.34, commenting on the term *bhisi*, "a float," occurring at *Sn.*, vs. 21, says, "Here, 'by a float [*bhisi*]' is called in the world a bound raft [*baddhakulla*], . . . but for a noble one this is a term for the noble path in this *dhamma* and training [*vinaya*]. Indeed, the noble path is illustrated variously as way [*magga*], path [*pajja*], course [*patha*], road [*pantha*], a straight way [*añjasa*], an approach road [*vaṭumāyānā*], a boat [*vāvā*], and a suspension bridge [*uttarasetu*], and a raft [*kulla*], a float [*bhisi*], a crossing [*saṃkama*] and also that which enables a long journey [*addhānaṃ pabhavo*].

[77] *S.* II. 106: "Bhikkhave addasaṃ purāṇaṃ maggaṃ purāṇañjasaṃ pubbakehi sammāsambuddhehi anuyātaṃ. Katamo ca so bhikkhave purāṇamaggo . . . ? Ayam eva ariyo aṭṭhaṅgiko maggo."

[78] *Ibid.*: "Tam anugacchiṃ." Again √*gam* is utilized, this time as aorist

called the middle course:

> There is, sirs, greed [*lobha*], which is bad [*pāpaka*], and also hatred [*dosa*], which is bad, and for the abandoning of greed as well as the abandoning of hatred there is the middle course [*majjhimā paṭipadā*] providing vision [*cakkhukaraṇī*], providing knowledge and it conduces [*samvattati*] to calm, to higher knowledge, to enlightenment [*sambodhi*], to *nibbāna*. And what, sirs, is this middle course. . . ? Just this noble eightfold way, namely, proper view [*sammādiṭṭhi*], proper purpose [*sammāsaṅkappa*], proper speech [*sammāvācā*], proper conduct [*sammākammanta*], proper livelihood [*sammā-ājīva*], proper effort [*sammāvāyāma*], proper mindfulness [*sammāsati*], proper concentration [*sammāsamādhi*].[79]

The commentary elaborates on the above passage with the following words:

> One extreme is greed; one extreme is hatred. The path does not approach, does not go to the two extremes; it is freed from the two extremes and therefore it is called the middle way. It is "middle" because it is in between them and "way" because it is to be put into practice [*paṭipajjitabbato*, "followed out"]. Although one extreme is the pursuit of sensual pleasures, one extreme is the pursuit of self-mortification;[80] one extreme is eternalism [*sassata*] and one extreme is annihilationism [*uccheda*][81]—it [the middle way] is to be explained in this context only by means of the former [sets or pairs, i.e., greed and hatred].[82]

And further, the commentary reads,

> In this passage, "just this [way]" is a statement of emphasis meaning refusing another way and showing the commonness

---

first person singular with the prefix *anu*. Compare this usage with "*tathāgata*".

[79] *M.* I. 15. The passage continues to speak of the middle course as it relates to the abandoning of anger (*kodha*), malice (*upanāha*), disparaging (of others, *makka*), envious rivalry (*paḷasa*; see *BHSD.*, *s.v. pradāsa* [°*śa*], p. 380a), envy (*issā*), selfishness (*macchera*), deceit (*māyā*), guile (*sāṭheyya*), stubbornness (*thambha*), quarrelsomeness (*sāramhba*), conceit (*māna*), arrogance (*atimāna*), infatuation (*mada*), and indolence (*pamāda*).

[80] See *M.* III. 230 where pursuit of sensual pleasures and self-mortification are noted as the two extremes.

[81] See *SA*.I.238 (on *S*.I.169) where the commentary glosses *majjhe*, "middle," by referring to this pair of extremes. See also *D.* I. 13 ff., 34 ff.

[82] *MA.* I. 104 (on *M.* I. 15).

[*sādhāraṇabhāvadassanatthañ ca*] of the Buddhas, *Paccekabuddhas* and disciples.[83]

There is an ancient way rediscovered by the Buddha, traveled by the *Tathāgata*, and one who enters into it participates in a process that on one level has a history and on another is timeless, in one sense can be talked about but primarily is to be realized. The commonness of which the commentary speaks leads one to infer that a disciple who enters into the way of salvation, even if he should live alone, becomes aware that he is not isolated in what he is doing. This absence of loneliness is, perhaps, better expressed metaphorically. Commenting on *dhammarahada*, "pond of *dhamma*," which term occurs in a *sutta* passage, a commentary provides a gloss in which the Buddha says, "There is for me no purpose with an external pond like Sundarika. Moreover, my pond is *dhamma* as the eightfold way and there I cause to bathe a hundred, a thousand, even eighty-four thousand beings at one stroke."[84]

A basic theme in Buddhist thought is represented in the triad of concepts, *sīla*, *samādhi* and *paññā*. Ideally, morality, concentration, and wisdom are to be maintained in complementary balance at all times. These three aspects of religious training permeate the eightfold way. Processes three, four and five of the eightfold way comprise the aspect of religious training known as "morality" (*sīla*); six, seven and eight form "concentration" (*samādhi*); and one and two fall under the aspect of "wisdom" (*paññā*).[85]

"One truth [reality?]! There is no second," one reads in the *Sutta-nipāta*.[86] The *Mahāniddesa*, an old commentary, considered

---

[83] *Ibid.*

[84] *SA.* I. 237 (on *S.* I. 169). The allusion in the *sutta* passage and in the commentary to ritual purification is unmistakable. *Dhammarahada* occurs at *Jā.* III. 290 and the *JāA.* takes it in that context comprehensively as the five and the ten moral precepts, the three modes of good conduct, the thirty-seven processes bearing on enlightenment and deathless great *nibbāna*. The verse commented upon, that occurs at *Jā.* III. 290, occurs also in the Sinhalese *PūjāV.*, p. 89. See also *JāAgp.*, p. 231, for a Sinhalese gloss on *JāA.*

[85] *M.* I. 301.

[86] *Sn.*, vs. 884: "Ekaṃ hi saccaṃ na dutīyam atthi."

canonical, dealing with the older portion of the *Sutta-nipāta*, notes:

> The cessation of *dukkha*, *nibbāna*, is called "one truth"; that which is the calming of all clustering forces [*saṃkhārā*], the putting away of all substrata [*upadhi*], the destruction of craving [*taṇhā*], the absence of passion [*virāga*], cessation [*nirodha*], *nibbāna*. Or, moreover, the truth of the way [*maggasacca*] is called "one truth"; it is the truth of leading on [*niyyānasacca*],[87] the practice [*paṭipadā*] going to the cessation of *dukkha*, the noble eightfold way....[88]

On reading the words "One truth! There is no second" one might anticipate the commentaries' bringing into their interpretation the central tenet forming the cornerstone of all the doctrinal statements that have been passed down in the Theravāda tradition. The words "or, moreover"[89] in the quotation from the *Mahāniddesa* might lead one to conclude that there was indecision involved in the interpretation that two truths are actually suggested in the *Mahāniddesa*. However, the way (*magga*) and the cessation of *dukkha*, or *nibbāna*, are two aspects forming one truth. This is made clear by a passage in the *Visuddhimagga*, a work by Buddhaghosa, the eminent Buddhist expositor of the fifth century A.D. Incorporating the same line from the *Sn.* on which the above quotation from the *Mahāniddesa* comments, Buddhaghosa wrote regarding the word "truth" (*sacca*): "Now this word *sacca* conveys many meanings." He continued, "[It is used] both with regard to *nibbāna*, truth in the highest sense [*paramatthasacca*], as well as *magga* in such passages as 'One truth! There

---

[87] See *SnA.*I.212 where *niyyāna*, occurring at *Sn.*, vs. 170, is explained in terms of *maggasacca*.

[88] *Nd.1.*II.292 (on *Sn.*, vs. 884).

[89] *Nd.1.*II.292: *Athavā* (initial). This indeclinable, formed of *atha* and *va*, carries the force of the English "or, moreover." *SnA.*II.555, no doubt following *Nd.1.*, says, "*Ekaṃ saccaṃ nirodho maggo vā.*" *Sdpj.*II.361, commenting on *Nd.1.*II.292, says, "*Ekaṃ saccaṃ nirodho, maggo vā.*" The learned Mahāthera A. P. Buddhadatta, who edited the *Sdpj.*, placed a comma where the original, of course, had none. The particle *vā* (enclitic) carries a disjunctive force and so used means "or." The Aristotelian rule of "the excluded middle" that often pivots on the English "or" does not weigh as heavily on *vā* and particularly is this the case in these commentarial passages.

is no second.'"[90] The *Paramatthamañjūsā*, a commentary (*tikā*) on the *Visuddhimagga*, elaborates:

> *Nibbāna* is truth in the highest sense because its *dhamma* is not vain. It is said, "*Nibbāna* has the *dhamma* of being not vain; that the noble ones know as truth." The knowing and penetration of that [*i.e.*, *nibbāna* has the *dhamma* of being not vain] and of the way that brings that about, although two, do not cause contradiction as truth is called in this verse "One truth!..."[91]

The way, in its most comprehensive sense, and *nibbāna* comprise one Truth and that Truth is saving Truth. The way without *nibbāna* is inconceivable and *nibbāna* without the way is meaningless.

The Buddha rediscovered an ancient way and traveled it. That way, the noble eightfold way mentioned above, is *dhamma* and it is considered as the fourth truth of the four noble truths, all four of which are *dhamma*. The Buddha awakened unto, thoroughly understood[92] what has been called in English "conditioned co-production" (*paṭiccasamuppāda*).[93]

> And what, *bhikkhus*, is *paṭiccasamuppada? Bhikkhus*, because of the condition of birth there is old age and death. Whether there

---

[90] *Vism.* XVI. 26: "Idhāyaṃ saccasaddo anekesu atthesu dissati.... 'Ekaṃ hi saccaṃ na dutiyan' ti ādisu paramatthasacce nibbāne c'eva magge ca."

I note the references to *Vism.* by chapter and paragraph drawn from *Visuddhimagga of Buddhaghosācariya*, ed. Henry Clark Warren, revised by Dharmananda Kosambi, "Harvard Oriental Series," Vol. XLI (Cambridge, Massachusetts: Harvard University Press, 1950). In some cases, cross-references to *The Visuddhi-magga of Buddhaghosa*, ed. C. A. F. Rhys Davids (London: Published for the Pali Text Society by Humphrey Milford, 1920), will be noted as *PTS* with volume and page numbers.

[91] *Pm.* II. 526: "Amoghadhammattā nibbāṇam paramatthasaccaṃ. 'Amoghadhammaṃ nibbāṇaṃ, tad ariyā saccato vidū' ti hi vuttaṃ. Tassa pana taṃ sampāpakassa ca maggassa pajānanā paṭivedho avivādakāraṇan ti dvayam pi 'ekaṃ hi saccaṃ...' imissā gāthāya saccan ti vuttaṃ."

[92] The verbal form of the word translated above as "thoroughly understood" occurs at *S.* II. 25 and *A.* I. 286 in the present tense. The Pāli word is *abhisameti* and in these passages follows immediately *abhisambujjhati*, "he awakes unto." *Abhisameti* is formed from the prefix *abhi* plus another prefix, *sam*, from √*i*, "to go." There is more to the activity suggested by this verb than the English term "understand" might convey.

[93] *S.* II. 25. See also *A.* I. 286.

> is an arising of *Tathāgatas* or whether there is no arising of *Tathāgatas*, this factor abides, this status of *dhamma*, this procedure of *dhamma*, this specific conditionality. The *Tathāgata* awakes unto, thoroughly understands that....[94]

A passage in the *Majjhima-nikāya* reads, "This was said by the *Bhagavan*, 'He who perceives *paṭiccasamuppāda* perceives *dhamma*. He who perceives *dhamma* perceives *paṭiccasamuppāda*.'"[95] The commentary on this passage mentions briefly, "'He who perceives *paṭiccasamuppāda*' means he who perceives causal relations. 'He who perceives *dhamma*' means he who perceives processes [*dhammā*] arisen together in dependence."[96] The commentator was, no doubt, aware of the use of *dhamma* in the accusative singular in the *Majjhima-nikāya* passage, and his use of *dhamme*, the accusative plural form, apparently represents neither an oversight nor an intentional variation,[97] but a forthright statement that one who perceives *dhamma* perceives processes (*dhammā*) that arise through conditional relations, in dependence.

The context of the passage under consideration presents Sāriputta demonstrating the five aggregates of an individual that form bases

---

[94] *S.* II. 25. Beginning with the second sentence of the quotation, the Pāli reads, "Uppādā vā Tathāgatānaṃ anuppādā vā Tathāgatānaṃ ṭhitā vā sā dhātu dhammaṭṭhitatā dhammaniyāmatā idappaccayatā. Taṃ Tathāgato abhisambujjhati abhisameti...." *Pm.*, p. 561, commenting on *Vism.* XVII. 25, warns that should one infer from the passage in *S.* II. 25 that *paṭiccasamuppāda* is permanent (*nicca*), one would misunderstand the regularity of modes of conditional relations (*paccayākāradhammatā*). *Paṭiccasamuppāda* would rightly be illustrated in terms of that inherent nature of a cause (*kāraṇa*) that is differentiated according to its own fruit or result. "The meaning of *paṭiccasamuppāda* is wrongly grasped by some who say 'without cessation, without arising.'"

[95] *M.* I. 190–191.

[96] *MA.* II.230: "Yo paṭiccasamuppādaṃ passatī ti yo paccaye passati. So dhammaṃ passatī ti so paṭiccasamuppanne dhamme passati."

[97] I assume this to be the case. The *PTS* editions of *M.* and *MA.* do not note textual variations of either the *sutta* or the commentary. The sutta in the *Majjhima-nikāya* under consideration is the *Mahāhatthipadopamasutta* considered to have been taught by Sāriputta. The quotation above beginning with "This was said by the *Bhagavan*..." has, to my knowledge, not been traced to a *sutta* passage in which the Buddha is recorded as speaking it.

for clinging (*ime pañc' upādānakkhandhā*). The desire for these five represents the genesis of *dukkha* (*dukkhasamudaya*) and the abandoning of desire for them represents the cessation of *dukkha* (*dukkhanirodha*). When the five aggregates are known as having originated through conditional relations they are perceived as having only penultimate value and through this realization one becomes aware that they were ill-suited objects for disorienting, inordinate desires.[98] This passage enables one to note the way in which the four noble truths and *paṭiccasamuppāda*, although formulated differently—the four noble truths being the more inclusive—represent the same state of affairs: things have not always been as they seem; there is a causal process at work; to recognize it and gain mastery of the situation is liberating. Hence, both formulations are *dhamma*.[99]

Paṭiccasamuppāda is expressed in a well-known statement, "When this is, this becomes; from the arising of this, this arises; when this is not, this does not become; from the cessation of this, this ceases."[100] The commentary on the *Udāna*, referring to this passage, reads:

> And is not "when this is, this becomes, etcetera" worthy to become a statement of the *Bhagavan* alone? No one but the Teacher is able to teach *paṭiccasamuppāda*. This is truth.[101]

We have noted that *paṭiccasamuppāda* is discussed in the context dealing with the five *khandhas*. It is more often mentioned in the

98 See *Ud.*, p. 1.

99 This relation is explicitly stated in the discussion at *MA.* II. 230: "Chandarāgavinayo chandarāgappahānan ti nibbānass' esa adhivacanaṃ. Iti tīṇi saccāni pāḷiyaṃ āgatān' eva. Maggasaccaṃ āharitvā gahetabbaṃ. Yā imesu tisu ṭhānesu diṭṭhi, saṅkappo, vācā, kammanto, ājīvo, vāyāmo, sati, samādhi, bhāvanāpaṭivedho, ayaṃ maggo ti." The *SnA.* I. 364–365, commenting on *Sn.*, vs. 368, demonstrates the relationship between the practice of psycho-physical analysis and the practice of the four truths. "Dhamman ti khandhāyatanādibhedaṃ yathābhūtañāṇena, catusaccadhammaṃ vā maggena viditvā."

100 *A.* V. 184; *M.* I. 262–263, 264, II. 32; *S.* II. 65.

101 *UdA.*, p. 29: "Nanu ca 'imasmiṃ sati, idaṃ hoti' ti ādi Bhagavato eva vacanaṃ bhavituṃ arahatī ti? Na hi Satthāraṃ muñcitvā añño paṭiccasamuppādaṃ desetuṃ samattho hotī ti. Saccam p' etaṃ."

context of the twelve *nidānas*, interrelated consequences,[102] and these *nidānas* are also referred to as *dhamma*.[103]

Again, one reads in the scriptures, "Whether there is an arising of *Tathāgatas*. . . this factor abides. . . all clustering forces [*saṃkhārā*] are impermanent."[104] The passage continues in identical phrasing but in the second case reads "all clustering forces are *dukkha*" and in the third case, "all *dhammas* are not-self [*anattā*]." These three characteristics (*tilakkhaṇa*) form another aspect of *dhamma*[105] and they represent three permeating characteristics of phenomena.[106]

---

[102] See *S.* II. 25.

[103] See *D.* II. 55 and *A.* II. 92.

[104] *A.* I. 286. The Pāli matches verbatim that relating to *S.* II. 25, except that after "dhammaṭṭhitatā dhammaniyāmatā," the *A.* passage reads "sabbe saṅkhāra [*read* saṅkhārā] aniccā" rather than "idappaccayatā." *AA.* II. 380 glosses *dhammaṭṭhitatā* and °*niyāmatā* by *sabhāvaṭṭhitatā* and *sabhāvaniyāmatā*, respectively.

[105] *Nd.1.* I. 94 (on *Sn.*, vs. 792); *SnA.* II. 550, 568.

[106] The commentarial tradition remains somewhat less than explicit about the scope of the *tilakkhaṇa* especially as the three phrases *sabbe saṅkhārā aniccā, sabbe saṅkhārā dukkhā, sabbe dhammā anattā* are concerned. There are four realms in the Buddhist world view: (1) *kāma*, (2) *rūpa*, (3) *arūpa*, (4) *lokuttara*. *AA.* II. 380 (on *A.* I. 286) glosses *sabbe saṅkhārā* as *catubhūmakasaṃkhārā*, that is, the impulses, clustering forces, active in the four realms; hence one would infer that even in the *lokuttara* sphere, where there are *saṅkhāras*, they would be *aniccā, dukkhā* and *anattā*. *SA.* II. 318, commenting on *S.* III. 133–134, notes, "Sabbe saṅkhārā aniccā ti, sabbe tebhūmakasaṅkhārā aniccā." The *S.* passage omits *dukkhā* but includes *sabbe dhammā anattā*, which *SA.* understands as "sabbe catubhūmaka-dhammā anattā," in which case, the *lokuttara* sphere would be considered *anattā*. The commentator ponders why *dukkha* was omitted and only two *lakkhaṇāni* were mentioned: because, he suggests, had *dukkha* been used, then *magga* and *phala*, which are considered *lokuttara*, would be seen as *dukkha*. This observation and the weight of Buddhist thought regarding the *lokuttara magga* and *nibbāna* would lead one to suggest that the commentarial gloss at *AA.* II. 380 represents an oversight on the part of the commentator or the editor. See *MA.* II. 112 (on *M.* I. 136) where it is stressed that *saṅkhāras* are pacified in *nibbāna*.

The three phrases under consideration occur also at *Dhp.*, vss. 277–279. *DhpA.* III. 405 commenting on *sabbe saṅkhārā* speaks of the *saṅkhāras* in terms of the *khandhas* that have arisen in *kāmabhava ādi* as ceasing, hence the term "*anicca*" is used. "*Sabbe dhammā*," it says, "means just the five *khandhas*." *Ibid.*, p. 407. One would infer that where there are *khandhas* the terms *anicca, dukkha, anattā* would be relevant, and there are *khandhas* even for one

The four noble truths are *dhamma*; the way is *dhamma*; morality (*sīla*), concentration (*samādhi*), and wisdom (*paññā*) are *dhamma*; *paṭiccasamuppāda* is *dhamma*; the *khandhas*, *āyatanas*, and *dhātus* are *dhamma*;[107] the *tilakkhaṇa* are *dhamma*. These terms represent *dhamma* put into words by the Buddha, the "one who has become *dhamma*."

In the *Samyutta-nikāya* there is recorded a conversation between one Vakkali and the Buddha. Vakkali mentioned that for some time he had sought to see the *Bhagavan* but was not strong enough in body to do so. When the Buddha heard this he said,

> Now hold on Vakkali! What is there for you with seeing this putrid body. Indeed, Vakkali, he who sees *dhamma* sees me. He who sees me sees *dhamma*. Indeed, Vakkali, the one seeing *dhamma* sees me; the one seeing me sees *dhamma*.[108]

The commentary on this passage draws the reader's attention to the *Tathāgata* as one having a *dhamma*-body (*dhamma-kāya*) and says that "body" (*kāya*) means the ninefold *dhamma* that transcends the world.[109] Elsewhere in the commentarial sources, the above passage is mentioned in close relation with *dhamma-kāya* and *dhamma-bhūta*. Three interpretations of *dhamma-bhuta*, "one who has become *dhamma*," are given in the commentaries: the *Bhagavan* is one who "has *dhamma* as his nature" (*dhamma-svabhāva*);[110] he is one who "has become *dhamma*" because of his rolling forth *dhamma* that is

in the *lokuttara magga*. *Sdpj.* I. 222 (on *Nd. 1.* I. 94) says, "Sabbe dhammā ti nibbānam pi antokaritvā vuttā." In this case, *nibbāna* also is *anatta*. *Pm.* I. 280 (on *Vism.*, p. 239; *PTS*, p. 290) discussing *anicca* sets the contrast with *nicca* and says, "Niccaṃ nāma dhuvaṃ sassataṃ—yathā taṃ nibbānaṃ. Na niccan ti aniccaṃ."

[107] See *SnA.* I. 364–365. See also *Thig.*, vss. 43, 69, 103.

[108] *S.* III. 120. See also *Itv.*, p. 91, and *Miln.*, p. 71.

[109] *SA.* II. 314 (on *S.* III. 120). See also *ItvA.*, p. 116 (on *Itv.*, pp. 90–91). *UdA.*, p. 311 (on *Ud.*, p. 58) says that the *dhammakāya* of the *Bhagavan* is seen by seeing the noble truths (*ariyasaccadassanena*). The passage from *S.* II. 120 occurs in *Ap.*, p. 467; *DhpA.* IV. 118; *UdA.*, p. 311; *Sdhs.*, p. 69; and *SdhRv.*, p. 1063.

[110] *AA.* V. 72 (on *A.* V. 226).

to be thoroughly learned, the authoritative teaching (*pariyattidhammappavattanato*), without distorting it; and "he has become *dhamma*" in the sense that he consists of *dhamma* that was uttered in words having reflected on it in his heart (*hadaya*).[111] Similarly, with regard to *dhamma-kāya*, a commentary says,

> Why is it said that the *Tathāgata* has a *dhamma*-body? The *Tathāgata*, having reflected on the *tepiṭaka* Buddha-word in his heart, sent it forth in words. Therefore his body is *dhamma* because of its consisting of *dhamma*.[112]

A further discussion of the relation between the Buddha and *dhamma* in the sense of *dhamma-kāya* falls beyond the scope of this study. One should note at this point that Siddhattha Gotama sought for *dhamma* and totally attained it, becoming at the moment of realization the Buddha who thereafter could not be dissociated from *dhamma* that he preached. The Pāli commentaries tend to utilize a *dhamma-kāya* notion not to suggest an ontological reality but to underline a continuity between the Buddha's holistic realization of *dhamma* and his teachings (*dhamma*), a continuity discerned to be at the basis of the soteriological process for Theravāda Buddhists. That which the Buddha spoke is in no way a distortion of that which he realized.

The Purpose for Which Dhamma Is Taught

The force of *dhamma* in the Pāli canon and commentarial literature might be noted further by considering the purpose for which *dhamma* was taught. When one perceives the relationship between the *Tathāgata* and the purpose for which he preached *dhamma* as consistent, one honors, reveres, praises and worships (*pūjeti*) him.

---

[111] *MA.* II. 76 (on *M.* I. 111); *SA.* II. 389 (on *S.* IV. 94); *Sdpj.* II. 295 (on *Nd.1.* I. 178 [on *Sn.*, vs. 834]). See also *ThagA.* II. 205 (on *Thag.*, vs. 491).

[112] *DA.* III. 865 (on *D.* II. 84). See also *DA.* I. 34 (on *D.* I. 1) and *SA.* I. 12 (related to *DA.* I. 34) where it is said that one who preaches *dhamma* as it was heard, saying, "Thus it was heard by me," makes manifest the *dhamma*-body (*sarīra*) of the *Bhagavan*.

> The *Bhagavan*, awakened, preaches *dhamma* for awakening; the *Bhagavan*, tamed, preaches *dhamma* for taming; the *Bhagavan*, at peace, preaches *dhamma* for calming; the *Bhagavan*, crossed over, preaches *dhamma* for crossing over; the *Bhagavan*, who has attained *nibbāna*, preaches *dhamma* for attaining *nibbāna*.[113]

Dhamma is preached for control (*saṃvara*) of the senses,[114] for the destruction of the defilements (*āsavas*),[115] for the destruction of all *dukkha*,[116] for the attaining of *nibbāna* and the release from all bonds (*gantha*),[117] for the pulling out of latent, biased dispositions (*anusaya*),[118] for calming composure (*assāsa*),[119] for the tranquilizing of all *saṅkhāras*,[120] for whatever is beneficial for someone,[121] for the abstinence from transgressing the five moral precepts,[122] for the suppressing of unwholesome *dhammas* and the development of wholesome *dhammas*,[123] for the attainment of arahantship (*arahatta*),[124] for the overcoming of birth and old age.[125]

> With higher knowledge, Uttiya, I preach *dhamma* to disciples for purification of beings, for transcending of grief and lamentation, for going to the end [*attha*] of *dukkha* and distress, for attaining of the method, for realization of *nibbāna*.[126]

---

[113] *M.* I. 235. *MA.* II. 282 glosses "awakening," *bodhi*, as "*bodhi* to the four truths." So also *DA.* III. 842, on the same passage occurring at *D.* III. 54–55. At *MA.* II. 134, the *sutta* passage is quoted as an example of giving praise, *namakkāra*. See also the Geigers' *PD.*, pp. 63–64, where references to passages in the Pāli canon on the purpose for which *dhamma* is preached are noted.

[114] *M.* I. 503; *MA.* III. 213; *Nd.1.* I. 243.

[115] *D.* III. 129–130; *MA.* II. 32 (on *M.* I. 71).

[116] *D.* III. 196; *D.* III. 4; *DA.* III. 817–818. See also *M.* I. 72; *A.* I. 187, II. 9.

[117] *D.* III. 272, as preached by Sāriputta. *DA.* III. 1054 notes that *dhamma* in this context is what Sāriputta heard.

[118] *M.* I. 213 as in the case of a learned *bhikkhu*.

[119] *Vin.* I. 236.

[120] *M.* I. 136. *MA.* II. 112 takes this as equivalent to *nibbāna*.

[121] *SnA.* I. 368 (on *Sn.*, vs. 378).

[122] *D.* III. 195. This *sutta* is the *Āṭānāṭiyasutta* which is one of the more important *suttas* in Sinhalese Buddhist *pirit* (Pāli, *paritta*) ceremonies.

[123] *D.* III. 57; *DA.* III. 843. See also *M.* I. 475.

[124] *Ud.*, p. 7.

[125] *Thig.*, vs. 192; *S.* I. 132; *Sn.*, vss. 1097, 1120, 1122.

[126] *A.* V. 194.

The commentarial tradition depicts the force of *dhamma* as it can be communicated through preaching and the value that it might have when lived. In providing the setting for the Buddha's statement in the *Dhaniyasutta* of the *Suttanipāta*, the commentary reads:

> Thus the *Bhagavan*, dwelling in Gandhakuṭi in the Jetavanamahāvihāra, heard with his hearing faculty that is pure and superhuman this *gāthā* [of Dhaniya, *Sn.*, vs. 18] as he was speaking and, having heard it, he, looking at the world with his Buddha-eye, saw Dhaniya and his wife. "Both of these are endowed with suitability [*hetusampannā*]. If, having gone, I shall teach *dhamma*, both, having gone forth [into the *saṅgha* as *bhikkhu* and *bhikkhunī*] will attain arahantship. If I shall not go, tomorrow they will be destroyed by a flood of water."[127]

The commentary on the *Majjhima-nikāya* mentions that the Buddha spoke two discourses to Saccaka and yet the latter neither attained a deep understanding nor did he go forth, nor did he become established in the refuges (*saraṇesu*). "Why did the *Bhagavan* preach *dhamma* to him?" the commentator asks; "For the sake of the impressions in future."[128] The Buddha, the commentary continues, was aware that two hundred years after his *parinibbāna* the *sāsana*, the instruction, would be established in Sri Lanka (Tambapaṇṇidīpa) and that there at that time the man Saccaka would attain arahantship and would be named Kāḷa-Buddharakkhita. "Having seen this, he taught *dhamma* for the sake of the impressions in future."[129]

These passages drawn from the canon and commentaries demonstrate that *dhamma* is preached not idly, not as a form of speculation, but rather for salvation with the assurance that it is not preached in vain.

Hearing and Penetrating Dhamma

Throughout the canon there are passages—in most cases repetitious, set phrases—that convey a confessional awareness on the part

[127] *SnA.* I. 29 (on *Sn.*, vs. 19).

[128] *MA.* II. 293: "Anāgate vāsanatthāya." [129] *Ibid.*

of one who has heard and perceived *dhamma* that was preached. In our bringing these passages together at this point in the study, the reader might note the close relation between the preaching of *dhamma* and the perception, realization of *dhamma* on the part of the hearer.

> Just as a clean cloth having dark stains removed would easily absorb dye, so also while on that seat the clear, spotless eye of *dhamma* [*dhammacakkhu*, vision of *dhamma*] arose for Upāli, a householder: "Whatever has as its *dhamma* arising, that has as its *dhamma* cessation." Then Upāli, a householder, [was] one who had seen *dhamma*, attained *dhamma*, known *dhamma*, plunged into *dhamma*; one who had crossed perplexity, without doubt; one who had attained confidence without relying on another in the Teacher's instruction [*sāsana*]. . . .[130]

The Buddha is viewed as having the capacity of perceiving in all levels of vision. The commentaries speak of him as being endowed with five eyes: "fleshly eye, heavenly eye, wisdom-eye, Buddha-eye, all-seeing-eye."[131] The Buddha's wisdom-eye (*paññācakkhu*) is glossed with *dhammacakkhu*, which is clear and spotless.[132] The Buddha-eye is interpreted as the knowledge of the faculties of others and knowledge of inclinations and dispositions. The all-seeing-eye represents knowledge that is omniscience. *Dhammacakkhu* is related to the knowledge of the three paths.[133]

Dhammacakkhu, *dhamma*-eye or vision of *dhamma*, is sometimes used to designate the four paths and also the four fruits,[134] or three paths, or the destruction of defilements in the case of an *arahant*,[135] but in most cases it designates the "path of stream attainment" in

---

[130] *M.*I.380. On Upāli, see Malalasekera, *DPPN.*I.411. On these statements beginning with *dhammacakkhu*, see also *Vin.*I.16, II.155; *D.*I.110; *M.*I.379, 501, II.145; *Ud.*, p. 49.

[131] See *Nd.1.*I.45 (on *Sn.*, vs. 776), II.488 (on *Sn.*, vs. 956); *ThagA.*II.177 (on *Thag.*, vs. 417).

[132] *Sdpj.*I.158 (on *Nd.1.*I.45), quoting the phrase found at *A.*IV.186; *S.*IV.46, 107. See also *Sdpj.*III.83 (regarding *Nd.2.* comments on *Sn.*, vs. 1120).

[133] *DA.*II.467 (on *D.*II.38).

[134] *SA.*II.392 (on *S.*IV.107).

[135] *MA.*III.92 (on *M.*I.380), but *VinA.*V.971 (on *Vin.*I.16) relates *dhammacakkhu* to the first three paths.

a process leading to salvation,[136] and has particular relevance to the thorough grasping of the four noble truths[137] in terms of their method (*ākāra*) that is expressed in the sentence, "Whatever has as its *dhamma* arising, all that has as its *dhamma* cessation."[138]

One reaches the point where *dhamma* is seen, perceived (*diṭṭha-dhamma*). The commentaries gloss this term in saying "*dhamma* as the four noble truths is seen."[139] One should keep in mind that the four noble truths represent a comprehensive means of stating what it is that *dhamma* as preached represents. In later Sinhalese commentarial glosses and translations, "*dhamma* that is seen" is taken in a comprehensive sense as well as in its highest sense. On the term *diṭṭhadhamma*, occurring in the commentary on the *Dhamma-pada*,[140] the Sinhalese glossary reads, "'one having seen the four truths,' or 'one having perceived *dhamma* that transcends the world.'"[141]

That one has attained *dhamma* (*pattadhamma*), known *dhamma* (*viditadhamma*), plunged into *dhamma* (*pariyogāḷhadhamma*), represents, for the commentators, not different stages in awareness, not a progression in grasping *dhamma*, but synonyms that, when taken with *diṭṭhadhamma*, represent a single thorough grasping of the four truths that is synonymous with knowledge of the first path.[142]

---

136 See *MA.* III. 92; *DA.* I. 237 (on *D.* I. 86), I. 278 (on *D.* I. 110); *UdA.*, p. 283 (on *Ud.*, p. 49); *VvA.*, p. 317 (on *Vv.*LXXXI, vs. 27, p. 74).

137 *AA.* II. 356 (on *A.* I. 242). 138 *MA.* III. 92 (on *M.* I. 380).

139 *DA.* I. 278 (on *D.* I. 110); *MA.* III. 92 (on *M.* I. 380).

140 *DhpA.* I. (2). 381.

141 *DhpAg.*, p. 111: "Diṭṭhadhammo, duṭu siyu sas ätiyē yi—nohot pasak kaḷa lovuturā dham ätiyē yi." *DhpAg.*, p. 66 glosses *tumhehi diṭṭhadhammassa* at *DhpA.* I. (2), pp. 197–198, with "tupa visin daknālada lovuturā dham ha ...." and *SdhRv.*, p. 229, translates the phrase at *DhpA.*, as "mumba vahansē duṭu nivan daham pasak kaṭa hemva"—"May I have a glimpse of *dhamma* as *nibbāna* seen by you sir." See also *SdhRv.*, p. 653—a translation of *DhpA.* III. 6 (on *Dhp.*, vs. 118)—where *nivan* is the term used to translate *dhamma* in the compound *diṭṭhadhamma*.

142 See *UdA.*, p. 285; *MA.* II. 92; *VinA.* V. 971. Note that the several terms are to be understood in the same way as *diṭṭhadhamma*.

The Pāli compounds that represent the thorough grasping of *dhamma* suggest that much more is involved in this awareness than one might, at first glance, think. The term *dhammacakkhu* is used to represent the arising of vision that is considerably more than knowing the constituents of the four noble truths. The vision mentioned is that in terms of which one is enabled to put one's life and the world and that which is both in the world and beyond into perspective.

The compounds, *diṭṭhadhamma*, *pattadhamma*, *viditadhamma*, and *pariyogāḷhadhamma* are what grammarians call *bahubbīhi* (Sanskrit, *bahuvrīhi*) and hence do not speak primarily of what Upāli did, but, rather, being adjectival, they communicate to the reader what Upāli became as a consequence of the arising of the *dhammacakkhu*: he was "one who had seen *dhamma*," *diṭṭhadhamma*, "one who had attained *dhamma*," *pattadhamma*.

Faith and the Hearing and Penetrating of Dhamma

> Wonderful, O Gotama, wonderful, O Gotama. Just as, O Gotama, one might raise up one who has fallen; or one might reveal that covered; or one might show the way to one confused; or one might hold up an oil lamp in the darkness that the sighted might see forms, just so *dhamma* has been proclaimed in many modes by the revered Gotama. I, myself, go to the revered Gotama as refuge and to *dhamma* and to the *bhikkhusaṅgha*.[143]

This passage frequently concludes *suttas* in the canon. Because it is often met, sometimes abbreviated in English translations because it is repetitious, one might fail to catch the force, the attitude that is being expressed on the part of the hearer about himself and about that which he has heard.

The commentary on the *Majjhima-nikāya* explains this passage:

> "Wonderful" means surpassing. Exceedingly pleasing, very

[143] *M.* I. 24. See also *M.* I. 501, where this passage follows immediately "*dhammacakkhuṃ . . . diṭṭhadhammo. . . .*"

> lovely, very beautiful is what is said. In this context he [the hearer] praises the preaching [*desanā*; implied, of course, is *dhammadesanā*] with the word "wonderful" at the same time [he expresses] his sense of being taken up [*pasāda*]. Now in this case, this is the meaning: Wonderful, O Gotama, is this preaching of *dhamma* [*dhammadesanā*] on the part of venerable Gotama, wonderful is my sense of being taken up [*mama pasādo*] because of this preaching of venerable Gotama. Or, moreover, he praises the saying [*vacanam*] of the *Bhagavan* himself each time on two counts. Because it destroys corruptness is the saying of venerable Gotama wonderful. It is wonderful because it is conductive to virtue. Thus, because it produces faith [*saddhā*], because it produces wisdom [*paññā*]; because of its meaning, because of its form [*sabyañjana*]; because the word is clear, because its meaning is profound; because it is pleasant to the ear, because it is heart stirring [*hadayaṅgama*]; because there is no self-exaltation, because there is no contempt for another; because it is refreshing with compassion, because it is pure with wisdom, because it is delightful in appearance, because it is patient and mild, because it is easy to hear, because it is beneficial when pondered over. So is it to be interpreted.[144]

The commentator on this passage in the *sutta* glosses the four similes and notes that they represent one's praise for the preaching about *dhamma*. The remainder of the passage is interpreted as follows:

> Just as someone would raise up something that had fallen, so by causing me, who had turned away from the *saddhamma* into that not *saddhamma*, to stand up from that not *saddhamma*; just as one would uncover that covered, so by uncovering the instruction [*sāsana*] that was covered by a jungle of perverse opinions [*micchādiṭṭhigahana*] since the disappearance of the instruction [*sāsana*] of *Bhagavan* Kassapa; just as one would describe the way for one confused, so by making manifest the way to heaven and release [*saggamokkhamagga*] for me who had followed along a crooked way, a perverse way [*micchāmagga*]; just as one would hold up an oil lamp in the darkness, so *dhamma* was proclaimed in many modes by venerable Gotama by holding the lamp of the preaching [*desanā*] that destroys that making the darkness of delusion that had covered this for me who was in the way leading to the dark-

---

[144] *MA*.I.130 (on *M*.I.24). See also *UdA*., p. 286 (on *Ud*., p. 49); *DA*.I.227–228 (on *D*.I.85).

ness of delusion not seeing the forms of the gems of the Buddha and so forth [i. e., *dhamma* and *saṅgha*].[145]

Such affirmation and joyous praise as noted in the *sutta* passage is primarily directed not to the Buddha but rather to *dhamma* that was preached. The preaching of *dhamma* by Mahā-Kaccāna,[146] Udena,[147] Kassapa,[148] and Ānanda[149] stimulated the same response on the part of their hearers.[150] This response on the part of the hearers represents an expression of faith. A recurring refrain elsewhere in the canon mentions persons acquiring faith in the *Tathāgata*, having themselves previously heard *dhamma*, and subsequently their decision to go forth from domestic life into the *saṅgha*.[151] The commentary on the *Dīgha-nikāya* draws attention to ways in which one might demonstrate this faith, having heard *dhamma*. Some, the commentary notes, are established in the refuges, some in the five precepts, and others, having made renunciation, go forth.[152] The force of the commentarial remarks suggests that by being "established [*patiṭṭhanti*]" in the refuges and moral precepts, persons respond not merely verbally

---

[145] *MA*. I. 130 (on *M*. I. 24).

[146] *M*. II. 90. [147] *M*. II. 162. [148] *D*. II. 353. [149] *D*. I. 210.

[150] In the first two cases, the hearers sought to go to Mahā-Kaccāna and Udena as refuge only to be told not to do so but, rather, to go to the *Bhagavan* as refuge just as the latter themselves had done. Subsequently, desiring to see the Buddha in order to go to him as refuge, but being told that he had attained complete *nibbāna*, the hearers then sought refuge in the *Bhagavan*, *dhamma*, and *saṅgha*. It appears that when the affirmation "wonderful etc." is expressed, refuge in *dhamma* to some extent has been realized. The remainder of the narratives reflect a concern within the early Buddhist movement; on a mundane level to avoid a possible fragmentation with each teacher claiming disciples who had taken refuge in him, and, on another level, to reaffirm that the three gems alone provide refuge that will enable one to be sustained in the midst of the pressures of mundane life by assisting one to see those pressures as, precisely, mundane.

[151] *D*. I. 62–63: "So taṃ dhammaṃ sutvā Tathāgate saddhaṃ paṭilabhati." *M*. I. 344, *M*. III. 33. *DA*. I. 180 (on *D*. I. 62–63) notes that "'He acquires faith in the *Tathāgata*,' means he acquires faith, having heard the thoroughly pure *dhamma*, in the master [*sāmin*] of *dhamma*, the *Tathāgata*, [saying] 'Indeed, Fully Enlightened One is the *Bhagavan*.'" This comment occurs also at *PugA*., pp. 234–235.

[152] *DA*. II. 360 (on *D*. I. 175).

or by adopting a creed, but, rather, they become totally involved in moral living—and this is a consequence of hearing *dhamma.*

A person is faithful (*saddho*) when he is endowed, infused—might one also say leavened?—with faith (*saddhāya samannāgato, saddhāsampanno*). In commentarial definitions of *saddhā,* a personal dimension provides the context in which the term is explained. Faith is fourfold, the commentaries tell us.[153] Among the beings set on omniscient enlightenment (*sabbaññubodhisattānaṃ*) there is "continuing faith" or "faith in the oncoming" (*āgamanasaddhā*)[154] or "faith in that which is to come" (*āgamanīyasaddhā*).[155] The nuance held in the commentarial ambiguity seems to suggest that the *bodhisattas* were not without faith since the time of, and including, their making their firm resolve to attain enlightenment. For one recalling some of the events in the many lives of the several *bodhisattas,* their faith might be understood in the sense of continuity of faith throughout those lives. For others, the faith of these *bodhisattas* might be understood primarily in terms of that for which they sought.[156] It will be noted below that a *sāvaka* "faiths" in the *bodhi* of the *Tathāgata.*

There is also faith in that which is attained or faith characterized by attainment (*adhigamana-saddhā,*[157] *adhigama*°[158]) "because of its being attained by penetration on the part of the noble disciples."[159] "When 'Buddha, *dhamma, saṅgha*' is said, there is serene joy

[153] *DA.* II. 529 (on *D.* II. 78), III. 1028–1029 (on *D.* III. 237); *AA.* III. 257 (on *A.* III. 65). See also *MA.* III. 325.

[154] *DA.*III.1028; *AA.*III.257. The passage at *DA.* reads, "Tattha sabbaññubodhisattānaṃ saddhā abhinīhārato paṭṭhāya āgamana-saddhā nāma." *AA.* reads the same until "*paṭṭhāya*" and continues, "āgatattā āgamana-saddhā nāma." *MA.* reads as *AA.*

[155] *DA.* II. 529; "Tattha āgamanīya-saddhā sabbaññubodhisattānaṃ hoti . . . ."

[156] The term *āgamana* could mean "authority of tradition" or the like, but its meaning this in a compound with *saddhā* and being ascribed to the *bodhisattas* seems dubious. The case might be otherwise should this aspect of faith have been ascribed to *sāvakas* or *bhikkhus.*

[157] *DA.* III. 1029–1030.

[158] *DA.* II. 529; *AA.* III. 257.

[159] *DA.* III. 1029–1030; *AA.* III. 257.

[*pasāda*] which is joyous faith [*pasāda-saddhā*]. Further, having resolved the act of 'faithing' [*saddahana*], having determined it, there is resolute faith [*okappana-saddhā*]."[160]

Faith is active in the process of salvation, is operative when one listens intently to *dhamma* being preached—either, following passages already noted, when one acquires faith having heard *dhamma*; or when one has faith and draws near to hear *dhamma*.

> Regarding this [i.e., gradual training], *bhikkhus*, one having faith arisen [*saddhājāto*] approaches; approaching, he sits down reverently [*payirupāsati*]; reverently sitting, he inclines his ear; having his ear inclined, he listens; having heard *dhamma*, he bears it in mind, he considers the meaning of the *dhammas* being borne in mind; considering the meaning, the *dhammas* are approved of and desire [*chanda*] arises; having desire arisen, he exerts; having exerted, he weighs the matter; having weighed it, he strives. Being one resolute he realizes individually [*kāyena*] the highest truth and having penetrated it through wisdom [*paññāya*], he sees.[161]

This passage continues, to state that in a case where there is no faith the whole process does not occur.[162]

A person who is faithful and becomes immersed in the instruction (*sāsana*) of the Teacher, the Buddha, realizes that though he does not understand fully the reason for the Buddha's having said to do this or that, he is prepared to follow the instruction because the Buddha

---

[160] *DA.* II. 529. The commentary mentions that the intention is twofold, namely, that *pasāda-saddhā* and *okappanasaddhā* both have bearing on the response to "Buddha, *dhamma*, *saṅgha*." *DA.*III.1029 and *AA.*III.257 speak of *okappanasaddhā* as being resolute (*okappana*) in the sense of being steadfast (*acalabhāvena*).

[161] *M.* I. 480, quoted at *SnA.* I. 144–145 and utilized in a comment at *SnA.* I. 235–236 (on *Sn.*, vs. 186).

[162] *M.* I. 480. *DA.* III. 954 (on *D.* III. 189) glosses "by one listening well" with "by one listening who has 'faithed,' for, indeed, one listening having not 'faithed' does not attain distinction"—"Sussūsāyā ti saddahitā savanena, assadahitvā [*read* assaddahitvā] suṇanto hi visesaṃ nādhigacchati." *MA.* IV. 171–172, in a narrative, notes, "They know neither to hear nor 'to faith.' Therefore there is no thorough understanding"—"N'eva sotuṃ na saddhātuṃ maññanti. Tato abhisamayo na hoti."

knew what he was doing,[163] that the instruction promotes growth and gives strength; hence, he is prepared to strive for that which is to be attained. The point is made that for a person living in such a manner there will either be knowledge in this life (*diṭṭhe va dhamme aññā*) or, should there be substrata remaining, the state of a non-returner.[164]

Faith has an important role in the life of a person who follows out the course that conduces to the attainment of wisdom (*paññā*).[165] Faith provides a dimension of reliance, of expectation, that what is called wisdom is rightly called, and what is called the way is the proper means.[166]

In an attempt to catch the force of "faith" (*saddhā*) one should avoid a pitfall presented by Western categories especially as seen in the so-called faith-and-reason problem. The English concepts "faith" and "reason" are held together in the Pāli term *saddhā* when the latter has to do with a reasonable person. *Saddhā* and *paññā* when taken together do not fit into "faith and reason." Rather, they express a dynamic process where *saddhā* is active in one wanting to know, coming to know in part and *paññā* becomes more pervasive in one coming to know and knowing fully, in truth.

In the process of salvation, faith arranges the necessary provisions for the journey;[167] faith is a person's second;[168] it is a possession that

---

[163] *M.* I. 480. The verb tense in the Pāli is present. "Satthā Bhagavā, sāvako 'ham—asmi; jānāti Bhagavā, nāham jānāmīti."

[164] Regarding the idiom *diṭṭhe va dhamme* or *diṭṭhe dhamme* coming to mean "in this life," Professor O. H. de A. Wijesekera has suggested to me a possible derivation from *dṛṣṭa janman*, which could, theoretically, have developed through *prakrit* into *diṭṭha dammam*; and the latter term, through analogy with *dhamma*, could have become itself *dhamma*. The commentarial tradition glosses *diṭṭhe va dhamme* by *imasmiñ ñeva attabhāve*.

[165] *SnA.* I. 235: "Evaṃ yasmā saddhāya paññā[ya]lābhasamvattanikaṃ paṭipadaṃ paṭipajjati. . . ."

[166] *Sdpj.* I. 214 (on *Nd. 1.* I. 85 [on *Sn.*, vs. 788]): "Ñāṇan ti paccetī ti paññā iti saddahati. Maggo ti paccetī ti upāyo ti saddahati."

[167] *S.* I. 44: "Saddhā bandhati pātheyyam."

[168] *S.* I. 25: "Saddhā dutiyā purisassa hoti." *SA.* I. 66: "'Faith is a person's

is best for a person,[169] by means of which one crosses the ocean of *saṃsāra*;[170] it is a sign-post for noble disciples,[171] and, like a seed, it leads to growth.[172]

Faith that is like a seed, the commentary on the *Sutta-nipāta* says,

> is characterized by composure [*sampasāda*], by reliance [*okappana*], or as having rejoicing as its essential property [*pakkhandanarasā*] in which resolve is present [*adhimuttipaccupaṭṭhānā*], in which no moral stains are present [*akālussiyapaccupaṭṭhānā*], being a distinguishing factor and proximate cause for stream attainment [*sotāpattiyaṅgapadaṭṭhānā*] or having as proximate cause *dhamma* that is to be "faithed in" [*saddahitabbadhammapadaṭṭhānā*], like the clearness [*pasāda*] of the mirror-like surface of water etcetera [*ādāsajalatalādīnaṃ*] it has brought about clearness of mind, like the water-clarifying gem for water, it causes clarification of the associated [psychic] processes [*sampayuttadhammānaṃ*].[173]

The scriptures make it clear that the Buddha did not consider

---

second' means faith of a person in the realm of gods and also in the human realm, of one going to *nibbana*; 'is a second' means it [faith] performs the task of a companion"—"Saddhā dutiyā purisassa hotī ti, purisassa devaloke manussaloke c'eva nibbānaṃ gacchantassa saddhā: dutiyā hotī ti, sahāyakiccaṃ sādheti."

[169] *S.*I.214: "Saddhīdha vittaṃ purisassa seṭṭhaṃ."

[170] *Ibid.*: "Saddhāya tarati oghaṃ."

[171] *A.*IV.109: "Saddhāsiko bhikkhave ariyasāvako akusalaṃ pajahati." The term *saddhāsiko,* if read as *saddhāyiko* would mean "one characterized by faith, faithful, trustworthy"—in Sinhalese script the "s" and "y" in manuscripts are often difficult to distinguish. However, *SnA.*I.143 and *AA.*IV.57 read *saddhesiko* and the latter text has noted one variant, *saddhāyika.* The gloss at *AA.* reads, "'One having faith as sign-post' means having made the sign-post firm. . . ." I follow Edgerton, *BHSD.*, p. 115b, *s.v. iṣika/iṣikā,* who takes it as "sign-post." *PTSD.*, p. 162b, *s.v. esika/esikā,* notes it as "a pillar, post."

[172] *Sn.*, vs. 77; *S.*I.172.

[173] *SnA.*I.144. In this passage, I have taken *sampasāda* as "composure" and *pasāda* as "clearness." *Pasāda,* also meaning "joy," I have translated elsewhere as "sense of being taken up." The imagery in the above passage depicts water being at rest, having silt settled, becoming still and clear; the surface becoming a mirror, smooth as glass. So is to be understood the mind, when, as I have tried to communicate in the translation, it becomes composed, calm, free from agitation, clear. This, too, is a quality of *saddhā,* faith.

himself to have attained the highest attainment by depending on others, adopting what they said, or solely through faith, but rather by thoroughly knowing *dhamma* for himself.[174] This pattern, prominent in the Theravāda tradition, of placing stress on personal realization entails a faith commitment, a commitment that man, the way in which he is put together, and *dhamma* are such that a personal realization of *dhamma* on the highest level is not only possible but worth pursuing. When total realization of *dhamma* as *nibbāna* has occurred and one sees in truth that which was previously not fully seen, one's faith is fulfilled and in becoming fulfilled is transcended.

Sāriputta, a leading disciple of the Buddha, made the statement that he did not go on faith in the *Bhagavan* regarding whether or not the five moral faculties or motivational forces—faith, energy, mindfulness, concentration, and wisdom—lead to that without death because he, Sāriputta, had known, seen, found out, realized this to be the case.[175] Citta, a householder, gave a similar response to a question posed by Nigaṇṭha Nātaputta, the Jain leader, on the matter of whether or not there is a way of concentration without directed and sustained thought, that brings these thinking processes to an end. Citta's reply was based on his knowing and seeing that this was the case (*evaṃ jānanto evam passanto*).[176]

The *Mahāniddesa*, commenting on a verse in the *Suttanipāta*, incorporates the above passage from the *Saṃyuttanikāya* where

---

[174] *M.* II. 211. The point of the passage is difficult to communicate in an English translation. Higher knowledge, *abhiññā* is not to be had in this life through report, *anussava*, or solely through faith, *kevalam saddhāmattaka*, but rather through higher knowledge, *abhiññāya*, having thoroughly known *dhamma* for oneself, *sāmaṃ yeva dhammaṃ abhiññāya*.

[175] *S.* V. 220–222. Sāriputta was asked by the *Bhagavan*, "Saddahāsi tvaṃ Sāriputta, saddhindriyam bhāvitaṃ bahulikataṃ amatogadhaṃ hoti amataparāyanaṃ amatapariyosānaṃ. . . ." *Ibid.*, p. 220. Sāriputta replied, "Na khvāham ettha bhante Bhagavato saddhāya gacchāmi saddhindriyam. . . ." *Ibid.*, p. 221.

[176] *S.* IV. 298: "Na khvāham ettha bhante bhagavato saddhāya gacchāmi . . . ." See also *Ibid.*, p. 299.

Sāriputta's response is noted.[177] The *Mahāniddesa* sets the passage in a context regarding one who is considered "not a faithful one" (*na saddho*) in the sense that he is one for whom *dhamma* is thoroughly known, is manifest (*sāmaṃ sayam abhiññātaṃ attapacchakkhaṃ dhammaṃ*).[178] The commentarial tradition seems to have maintained an awareness of the value of properly directed faith in the religious life.

> "Faithful [*saddho*]" means one endowed with deepening composure [or unalterable joy, serenity; *aveccappasāda*][179] that is possessed of all modes [of knowing the three gems] because of the fact of having abandoned dependence on another with regard to the Buddha and so forth [i.e., *dhamma* and *saṅgha*], not by going along in a prescribed way through faith in another; as it was said, "On this, I do not go on faith in the *Bhagavan*."[180]

The commentary on the *Dhammapada* draws on the *sutta* passage dealing with Sāriputta's response and in its discussion of the term *assaddho*, "one without faith," notes that some *bhikkhus* thought Sāriputta to have gone astray, to lack faith in the Fully Enlightened One. The Teacher, the Buddha, on hearing this said that the con-

---

[177] *Nd.1.*I.236 (on *Sn.*, vs. 853) quoting *S.*V.220–221.

[178] *Nd.1.*I.235.

[179] K. N. Jayatilleke, *Early Buddhist Theory of Knowledge* (London: George Allen & Unwin Ltd., 1963), p. 386, notes that *avecca* at *Sn.*, vs. 299, "seems to mean 'having understood'" and that the compound *aveccappasāda* might originally have meant something like "faith based on understanding." He notes the standard commentarial gloss, *acala*, "unshaken," for *avecca* in *aveccappasāda*. Pāli verbal roots of motion are frequently used to designate a process of knowing through acquaintance and, assuming *avecca* to be a gerund from *ava* and √*i*, one could very well agree with Jayatilleke. At *MA.*I.130 (on *M.*I.24) it is said, "Yesaṃ hi dhātūnaṃ gati-attho, buddhi pi tesaṃ attho. Tasmā gacchāmī ti imassa jānāmi, bujjhāmī ti ayam attho vutto"—"Whatever roots convey the meaning of going, those roots convey the meaning of understanding. Hence for this [expression] 'I go' the meaning expressed is 'I know,' or 'I understand.'" I have taken *ava* and √*i* in the sense of "deepening," which conveys the sense of deepening awareness. See also *MA.*I.172 (on *M.*I.37) where *avecca* is glossed by *acala*, "unshaken, steadfast," and *accuta*, "immovable."

[180] *SnA.*I.365 (on *Sn.*, vs. 371), quoting from *S.*V.221 and perhaps also *S.*IV.298.

versation he had had with Sāriputta was concerning whether or not Sāriputta "faithed"; that when the five moral faculties were cultivated and tranquility and insight were increased, one was able to realize the ways and fruits (*maggaphalāni sacchikātuṃ*); and that Sāriputta had replied that since he was one realizing such, he did not "faith."[181] Sāriputta, the passage continues, did not say that he did not "faith" in the fructifying recompense of that given or done and in the qualities of the Buddha, *dhamma*, and *saṅgha*.[182]

The canon mentions the acquiring of faith following the hearing of *dhamma*, and the drawing near to hear *dhamma* by those who have faith. Further, a faithful one "faiths" in the awakening of the *Tathāgata*.[183] This focusing of faith on the *bodhi* of the *Tathāgata*, his rediscovery of and perfect realization of *dhamma*, provides the bedrock upon which Buddhists for centuries have chosen to build their lives religiously. If there were no *bodhi* of the *Tathāgata*, if "Buddha" were to be a misapplied epithet, if *dhamma* had not been perfectly realized, faith would have been in vain.[184]

"*Bodhi*," the commentaries tell us,

> means knowledge of the four ways.[185] He "faiths" [*saddahati*]

---

[181] *DhpA.* II. 187 (on *Dhp.*, vs. 97): "'"Evaṃ sacchikaronto atthi nāmā" ti na saddahāmi bhante' ti kathesi."

[182] *Ibid.*: "Na 'dinnassa vā katassa vā phalavipākaṃ na saddahasi nāpi buddhādīnaṃ guṇaṃ na saddahasī' ti. . . ."

[183] *M.* II. 95: "bhikkhu saddho hoti saddahati Tathāgatassa bodhim: 'Iti pi so Bhagava. . . .'" The phrase is repeated in *M.*I.356; *D.*III.237; *A.*III.65. See also *CpA.*, p. 311.

[184] At *D.* II. 115, in the *Mahāparinibbāna Sutta*, Ānanda requested that the *Tathāgata* remain for a *kalpa* for the sake of gods and men. In response to the first two requests made by Ānanda, the *Tathāgata* mentioned, "Now is not the time for such request." After Ānanda made the request the third time, the *Tathāgata* asked, "Do you, Ānanda, 'faith' in the *bodhi* of the *Tathāgata?*" "Yes," was the reply. "Then why did you, Ānanda, trouble the *Tathāgata* the third time?" The following portion, *D.* II. 115. line 17, to p. 118, line 26, appears to be a later insertion. *D.* II. 118.26 ff., picks up the train of thought with the *Tathāgata* reminding Ānanda that one must be prepared to sever that which is dear to one and that the *parinibbāna* of the *Tathāgata* was near at hand. See also *DA.* II. 563.

[185] Knowledge of the four ways represents the knowledge active on the

"that [knowledge of the four ways] is well penetrated by the *Tathāgata*." This has to do with the category of the preaching, but also, in this way, faith in the three gems is intended. Exertion and energy prosper for one who is composed [*pasādo*], firm with regard to the Buddha etcetera [i.e., *dhamma* and *saṅgha*].[186]

Faith is present when one views one's life in terms of *kamma*. *Kamma*—volition and action done with an assurance that justice permeates the way to salvation and ideally should penetrate all aspects of social interaction, that what one does in thought, word, and deed has a scope of significance that reaches far beyond the stages of birth and death—at one and the same time provides meaning for inexplicable moments and conditions in this life and, through a concern for life more abundant now and in future, provides motivation for wholesome action. *Kamma* is such that a man living life with compassion is assured that by so living he will ultimately not be crushed. To the extent that *kamma* is *dhamma*, to that extent *kamma* is a fact, and to the extent that *kamma* is considered outside the sphere of *dhamma*, to that extent *kamma* is a theory only.

The commentarial tradition stresses that volition and action (*kamma*) and recompense of volition and action are expressions of

---

way to salvation and the four ways form part of one of the most important interpretations of *dhamma*.

[186] *MA*.III.326; *DA*.III.1029; *AA*.III.65: "Bodhin ti catumaggañāṇaṃ; taṃ suppaṭividdhaṃ Tathāgatenā ti saddahati. Desanāsīsam eva c' etaṃ; imina pana aṅgena tīsu pi ratanesu saddhā adhippetā; yassa hi buddhādisu pasādo balavā tassa padhānaṃ [*AA*. omits and reads *pana*] viriyaṃ ijjhati." It is said in *AA*.III (on *A*.II.44), "Saddho ti buddha-dhamma-saṃgha-guṇānaṃ saddahanatāya saddho"—"'Faithful one' means one faithful because of faithfulness in the qualities of the Buddha, *dhamma* and *saṅgha*." *DA*.III.864 (on *D*.III.84) comments, "Niviṭṭhā ti abhiniviṭṭhā acala-ṭṭhitā. Kassa pana evarūpā saddhā hotī ti? Sot'āpannassa. So hi niviṭṭhasaddho asinā sīse chijjamāne pi Buddho abuddho ti vā Dhammo adhammo ti vā Saṃgho asaṃgho ti vā na vadati"—"'Established' means well established, made firm. Of whom is there such faith? Of the one who has attained the stream. One having faith established does not say, 'Buddha is not buddha,' or '*Dhamma* is not *dhamma*,' or '*Saṅgha* is not *saṅgha*,' even while his head is being severed with a sword." *PugA*., p. 185, interprets "those without faith" (*assaddhā*) as "those without faith in the Buddha, *dhamma* and *saṅgha*," as does *MA*.I.152.

faith. One "faiths" in *kamma* and *kammaphalaṃ*;[187] and gifts given through faith are given by one

> having "faithed" in *kamma* and *phala*, in this world [*idha-lokam*] and the other world [*para-lokam*, or next world]. The meaning is that they are not given to thinking thusly, "This one is my relative or friend," or "This he will do in return," or "This was done previously by him for me." Things given thusly are not those things that are given through faith.[188]

A person steps forward in the process of salvation with faith active in his being aware that this way leads to release from old age and death;[189] that faith precedes in the quest for insight;[190] that faith is wealth that leads to the wealth of wisdom [*paññā*], which is the best of all;[191] that through wisdom one coming to learn of bad acts of bad *bhikkhus* does not lose one's faith, knows it is not diminished;[192] that when he hears "This was heard by me" at the beginning of a *sutta*, his faith in the instruction (*sāsana*) increases.[193]

In Buddha, *dhamma* and *saṅgha* a Buddhist places his faith[194] and through faith he goes to these three gems[195] for refuge (*saraṇa*). The statement of going for refuge in the three gems frequently follows the expression of wonder upon hearing the preaching of *dhamma*.

> Having praised the discourse [*desanā*] thusly, he, having a

---

[187] *ThagA.*III.41: "kammaṃ kamma-phalaṃ...saddahitvā." *ThagA.*II.102: "kamma-phalāni...saddahitvā." *KhpA.*, p. 183; "kammañ ca kammavipakañ ca saddahitvā...." See also *ThagA.*II.128.

[188] *DA.*I.81 (on *D.*I.5). See also *KhpA.*, p. 183.

[189] *ThagA.*I.143 (on *Thag.*, vs. 59).

[190] *Nd. 2.*, p. 228, no. 512 (on *Sn.*, vs. 1146); *SnA.*II.606. See also *Sdhp.* III.94.

[191] *DA.*III.1038 (on *D.*III.251).

[192] *SnA.*I.166 (on *Sn.*, vs. 90).

[193] *DA.*I.31 (on *D.*I.1).

[194] *AA.*III.84; *ThagA.*II.102, III.41. See also *ThagA.*II.71; *PugA.*, p. 185; *DA.*III.864; *MA.*I.152.

[195] Pāli *ratana*, "gem or jewel." *KhpA.*, p. 170 (on the *Ratanasutta* [see also *Sn.*, vs. 224]); "*Ratana* is a synonym for that which induces, brings, produces, increases delight [*rati*]—for whatever is valued, very costly, inestimable, rarely seen, having incomparable enjoyment for beings."

gladdened heart [*pasannacitta*], by means of this discourse on the three gems, making a gladdened condition [*pasannākāra*] said firstly, "I myself" [*esāham*]. Here *esāham* means "this I" [which has the force of "I myself"]. "I go to the venerable Gotama as refuge" means venerable Gotama is a refuge [*saraṇa*] for me, a support [*parāyana*], he is the slayer of grief [*aghassa hantā*], and of benefit [*hitassa*], he is the provider [*vidhātā*]. Hence, with this attitude [*adhippāya*] I go to venerable Gotama as refuge, I follow [in his wake, *bhajāmi*], I serve, I attend on [*payirupāsāmi*], thus I come to know, I understand. Whatever [philological] roots convey the meaning of "going" convey also the meaning of "knowing" [*buddhi*]. Hence, for this [expression] "I go" the meaning "I know, I understood" is expressed. Regarding "to *dhamma* and *bhikkhusaṅgha*": *dhamma* is used in the sense that it supports [*dhāreti*] those who have attained the path, who have realized cessation (*sacchikatanirodha*], who are following along accordingly, who are not falling into the four hells. In effect it [*dhamma*] is both the noble way and *nibbāna*. Indeed this explanation was given by the *Bhagavan*. "O *bhikkhus*, of the *dhammas* that are conditioned [*saṅkhatā*], the noble eightfold way is proclaimed the foremost." [*A*. II. 34] Not only [is *dhamma*] both the noble way and also *nibbāna* but also *dhamma* as authoritative teaching [*pariyattidhamma*] together with the noble fruits. Thus it is said in the *Chattamāṇavakavimāna* [*Vv*., p. 51],

> "I go for refuge to this sweet, learned, well apportioned *dhamma*;
> Free from lust of passion, free from desires, free from sorrow, *dhamma* not conditioned, without disgust."

Here, "without lust of passion" is the way that is described. "Free from desires, free from sorrow" is the fruit. "*Dhamma* that is not conditioned" is *nibbāna*. "Without disgust, sweet, learned, well apportioned" means the collections of *dhamma* divided into the three *piṭakas* [i.e., *sutta* (or *dhamma*), *vinaya*, and *abhidhamma*]. As for the *saṅgha* it is so called because it is compact with the accumulation of [proper] views and moral virtues. In effect it is the group of eight noble persons.[196]

In this passage from the *Majjhima-nikāya* commentary one notes

---

[196] *MA*. I. 130–131 (on *M*. I. 24, lines 7 ff.). This commentarial explanation is given also in *AA*. II. 107–108. See also *UJ*., c. I. 67–68. The *MA*. passage under consideration has been rather freely translated into English by Nyanaponika Thera as *The Threefold Refuge*, in "The Wheel Series," number 76 (Kandy, Ceylon: Buddhist Publication Society, 1965 [first published by the "Servants of the Buddha," 1949]), pp. 1–2.

the manner in which *dhamma* is etymologically explained in terms of soteriological considerations. The term *dhamma* is derived from √*dhṛ* and the force of *dhamma* is presented through the causative form of the verb from √*dhṛ*, "to hold, bear, support,"[197] as well as through a verbal noun of secondary derivation, *dhāraṇa*, "holding, bearing, supporting, sustaining."[198]

The commentary on the *Khuddakapāṭha* differs slightly from the *Majjhima-nikāya* commentary when it reads,

> Some say *dhamma* means ways, fruits, and *nibbāna*. Our preference is to take *dhamma* in the sense of way and the absence of passions [*maggavirāga*] because of the sustaining [*dhāraṇato*] of those who have cultivated the way [*bhāvitamaggānaṃ*] and those who have realized *nibbāna* in the sense that there is no falling into hells and because of the providing of the highest consolation [*paramassāsavidhānato*].[199]

When one takes refuge in *dhamma*, one is told that by living thusly one will not fall because *dhamma* supports, sustains.

The notion of refuge, *saraṇa*, is analyzed in the commentaries in a sevenfold classification:

---

[197] See also *Sdpj.* I. 146 (on *Nd.1.* I. 40 [on *Sn.*, vs. 775]): "Attano kārakaṃ apāyesu apatamānaṃ dhāretī ti dhammo"—"*Dhamma* is so called because 'it holds its doer as one not falling into hells.'"

[198] *UdA.*, p. 268 (on *Ud.*, p. 46): "yathānusiṭṭhaṃ paṭipajjamānaṃ saṃsāra-dukkha-pātato dhāraṇena . . ."—"by a sustaining of those following along accordingly from a fall into *dukkha* of *saṃsāra*." *MA.* I. 173 (on *M.* I. 37): "Dhāraṇato Dhammo. Vinipatituṃ appadānato ti vuttaṃ hoti"—"*Dhamma* is so called because of sustaining, which is to say, because it does not allow one to fall."

[199] *KhpA.*, p. 19. The *Khp.* and *KhpA.* are admirably translated into English by Bhikkhu Ñāṇamoli in the Pali Text Society translation series, number 32, as *The Minor Readings and the Illustrator of Ultimate Meaning* (London: Luzac & Co., Ltd., 1960). I differ with this able translator when he takes *maggaphalanibbānāni* as "the Path, its Fruit and Extinction." There are four paths or ways, four fruits, and *nibbāna*; and it appears that this is the way in which the compound is most frequently used. Further, *maggavirāga* which Ñāṇamoli takes as meaning "the fading of lust, which is the Path" seems rather to be a *dvanda* compound with *virāga* used synonymously for *nibbāna* since the passage speaks of those who have cultivated the *magga* and those who have realized *nibbāna*. This observation remains inconclusive since *VvA.* 233 (on *Vv.*, p. 51) interprets *rāgavirāga* as *ariyamagga*.

For the sake of proficiency in the acts of going for refuge, this classification should be understood; namely, refuge, the going for refuge, he who goes for refuge, the mode of going for refuge, the effect of going for refuge, defilement, and breach [of the going for refuge.].[200]

The commentary on the *Majjhima-nikāya* continues:

"Refuge" [*saraṇa*] is so called because it slays [*hiṃsati*], such is the force of the term [*padattha*]. Of those who have gone for refuge, by just this act of going for refuge, it [i.e., *saraṇa*] slays, it destroys fear, affliction, *dukkha* and misery of unsatisfactory [future] abodes. This [i.e., *saraṇa*] is a synonym for the three gems themselves. In other words, the Buddha, by causing the performance of what is beneficial and by causing one to turn from what is not beneficial, destroys fear on the part of beings. And *dhamma*, by causing one to cross over the wilderness of becoming, by giving consolation [destroys fear], and *saṅgha* by causing even those who have done little to derive great benefits [destroys fear]. Therefore, in this manner are the three gems a refuge.[201]

The act of going for refuge [*saraṇagamana*] is

the arousing of thoughts that are gladdened by it [i.e., refuge in the three gems] and respect it, that are free from defilement, that are activated by reason of being inclined to it.[202]

And a being [*satta*] endowed with this going for refuge is one who goes for refuge.[203]

The act of going for refuge is twofold, transcendental or supramundane (*lokuttara*) and customary or "mundane" (*lokiya*). The transcendental manner is seen when one has had a vision of the four truths at the moment that he attains the way or path (*maggakkhaṇa*), by the uprooting of whatever might harm the going for refuge, and this manner has *nibbāna* as objective and has the function of flourishing in all of the three gems. The customary manner of going for refuge is seen when an average person arrests whatever might harm

---

[200] *MA.* I. 131–132. See also *AA.* II. 108–112 and *KhpA.*, pp. 16–17. I have chosen to follow *MA.* (which is the same as *AA.*) because it is more concise than *KhpA.*

[201] *MA.* I. 132. [202] *Ibid.* [203] *Ibid.*

the going for refuge and when the qualities of the Buddha etcetera become the objective and so it, too, flourishes. Regarding the customary manner of going for refuge, it is said, "In effect it means the attainment of faith in the Buddha and the other subjects [i.e., *dhamma* and *saṅgha*]."[204]

It is not necessary to continue the discussion[205] provided by the *MA.* on refuge since the primary concern is to note the presence of *dhamma* in the three gems and the manner in which it is interpreted. Regarding the supramundane going for refuge one should note the presence of *magga* and *nibbāna* and the manner in which they are held together soteriologically—one entering the path having *nibbāna* as his objective. *Dhamma*, it will be remembered, means both way and *nibbāna*. When one focuses on the qualities or characteristics of the three gems one is participating in a customary going for refuge. But when one settles on that for which the three gems stand, one is involved in a transcendental going for refuge, a process of discovering that leads to a perfect, complete realization of *dhamma*. Faith in the former case is transcended in the latter.

The passages from the *suttas* and commentaries discussed in this chapter show the foundation of a religious tradition based on that for which Siddhattha Gotama sought; on that which he as the Buddha rediscovered; on that which he revered and about which he preached; on that about which men heard and which they perceived; on that which men, while living accordingly, were assured would not fail; on that which was a refuge in a world of flux—*dhamma*.

---

[204] *Ibid.*

[205] I have utilized some of the material presented in this discussion and have developed more fully the weighty matter of refuge, in "The Notion of Refuge (*saraṇa*) in the Theravāda Tradition," forthcoming in a volume in memory of J. Kaśyap, under the general editorship of A. K. Narain.

CHAPTER III

RECOLLECTION OF *DHAMMA* IN THE *VISUDDHIMAGGA*

When the eminent fifth century Buddhist commentator Buddhaghosa wrote his great work, the *Visuddhimagga*,[1] he brought together into topical considerations passages scattered throughout the Pāli canon; and by including interpretations apparently considered established or traditional at the time that he wrote, provided a comprehensive manual on which many subsequent interpretations of the canon by Theravāda Buddhists are based.

---

[1] The biographical information on this person is a matter of considerable uncertainty—whether he was from India, as is the general consensus, or whether he was from lower Burma, as was suggested by A. P. Buddhadatta in his article, "Who was Buddhaghosa?" *UCR.*, Vol. II, Nos. 1 and 2 (October, 1944), pp. 77–85. In any case, he was not a Sinhalese. He is said to have composed the *Visuddhimagga*, his first literary work in Sri Lanka, while in residence at the Mahāvihāra in Anurādhapura.

It is difficult to determine how original Buddhaghosa was in his *Visuddhimagga*. It appears that he saw himself as one who was in position to summarize the Pāli *tepiṭakas*, Sinhalese commentaries, and the opinions of the ancients. See the brief but informative comments by E. W. Adikaram, *Early History of Buddhism in Ceylon* (Colombo: M. D. Gunasena & Co., Ltd., 1953), pp. 2–8.

In the discussion that follows, I will note references to the *Visuddhimagga* by chapter and paragraph drawn from the "Harvard Oriental Series," Vol. 41, edited by Warren and Kosambi. Cross-references to the *PTS.* edition will be noted by *PTS.*, volume number and page number. A splendid English translation of this work is *The Path of Purification* (*Visuddhimagga*) *by Bhadantācariya Buddhaghosa*: translated from the Pāli by Bhikkhu Ñyāṇamoli (Colombo: Published by A. Semage and printed at M. D. Gunasena & Co. Ltd., 1964 [2nd edition of the work first published in 1956]). The Sinhalese *sanya* on chapter seven, paragraphs 66–88 in *Vism.* provides straightforward Sinhalese translations for several Pāli words in *Vism.* not mentioned in *Pm.* The more elaborate comments in the *sanya* follow closely those given in *Pm.* See *Viśuddhimārga* . . . *Parākramabāhu mahīpālayan visin liyū mahā sanya sahitayi*, edited by Bentara Śraddhātiṣya (Kalutara, Ceylon: K. J. Piris, Vidyātilaka Yantrālaya, 1950), II. 516–534.

The seventh chapter of the *Visuddhimagga* containing a discussion of the six recollections, namely, recollections on the Buddha, *dhamma*, *saṅgha*, morality (*sīla*), generosity (*cāga*), and deities (*devatā*),[2] will provide the foundation for the discussion that follows. Of primary interest will be the recollection or reflection on *dhamma* which Buddhaghosa tells us is mindfulness, being immediately aware, of the qualities (*guṇa*) of *dhamma*.

In keeping with the accepted commentarial style, Buddhaghosa, in his discussion of the qualities of *dhamma*, quotes a standard phrase found throughout the canon and lets a word by word analysis of the phrase provide the structure for his presentation. He quotes,

> Well proclaimed by the *Bhagavan* is *dhamma* that is visible, timeless, characterized by [the imperatives] "Come! Look!", leading on, to be known personally by the wise.[3]

Now these characteristics pertain to *dhamma* as that which is to be thoroughly learned, the authoritative teaching (*pariyatti*) and to *dhamma* as the ninefold supramundane *dhamma* or ninefold *dhamma* that transcends the world (*navavidhalokuttaradhamma*). However, as Buddhagosa notes, whereas "well proclaimed" describes both these dimensions of *dhamma*, the remainder of the characteristics have to do only with *dhamma* that transcends the world.[4] Straightway, Buddhaghosa mentions two levels in *dhamma*: the one being *dhamma* that is to be thoroughly learned, memorized, mastered and taken as the authoritative teaching; the other being *dhamma* that is to be realized. The latter is that about which the former speaks.

Woven into the discussion of *dhamma* as "well proclaimed" is another phrase frequently met in the canon:

---

[2] *Vism.* VII. 1.

[3] *Vism.* VII. 68, *PTS.* I. 213; quoting a sentence occurring at *D.* II. 93, 217; II. 5; *M.* I. 37, 265; *S.* I. 10–11; *A.* III. 285. See also *M.* I. 141; *S.* II. 28. The Pāli passage at *Vism.* VII. 68 reads, "Svākkhāto Bhagavatā dhammo sandiṭṭhiko akāliko ehipassiko opaneyyiko [*or* opanayiko] paccattaṃ veditabbo viññūhi."

[4] *Vism.* VII. 69: "Svākkhāto ti imasmiṃ hi pade pariyattidhammo pi saṅgahaṃ gacchati, itaresu lokuttaradhammo va."

because it [*dhamma*] is admirable in beginning, middle, and end and because it illustrates with general meaning and in detail the higher life that is thoroughly complete and completely pure.[5]

Taking the latter phrase as a means of describing *dhamma* in the sense of its being "well proclaimed," Buddhaghosa writes that the authoritative teaching (*pariyatti*), whether considered as a small unit, a verse, or in larger units of simple and complex *suttas*, is admirable in the beginning, middle, and end. Moving to what appears to be another level, Buddhaghosa mentions that *pariyatti* is admirable in the beginning in that it provides the setting and situation for the discourse, in the middle "because it is relevant for those who are ready to be taught, is unequivocal in meaning and is furnished with cause and example."[6] *Pariyatti* is "admirable in the end with its conclusion that produces the acquiring of faith."[7] In this way, Buddhagosa illustrates a progression as it pertains to *dhamma* as *pariyatti* and on every count it, *dhamma*, is admirable.

Furthermore, *dhamma* as the entirety of the instructions (*sāsana*)[8] is similarly admirable throughout. Beginning with morality, progressing through tranquility and insight, and paths and fruits, and ending in *nibbāna*, *dhamma* as instruction is admirable.

Dhamma,[9] the authoritative teaching (*pariyatti*), that pertains to the higher life in the instruction and the higher life in the path(s)

---

[5] *Ibid.*: "Ādi-majjha-pariyosanakalyāṇattā, sāttha-sabyañjana-kevalaparipuṇṇaparisuddhabrahmacariyappakāsanattā ca." See *D.*I.62; *M.*I.285; *S.*I.105; *A.*II.47; *DA.*I.175 (on *D.*I.62).

[6] *Vism.*VII.69. *PTS.*I.213.

[7] *Ibid.*: "Sotūnaṃ saddhāpaṭilābhajananena nigamanena ca pariyosānakalyāṇaṃ."

[8] *Vism.*VII.70. The phrase, "*Sakalo pi sāsanadhamma*," is taken by Ñyāṇamoli as "Also the entire Dhamma of the Dispensation," *Path of Purification*, p. 231. I follow *Pm.*I.221, which provides the following gloss: "Evaṃ suttavinayavasena pariyattidhammassa ādi-majjha-pariyosānakalyāṇataṃ dassetvā idāni tīṇi piṭakāni ekajjhaṃ gahetvā taṃ dassetuṃ—sakalo pī ti ādi vuttaṃ." Then, quoting *Dhp.*vs.183, *Pm.* continues, "Evaṃ vuttassa satthusāsanassa pakāsako pariyattidhammo sīlena ādikalyāṇo—sīlamūlakattā sāsanassa."

[9] *Pm.*I.224 (on *Vism.*VII.72, *PTS.*I.214) glosses *dhamma* with *tanti*. See also *Pm.*I.225.

is "with meaning" in the sense that it is communicative and "with detail" in the sense that language is involved. It is "with meaning" because of the profundity of penetrating knowledge (*paṭivedha*) of the meaning in *pariyatti* and of *pariyatti* itself; "with detail" because of the profundity of the *pariyatti* and the preaching. Buddhaghosa continues with the dual analysis of "with meaning" and "with detail" in order to demonstrate the levels in which *dhamma* as *pariyatti* is viewed.

> It is "with meaning" in the sense that it is a source of joy for suitable people [*sarikkhaka-janappasādakam*][10] because it is to be known by the wise. It is "with detail" in the sense that it is a source of joy for ordinary people [*lokiya-janappasādakam*] because it is to be "faithed in" [*saddheyyato*].[11]

Dhamma as the authoritative teaching (*pariyatti*), is "completely pure because it is present for the purpose of crossing over [the whirl of life as usually considered] and because it does not concern mundane material matters [*lokāmisanirapekkhato*]."[12] *Dhamma* as *pariyatti* is complete; nothing need be added or deleted and whatever therein is designated as factors that impede the religious life and factors that lead on are accurately described. "The meaning of *dhamma* among other religious leaders [*aññatitthiyānaṃ dhammassa attho*]," Buddhagosa mentions, "exhibits distortion."[13]

Moving to a discussion of *dhamma* that transcends the world (*lokuttaradhamma*), Buddhaghosa sets clearly before the reader two dimensions:

> *Dhamma* that transcends the world is well proclaimed because

---

[10] Mention should be made of an alternate reading, *parikkhaka°*, in which case the compound would read, "a source of joy for people of discretion."

[11] *Vism.* VII. 72. I have forced customary English usage by suggesting "faithed in." I am in splendid company with Ñyāṇamoli who, apparently aware of the limitation of English and not Pāli, translates *saddheyyato* rather loosely as "being a fit object of faith." *Path of Purification*, p. 232.

[12] *Vism.* VII. 72.

[13] *Vism.* VII. 73; *PTS.* I. 214.

> of the proclamation of the practice [*paṭipatti*] that conforms with *nibbāna* [*nibbānānurūpa*] and of *nibbāna* that conforms with the practice. As it is said, "Indeed the mode of progress [*paṭipadā*] going to *nibbāna* is well demonstrated by the *Bhagavan* to the disciples; both *nibbāna* and the mode of progress merge [*saṃsandati*]. Just as the water of the Ganges merges, comes together [*sameti*] with the water of the Yamunā, just so the mode of progress going to *nibbāna* is well demonstrated by the *Bhagavan* to the disciples; both *nibbāna* and the mode of progress merge"[14]

Or, viewed another way, *dhamma* that transcends the world is comprised of the noble way (*ariyamagga*) that is a middle course (*majjhimā paṭipadā*) between extremes; the fruits of samaṇaship or the state of one striving for inner calm (*sāmaññaphalāni*); and *nibbāna* "whose nature is eternal, without death, a protection, a shelter and so forth [*sassatāmatatāṇaleṇādi-sabhāvam*]."[15]

The ninefold transcendent *dhamma* is held to be present, visible (*sandiṭṭhika*), because it is to be seen (*daṭṭhabba*) by a noble person himself who is bringing about the absence of desire and the like in his own stream of consciousness.[16] When it is attained (*adhigata*) it is to be seen for oneself through reviewing knowledge, having put aside whatever is said to be grasped through faith in another. In

[14] *Vism.* VII. 74; *PTS.* I. 215. Buddhaghosa quotes from *D.* II. 223. *DA.* II. 652 (on *D.* II. 223) reads, "'The water of the Ganges with the water of the Yamunā' means the water at the confluence [*samāgama-ṭṭhāna*] of the Ganges and Yamunā 'merges, comes together' in color, smell, and also taste. It becomes [*hoti*] just like one [*eka-sadisam eva*], like gold that is split in the middle; not dissimilar as on the occasion when it [i.e., fresh water] is mixed with the water of the great ocean [at an estuary]." See the comment regarding truth as one, that is, *magga* and *nibbāna*, at *Vism.* XVI. 26, *PTS.* II. 497 and also *Pm.* II. 526 where it is noted that in speaking of these two dimensions as one truth there is no contradiction. I have translated the passage in the text and the one in this note in an article sharing, generally, some of the findings of this study. See John Ross Carter, "*Dhamma* as a Religious Concept: A Brief Investigation of Its History in the Western Academic Tradition and Its Centrality within the Sinhalese Theravāda Tradition," *Journal of the American Academy of Religion*, Vol. 44, no. 4 (December, 1976), pp. 661–674.

[15] *Vism.* VII. 75; *PTS.* I. 215.

[16] *Vism.* VII. 76.

this sense, too, it is visible, actual (*sandiṭṭhika*).[17] The term *sandiṭṭhika* is further interpreted by Buddhaghosa in the sense of proper view, recommended view (*pasatthā diṭṭhi*), and as such this view, being associated with the noble way (*ariyamagga*), being a cause for noble fruit (*ariyaphala*), having as its objective *nibbāna*, conquers defilements. In this sense the ninefold transcendent *dhamma* is characterized by proper view (*sandiṭṭhika*).[18]

Moreover, *dhamma* that transcends the world is worthy of being seen. When it is being seen in the sense of a thorough understanding by mental cultivation (*bhāvanābhisamaya*) and a thorough understanding of that which is to be realized (*sacchikiriyābhisamaya*), it puts a stop to fear of the whirl of mundane existence (*vaṭṭabhayaṃ nivatteti*).[19]

Dhamma that transcends the world is immediate, timeless (*akālika*) in the sense that there is no time lag in the giving of its fruit.[20] Moreover, *dhamma* that is ordinary wholesome conduct (*lokiya kusaladhamma*)[21] requires a certain period of time to elapse before its fruit is attained—some days, perhaps, or even in the next life and beyond. But with the way (*magga*) the fruit is immediate.

Dhamma is such that one can say regarding it, "Come! Look!" (*ehi passa*). Buddhaghosa elaborates that such directives are applicable because *dhamma* is found and because it is pure.[22] When one speaks of *dhamma* as being characterized by "Come! Look!" (*ehipassika*),

---

[17] *Ibid.*, VII. 77. In paragraphs 76 and 77, Buddhaghosa interprets *sandiṭṭhika* firstly in terms of *sāmaṃ daṭṭhabba* and then *sayaṃ daṭṭhabba* stressing thereby the personal awareness that is involved in this seeing.

[18] *Ibid.*, VII. 78.

[19] *Ibid.*, VII. 79. *Pm.* I. 227 glosses *bhāvanā°* with *maggadhamma* and *sacchikiriya°* with *nibbānadhamma*.

[20] *Vism.* VII. 80.

[21] *Ibid.*, VII. 81. See above, n. 71, Chapter II.

[22] *Vism.* VII. 82. *Pm.* I. 227 notes, "'Because of its being found' means because of its being obtained in the highest sense. 'Because of its complete purity' means because of its purity in every way by being without defilements and stains"—"Vijjamānattā ti paramatthato upalabbhamānattā. Parisuddhattā ti kilesamalavirahena sabbathā visuddhattā."

as being found and being pure, it appears that *dhamma* is that the sight of which, the perception of which, is worthy to be shared.[23]

Dhamma is characterized as leading on (*opaneyyika* or *opanayika*). Buddhaghosa discusses this characteristic of *dhamma* in the sense of the verb *upa* + √*nī*, "to induce," "to lead on." Of the ninefold *dhamma* the first eight factors are considered compounded (*saṅkhatā lokuttaradhammā*) and they are worthy of being led to one's mind (*citte*) through mental cultivation (*bhāvanā*). The ninth is considered uncompounded (*asaṅkhata*) and is worthy of being led to by one's mind (*cittena*) through realization, manifestation (*sacchikiriyā*).[24] The noble way leads on to *nibbāna*, and *dhamma* as fruit and *nibbāna* ought to be led on to realizability (*sacchikātabbatam*).[25]

The sixth characteristic of *dhamma* is that it is to be known personally by the wise (*paccattaṃ veditabbo viññūhi*). Buddhaghosa explains that *dhamma* has been known when one is able to say, "'The way has been cultivated by me, the fruit has been attained, cessation [*nirodha*] has been realized.'"[26] One can in no way claim for oneself the attainments of one's preceptor. Rather, *dhamma* is to be regarded in one's own mind (*attano pana citte yeva daṭṭhabbo*).[27]

In view of the discussion in the *Visuddhimagga*, *dhamma* means the ninefold *dhamma* that transcends the world together with *dhamma* as the authoritative teaching (*pariyatti*).[28] In the *Upāsakajanālaṅkāra*, *dhamma* is defined in the following manner:

> *Dhamma*: Here, it is *dhamma* [because] it supports [*dhāreti*] those who have attained the path, those who have realized cessa-

[23] It is obvious for the reader, I suppose, that I tend to refrain from following a vogue among some interpreters, that the point of this characteristic is that *dhamma* is in principle capable of being empirically verified, an interpretation that extends the generally accepted understanding of "empirical" in philosophical discourse such that the interpretation is merely stating the obvious. Of course *dhamma* can be known and this knowledge can be shared, and mutual agreement can be reached.

[24] *Vism.* VII.83. [25] *Ibid.*, VII.84. [26] *Ibid.*, VII.85. [27] *Ibid.*

[28] And so, *Pm.* I.180 (on *Vism.* VII.1; *PTS.* I.197) glosses *dhamma* thusly: "Dhamman ti pariyattidhammena saddhiṃ navavidham pi lokuttara-dhammaṃ."

tion, those following along accordingly—having made them ones not falling into the sorrows of hells [*apāya*] and also into the sorrows of the whirl [of life in *saṃsāra*]. This *dhamma* is tenfold [*dasavidha*] in the sense of the four noble paths, the four fruits of the state of one striving for inner calm [*sāmaññaphala*], *nibbāna*, and *dhamma* as *pariyatti*.[29]

Dhamma interpreted as the ninefold *dhamma* that transcends the world came to represent in the Theravāda movement one of the central doctrinal concepts. Precisely when this interpretation of *dhamma*, formally structured as *navavidha-lokuttaradhamma* or *nava-lokuttarā dhammā*, became current is difficult to determine. The four ways and corresponding fruits and *nibbāna* are called *dhammas* that transcend the world in the later portion of the *Sutta-piṭaka* and in the *Abhidhamma* literature,[30] but to my knowledge are not called *navavidhalokuttaradhamma* in the *Sutta* and *Vinaya-piṭakas*. For the commentators, *navavidhalokuttaradhamma* frequently represents the meaning of *dhamma* in the *suttas*.[31]

---

[29] *UJ*. c.I.66. See also *Vaṃsatthappakāsinī* (the commentary on the *Mahāvaṃsa*), I.308. The context in which *dhamma* is so interpreted has to do with the *tisaraṇa*. *UJ*. c.I.66 reads, "Dhamman ti ettha adhigatamagge sacchikatanirodhe yathānusiṭṭhaṃ paṭipajjamāne ca apāyadukkhesu c'eva vaṭṭadukkhesu ca apatamane katvā dhāretī ti dhammo. So pana atthato catunnaṃ ariyamaggānaṃ catunnañ ca sāmaññaphalānaṃ nibbānassa ca pariyattidhammassa ca vasena dasavidho, tam dhamman ti attho."

[30] *Dhs*.1447, p. 245; "Cattāro maggā apariyāpannā, cattāri ca sāmaññaphalāni nibbānañ ca—ime dhammā lokuttarā." See also *Dhs*.992, p. 181; 1094, p. 193; 1101, p. 196. At *Pṭs*. (a part of the *Khuddaka-nikāya*) II.166, what came to be called *bodhipakkhiyadhammā* are called, along with "cattāro ariyamaggā cattāri ca sāmaññaphalāni, nibbānañ ca," *lokuttarā dhammā*.

[31] See for example, *DA*.I.76 (on *D*.I.4), II.377 (on *D*.I.188), II.378 (on *D*.I.190), III.701 (on *D*.II.265), III.865 (on *D*.III.84), III.903 (on *D*.III.115), III.915 (on *D*.III.136), III.916 (on *D*.III.137), III.1061 (on *D*.III.287). See also *DA*.III.1019–1020 (on *D*.III.226); *MA*.II.232 (on *M*.I.197); *SA*.II.200 (on *S*.II.221), II.239 (on *S*.II.280), II.267 (on *S*.III.40); *AA*.*I*.52 (on *A*.I.5), II.147 (on *A*.I.73), II,203 (on *A*.I.131), III.90 (on *A*.II.51), III.190 (on *A*.II.209), IV.119 (on *A*.IV.228); *ThagA*.I.58 (on *Thag*., vs. 11), I.206 (on *Thag*., vs. 94), see also I.55 (on *Thag*., vs. 9), II.140 (on *Thag*., vs. 331); *SnA*.I.123 (on *Sn*., vs. 69), I.328 (on *Sn*., vs. 316). See also I.331 (on *Sn*., vs. 323); *Sdpj*.II.385 (on *Nd*. *1*.II. 360). See also *Sdpj*.II.257 (on *Nd*. *1*.I.132) and *UdA*., p. 97 (on *Ud*., p. 8); *DhpA*.I.230 (on *Dhp*., vs. 22), II.126 (on *Dhp*., vs. 79), II.278 (on *Dhp*., vs. 115), III.123 (on *Dhp*., vs. 151), III.288

The four paths (*maggas*) represent four stages in the process of salvation, the first being the stage of *sotāpatti*, "stream-attainment." One who has attained the stream is a *sotāpanna*, "stream attainer." A person who has attained the second path is called a *sakadāgāmin*, a "once returner" and he who has attained the third path is an *anāgāmin*, a "non-returner." One who has attained the fourth path is one whose impurities (*āsavas*) are destroyed and such person is considered an *arahant*, "worthy one."[32]

A passage in the *Dīgha-nikāya* reads,

> Now, Mahāli, a *bhikkhu*, by the complete destruction of three fetters, is one who has attained the stream [*sotāpanna*], having as *dhamma* not falling, assured, having enlightenment as final goal.[33]

One who attains the stream has as his *dhamma* not falling into the four hells or states of woe.[34] When it is said that such is one's *dhamma* what is meant is that one's nature is such, has become such, that one does not fall.[35] One is assured, certain of one's objective because of the regularity of *dhamma*[36] or by the propriety that pertains to the first path.[37]

(on *Dhp.*, vs. 217), IV.95 (on *Dhp.*, vs. 364. See also *ThagA.*III.119 [on *Thag.*, vs. 1032]), IV.152 (on *Dhp.*, vs. 393); *ApA.*, p. 294 (on *Ap.*, p. 48); *JāA.*II.56, 185, III.128, 404.

[32] The most comprehensive study in English of the stages leading to arahantship is the work by I. B. Horner, *EBTMP*.

[33] *D.*I.156: "Idha Mahāli bhikkhu tiṇṇaṃ saṃyojanānaṃ parikkhayā sotāpanno hoti avinipāta-dhammo niyato sambodhiparāyano." The three fetters are "preoccupying opinions about the reality of one's individuality" (*sakkāyadiṭṭhi*), "doubt" (*vicikicchā*), "doting on precepts and practices" (*sīlabbataparāmāsa*). The three fetters are listed at *D.*III.216.

[34] *DA.*I.313 (on *D.*I.156): "Sotāpanno hotīti maggasotaṃ āpanno hoti. Avinipāta-dhammo ti catusu apāyesu apatana-dhammo. Niyato ti dhamma-niyāmena niyato."

[35] *MA.*I.162 (on *M.*I.34): "Avinipātadhammo ti vinipātetī ti vinipāto; nassa vinipāto dhammo ti avinipātadhammo. Na attānaṃ apāyesu vinipātanasabhāvo ti vuttaṃ hoti." *SA.*II.73 (on *S.*II.68) reads, "Avinipātadhammo ti, na vinipātasabhāvo." See also *UdA.*, p. 290 (on *Ud.*, p. 50).

[36] *DA.*I.313 (on *D.*I.156): "Niyato ti dhamma-niyāmena niyato." See also *DA.*II.544.

[37] *SA.*II.73 (on *S.*II.68): "Niyato ti, paṭhama-maggasankhātena sammatta niyāmena niyato." See also *SnA.*I.106 (on *Sn.*, vs. 55).

By reflecting thoroughly on each of the four noble truths, their interrelation, and by perceiving the vision for which the truths are designed, the three fetters are abandoned.[38] The path of stream attainment (*sotāpattimagga*) according to the commentary on the *Majjhima-nikāya* involves this vision "because [in it] there is the first glimpse of *nibbāna*."[39] The characteristic of reflecting thoroughly (*yonisomanasikāra*) is the third of four factors of stream attainment (*sotāpattiyaṅga*). The other three are associating with good persons, hearing *saddhamma* and practicing according to *dhamma*.[40] Four other factors of stream attainment are noted elsewhere.[41] They are serene joy (*aveccappasāda*) in the Buddha, *dhamma*, and *saṅgha*, and moral behavior that delights noble ones.

Stream attainment is not limited to those who have gone forth into the *saṅgha*. A householder who has trained himself properly can announce privately to himself:

> I am one for whom *niraya* hell is destroyed, for whom birth among crawling animals is destroyed, the realm of tormented spirits is destroyed, falling into the bad bourne of *apāya* hells is destroyed; I am one who has attained the stream, having as *dhamma* not falling, assured, having enlightenment as final goal.[42]

When the mind (*citta*) is freed from obsessive preoccupation

---

[38] *M.*I.9.

[39] *MA.*I.74 (on *M.*I.9): "Dassanā pahātabbā ti dassanaṃ nāma sotāpattimaggo, tena pahātabbā ti attho. Kasmā sotāpattimaggo dassanaṃ? Paṭhamaṃ nibbānadassanato." This commentary reflects *Sn.*, vs. 231, *Khp.*, p. 5, where it is said that by attainment of vision one abandons *sakkāyadiṭṭhi*, *vicikicchā*, and *sīlabbataparāmāsa*. The technical terms *saṃyojana* and *sotāpatti* are not present. The verse in *Sn.* and *Khp.*, the tenth verse of the *Ratana Sutta*, seems to represent an early stratum.

[40] *S.*V.347. The passage at *S.*V.347 is quoted at *MA.*I.162 (on *M.*I.34) as an explanation of *sotāpanna*. See the *sotāpatti-saṃyutta*, *S.*V.342–413. In *S. V.*410–413, it is said that these four factors, if cultivated and made much of, conduce to the realization of the fruit of stream attainment (*sotāpattiphalasacchikariyā*), to the fruit of a "once returner," to that of a "non-returner," to that of arahantship and several others.

[41] *S.*II.69–70. See also *D.*II.217–218; *D.*III.227; *SA.*III.289 (on *S.*V.384).

[42] *A.*III.213.

(*pariyuṭṭhāna*); when one gains calm (*samatha*) and allayment (*nibbuti*) and knows that such is only to be found in stream attainment; when one is of such nature that one quickly sets right any transgression, strives for higher training in morality, higher training of the mind, and higher training in wisdom; when one listens intently while *dhamma* and *vinaya* proclaimed by the *Tathāgata* are being preached and in so listening attains a knowledge of the goal (*attha*), a knowledge of *dhamma* and delight that is associated with *dhamma*, one is endowed with the fruit of stream attainment (*sotāpattiphala*).[43]

> More noble the fruit of stream attainment
> Than an empire on the earth,
> Than going to heaven,
> Than sovereignty over the whole world.[44]

A person who has reached the second path is called a "once-returner" (*sakadāgāmin*).

> And further, Mahāli, a *bhikkhu*, by the complete destruction of three fetters, by the diminution of passion, hatred, and delusion is a once-returner who, having come to this world just once more, makes an end of sorrow.[45]

A "once-returner" is one

> who, having cultivated the path here, comes into the world of gods; having remained there a life span, having arisen again right here, attains *parinibbāna*.[46]

The canon mentions "the fruit of a once-returner" (*sakadāgāmi-phala*)[47] but does not provide a concise explanation of what *phala*,

---

[43] *M.*I.323–325. These characteristics are noted as *sattaṅga*, seven factors, and are interpreted as seven knowledges born of reflection at *MA.*II.404.

[44] *Dhp.*, vs. 178.

[45] *D.*I.156: "'Puna ca paraṃ Mahāli bhikkhu tiṇṇaṃ saṃyojanānaṃ parikkhayā rāga-dosa-mohānaṃ tanuttā sakadāgāmī hoti, sakid eva imaṃ lokaṃ āgantvā dukkhass' antaṃ karoti.'"

[46] *MA.*I.163 (on *M.*I.34): "Yo pana idha maggaṃ bhāvetvā devaloke nibbatto, tattha yāvatāyukaṃ ṭhatvā puna idh'eva uppajjitvā parinibbāti...." See also *PugA.*, pp. 197 ff.

[47] *D.*I.229; *S.*III.168, V.411; *A.*I.23, 44, III.272, IV.204, 276, 292, 293, 372.

"fruit," in this context entails. It appears that *phala* means a fructification involving a total realization that one has indeed reached a stage wherein the breaking free from the three fetters and the waning of passion, hatred and delusion have in fact occurred.

A person who has reached the third path is called a "non-returner" (*anāgāmin*).[48] The passages in the *Suttapiṭaka* that speak of four stages in terms of fetters that are broken mention "stream-attainer" and "once-returner" but do not use the term *anāgāmin* to designate the third stage.

> And further, Mahāli, a *bhikkhu*, by the complete destruction of the five fetters that pertain to the lower [realms], is one of spontaneous uprising, one who attains *parinibbāna* there [in pure abodes], having as *dhamma* not returning from that world.[49]

Anāgāmin occurs along with "stream-attainer," "once-returner" and the state of arahantship in several canonical passages but in most such cases the fetters are not set as a criterion for differentiating the paths and fruits; rather, the terms are, for the most part, merely listed.[50] In one passage, for example, *anāgāmin* occurs with the other terms designating the paths and fruits with the five aggregates of grasping (*pañca-upādānakkhanda*)[51] providing a means of differentiation.[52] And again, *anāgāmin* occurs with the other terms, but the five guiding principles (*pañca-indriya*)[53] provide the criteria by means

---

[48] See the references in the previous note.

[49] *D.*I.156: "'Puna ca paraṃ Mahāli bhikkhu pañcannaṃ orambhāgiyānaṃ saṃyojanānaṃ parikkhayā opapātiko hoti tatthaparinibbāyī anāvattidhammo tasmā lokā.'" The five fetters are the three noted with regard to the "stream-attainer" and the "once-returner" plus sensuality (*kāma*) and ill-will (*byāpāda*). See also *D.*II.92, III.107. At *Itv.*, p. 95, persons are classified in three categories: *āgāmin*, *anāgāmin*, and *arahant*.

[50] *D.*I.229; *S.*III.168; *Vin.*II.240; *A.*I.23.

[51] These five are matter (*rūpa*), feeling (*vedanā*), perception (*saññā*), psychophysical coefficients of consciousness (*saṅkhārā*), consciousness (*viññāṇa*).

[52] *S.*III.168.

[53] These five are faith (*saddhā*), energy (*viriya*), mindfulness (*sati*), concentration (*samādhi*) and wisdom (*paññā*).

of which one's position in the paths is determined.[54]

When the term *anāgāmiphala*, "the fruit of non-returner," is used, it is usually placed as the third *phala* in the list of four including *sotāpattiphala*, *sakadāgāmiphala*, and *arahattaphala*[55] However, in two passages,[56] *anāgāmiphala* is used to designate the accomplishment of householders (*gahapati*) who live at ease in the four bases of mindfulness (*satipaṭṭhāna*)[57] and who have abandoned the five fetters that pertain to what is lower.

The fourth path is *arahattamagga*, the path leading to the state of a worthy one. This term is frequently listed with the previous three *maggas*, but also, in a few passages, stands in relation only to *arahant* in considering whether one is on the path leading to the state of a worthy one or is in fact a worthy one.[58] The fruit of the state of a worthy one, *arahattaphala*, is listed in several passages with the first three *phalas*[59] and forms the eighth category with the four stages and four fruits.[60]

> And further, Mahāli, a *bhikkhu*, by the destruction of defilements [*āsava*], dwells, having realized, having attained the release of mind, release through wisdom that is without defilement [*anāsava*], in this very life.[61]

---

[54] *S.*V.200. See also *A.*I.63–64, where an *anāgāmin* is contrasted with an *āgāmin*, one who returns. See also *Itv.*, p. 95, and *ItvA.*II.123.

[55] *D.*I.229; *Vin.*II.240; *S.*III.168, V.411; *A.*I.23, 44.

[56] *S.*V.177, 178.

[57] These four are mindfulness or immediate awareness of the body (*kāya*), feeling (*vedanā*), thought (*citta*), and psycho-physical processes that can be known by the mind or *manas* (*dhammā*).

[58] See *S.*I.78; *A.*III.391; *Vin.*I.39, 41. See also *A.*I.120 where *sakadāgāmin*, *anāgāmin*, and *arahattāya paṭipanno* (one who is following along for the state of a worthy one) are differentiated. Incidently, the point of this passage is that one who is set free through faith (*saddhā-vimutta*), one who has gained personal perception (*kāyasakkhin*), and one who has attained to proper vision (*diṭṭhippatto*), might each be on any one of the three stages noted.

[59] *Vin.*I.293, III.93. See *D.*III.227 where the four *phalas* are called *sāmañña-phalāni*, fruits of the state of one striving for inner calm—so also at *D.*III.277. See also *A.*I.23, 44–45, III.272, IV.276; *S.*V.411.

[60] *S.*III.168.

[61] *D.*I.156. See also *A.*I.232.

One notes the absence of the term *arahant* in this passage but one might not be inaccurate should the destruction of the *āsavas* be understood as synonymous with the attainment of the state of *arahant*. So, it seems to have followed that an *arahant* was one who had abandoned not only the first five *saṃyojanas* but also five more,[62] for in a later portion of the canon it is said that at the moment of entering the path to arahantship the latter five fetters are abandoned.[63]

It is not necessary to pursue further the lengthy and involved matter of the four paths and fruits. Their importance in the process of salvation should be noted and the fact that they comprise a means of conceptualizing an aspect of *dhamma* that transcends the world should be kept in mind. In the development of the scheme of the four paths and fruits one can distinguish a tendency to classify, harmonize, arrange—in a manner that depicts spiritual development from nescience to *nibbāna*—the instructions or teachings of the Buddha.

What the Buddha rediscovered is *dhamma*; what he taught is *dhamma*; that to be mastered is *dhamma*; the paths and fruits are *dhamma*, and, of course, *nibbāna* is *dhamma*. It was noted that in the *Dhammasaṅganī*[64] the four paths that are not limited to, restricted by the mundane sphere and the four fruits of the state of one striving for inner calm and *nibbāna* were called *dhammas*, supportive processes that can be known, that transcend the world. We have, then, four paths and four fruits and *nibbāna*, which classification leads to the use of *nava*, "nine," to describe these stages.[65] In the *Visuddhimagga*

[62] The ten *saṃyojanas* are listed at *S*.V.61 and *A*.V.17. The last five, considered as "belonging to the upper [realms]," *uddhambhāgiya*, are abandoned by the *arahant*. They are inordinate desire for the realms of form (*rūparāga*), for the formless realms (*arūparāga*), pride (*māna*), agitation (*uddhacca*) and ignorance (*avijjā*).

[63] *Pṭs*.II.84; *Pug*.I.50, p. 18.

[64] *Dhs*. 1447, p. 245. See above, note 30.

[65] *Nava* is not so used in the contexts dealing with the paths and fruits and *nibbāna* in the *Dhs*.; consequently, the *PTSD*., p. 588a, is inaccurate in using the term *nava* in reference to *Dhs*. 1094.

and in the commentaries one notes the prevalent use of *nava* and *navavidha*, "ninefold."

When *navavidha* "ninefold," became established as the first member of the compound *navavidhalokuttaradhamma*, *dhamma* was frequently used in the singular, which communicates a subtle and remarkably insightful discernment that there is a conceptual unity in diversity, a continuity in the soteriological process. *Navavidhalokuttaradhamma* means "ninefold *dhamma* that transcends the world." Now *nibbāna* is considered to be uncompounded (*asaṅkhata*)[66] and to this extent it is to be differentiated from the four paths and four fruits, which, though not included (*apariyāpanna*) in the mundane realms are nevertheless not themselves uncompounded. Yet, Buddhaghosa, in the *Visuddhimagga*, Dhammapāla, in the *Paramatthamañjūsā*, and the authors of the commentaries understood *dhamma* to include both the paths and fruits together with *nibbāna*, like two rivers joining, like gold cracked in the middle, as one *truth* (reality?).

The author of the *Upāsakajanālaṅkāra* speaks of *dhamma's* being tenfold and in doing so he includes *pariyatti*, "the authoritative teaching,"[67] and follows the lead of Buddhaghosa's discussion in the seventh chapter of the *Visuddhimagga*.

---

[66] As, indeed, is noted at *Dhs*. 1094, p. 193: "Apariyāpannā maggā ca maggaphalāni va asaṅkhatā ca dhātu-ime dhammā lokuttarā."

[67] *UJ*., c. I. 66.

CHAPTER IV

DHAMMA: ONE AND MANIFOLD

In Chapter III, *dhamma* understood as paths, fruits, and *nibbāna* together with the authoritative teaching (*pariyatti*) was discussed. This interpretation, as we shall have occasion to note below, continued to be a central doctrine in the Sinhalese Buddhist tradition.

There developed, however, another way of interpreting *dhamma*, wholly consonant with other tenets, and this also rather early, at least by the time of the Pāli commentaries.

In the old commentary, considered canonical, on the latter portions of the *Sutta-nipāta*, the word *sāsana*, "instruction," is glossed in terms of *pariyatti*, "the authoritative teaching," and *paṭipatti*, "practice."[1] Elsewhere in the commentaries, *dhamma* is understood in the sense of *pariyatti* and *paṭivedha*, "penetration."[2] A threefold classification is mentioned in the commentary on the *Aṅguttara-nikāya: pariyatti*, "the authoritative teaching," which is understood as the words of the Buddha; *paṭipatti*, "practice," being proper conduct, morality, *samādhi*, and insight; and, lastly, *adhigama*, "attainment," which refers to the ninefold *dhamma* that transcends the world.[3] The same threefold classification appears elsewhere in this commentary in a discussion of a disappearance of *saddhamma*.[4] It is there suggested that a disappearance will not occur as long as *pariyatti* remains. A decision of the elders that the authoritative teaching, the words of the Buddha as they had been passed down

---

[1] *Nd. 1.*I.143 (on *Sn.*, vs. 815). See also *SnA.*II.536; *Sdpj.*II.270 (on *Nd. 1.*I.143).

[2] *AA.*III.325 (on *A.*III.249); *UdA.*, p. 326 (on *Ud.*, p. 63); *SA.*III.253 (on *S.*V.261); *SnA.*I.329 (on *Sn.*, vs. 318); *ThagA..*II.153 (on *Thag.*, vss. 360-363); *UdA.*, p. 293 (on *Ud.*, p. 50).

[3] *AA.*V.33 (on *A.*V.70). [4] *AA.*I.87 ff.

from generation to generation (*pariyatti*), and not practice (*paṭipatti*) formed the basis with regard to the Teacher's instruction, provided the authority for this tradition.[5]

The commentary on the *Dīgha-nikāya*, in a discussion of the reasons for there being only one Buddha at a time, mentions *pariyatti*, *paṭipatti*, and *paṭivedha*, "penetration." It notes that as long as the *pariyatti* remains, the *sāsana*, the Buddha's instruction, remains.[6] This same classification is related to *dhamma* in the commentary on the *Dhammapada*[7] and appears in the Sinhalese glossary of this commentary.[8] This Sinhalese glossary, *Dahampiyā Aṭuvā Gätapadaya*, elsewhere, says:

> *Saddhamma* is twofold, religious texts [*āgama*] and attainment [*adhigama*]. The sayings of the Buddha constitute *saddhamma* that is religious texts. The paths, fruits and *nirvāna* constitute *saddhamma* that is attainment. Both are taken as *saddhamma*; *saddhamma* that is *dhamma* of the good [ones (*sat*)] and also *saddhama* that is good, pleasing [*sat*].[9]

Three aspects of the Buddha's instruction (*sāsana*) or three dimensions of *dhamma* are represented in the above sources and may be summarized as follows:

Authoritative Teaching or Religious Texts	Practice	Realization or Attainment	
pariyatti	*paṭipatti*		(*Nd*.1; *SnA*)

[5] *AA*.I.91–93. See *Thag*., vs. 1027, where "that heard" or *suta* is considered the basis of the higher life (*brahmacariya*).

[6] *DA*.III.898 (on *D*.III.114). This commentary glosses *pariyatti* as the "three *piṭakas*."

[7] *DhpA*.II.31 (on *Dhp*., vs. 64).

[8] *DhpAg*., p. 124 (on *DhpA*.II.31).

[9] *DhpAg*., p. 2: "Saddhamma devē. Āgama adhigama visin budu vadan āgama saddhamma veyi. Maṅgaphala nivan adhigama saddhamma vē. Dej, sataṃ dhammo saddhammo santo pasattho dhammo ti pi saddhammo, yi gaṇanē."

pariyatti		*paṭivedha*	(*AA.*, *UdA.*, *SA.*, *SnA.*, *ThagA.*)
pariyatti	*paṭipatti*	*adhigama*	(*AA.*)
pariyatti	*paṭipatti*	*paṭivedha*	(*DA.*, *DhA.*, *DhpAg.*)
āgama		*adhigama*	(*DhpAg.*)

These represent the authoritative teaching, living life accordingly, and realization of that about which the authoritative teaching speaks and for which life is so lived. The Buddha preached *dhamma* and because of this his instruction, *sāsana*, is to be taken with utmost seriousness.

In later Sinhalese Buddhist literature the threefold classification of *pariyatti*, *paṭipatti*, and *paṭivedha* becomes standard and is frequently met.[10]

The *Saddharmālaṅkāra*, written in the fourteenth century and drawing on the discussion in *AA.* I. 92–93, reads:

> *Dharma* that is characterized as the *śāsana* of our Buddha is threefold such as the authoritative teaching, practice and penetration. These are also called the threefold *śāsana*. Of them, *dharma* that is the authoritative teaching is all the words of the Buddha brought together in the three *piṭakas*. *Dharma* that is practice means the thirteen ascetic qualities, the fourteen practices in the *Khandhaka* [of the *Vinayapiṭaka*], the eighty-two major practices, morality, concentration [*samādhi*] and insight. Further, the nine *dharmas* that transcend the world, such as the four paths and the four fruits and *nirvāna*, that is, stream attainment and so forth, are called *dharma* that is penetration. These [last nine] are also called *saddharma* that is attainment. Further, of this threefold *dharma* only *dharma* that is the authoritative teaching is the basis [*mul*] for the *śāsana* of the Omniscient One.[11]

---

[10] See, for example, *Sdhs.*, p. 65; *MhvT.* I. 151 (on *Mhv.*, c. III, vs. 38); *SdhRv.*, p. 458; *SdhRk.*, p. 63; *SdhAl.*, pp. 20–22; *SSdhAv.*, pp. 2, 10, 249. For full reference, titles and approximate dates, see Carter, "*Dhamma* as a Religious Concept . . .," *op. cit.*, p. 669, note 42.

[11] *SdhAl.*, p. 20: "Apa budungē śāsanika dharmaya nam̱ paryāpti dharmaya, pratipatti dharmaya, prativedha dharmaya yi tun vädārum veyi. Ema trividha śāsana namudu veyi. Eyin tun piṭakayehi sangṛhita vū siyalu buddha vacanaya paryāpti dharma nama. Terasa dhutaguṇaya vuddasa khandhakavṛttaya, deyāsūmahāvṛttaya, sīla samādhiya, vidarśanāya yana mē pratipatti dharma nama. Tavada śrota apatyādi satara mārgaya da satara phalaya da nirvāṇaya da yana mē lokottara dharma navaya prativedha

The threefold classification represents another way of viewing *dhamma* and is parallel to the interpretation recorded by Buddhaghosa in the seventh chapter of the *Visuddhimagga*: Buddhaghosa there wrote of the ninefold *dhamma* that transcends the world together with the authoritative teaching, and the author of the *Upāsakajanālaṅkāra* subsequently considered *dhamma* as tenfold. The author of an eighteenth century Sinhalese work, the *Śrī Saddharmāvavāda Saṃgrahaya*, having mentioned the Buddha, continued to express his praise:

> *Saddharma* in ten modes, that is, paths, fruits, *nirvāṇa* together with the textual *dharma* [*pāli dharmaya*] that is characterized by qualities such as "well proclaimed" etcetera, because it was taught by that noble *Bhagavan*, and also the *saṅgha* of the eightfold noble persons who are called *saṅgha* because they are composed of proper views, morals, practices of *śramaṇas*, who are following along well, consisting of virtuous qualities, who are children of the Conqueror, custodians of the threefold *saddharma* considered as the authoritative teaching, practice, penetration, who are an incomparable field of merit for the inhabitants of the entire world.[12]

Dhamma as the ninefold *dhamma* that transcends the world continued to be one of the central concepts of the Theravāda tradition among Sinhalese[13] and often, especially when *dhamma* is understood

---

dharma nama. Ema adhigama saddharma namudu veyi. Tavada ē tun vädā̄rum vū dharmayan aturen paryāpti dharmaya ma sarvajña śāsanayaṭa mul veyi."

[12] *ŚSdhAv.*, p. 2: "Ē bhāgyavatun vahansē visin desita heyin svakkhātatādi guṇopalakṣita mārga phala nirvāṇaya hā pāli dharmaya sahita vū daśa prakāra saddharmaya da, manā dṛṣṭi śīla śrāmaṇyādi guṇa samūhayaňgē saṃghaṭita bhāvayen saṃgha nam vū supratipanna guṇa gaṇāňga saňgata jīnorasa paryāpti pratipatti prativedha saṃkhyāta trividha saddharmānupālita samasta loka vāsīňgē niruttara puṇyakṣetra vū aṣṭāryya pudgala saṃghayā da. . . ."

[13] See, for example, *AmāV.*, p. 64 (*ca.* 1200 A.D. [see also *AmāVgpv.*, pp. 38, 134 on *AmāV.*, p. 198]); *JāAg.*, p. 207 (twelfth century [on *JāA.*III.128]); *JāAg.*, p. 422 (on *JāA.*V.251, 252); *DahamS.* (twelfth century [?]), pp. 45, 91, 207; *SdhRv.* (thirteenth century), pp. 34, 138–139, 386–387 (see *DhpA.*I.382–383), 458 (see *DhpA.*II.32), 520 (for *dhamma* at *DhpA.*II.118), p. 712 (see *DhpA.*III.80), p. 746 (for *sappurisadhamma* at *DhpA.*III.122), p. 1037; *SdhAl.* (fourteenth century), pp. 19, 93, 105–106, 229 (see *RasaV.*, p. 47), p. 418 (see

as one of the three refuges, *dhamma* is interpreted as the ninefold *dhamma* and the authoritative teaching.[14]

Whether *dhamma* is considered as twofold, threefold, ninefold or tenfold, it can be heard, handled, practiced, followed, penetrated, realized.

RasaV., p. 107), p. 780; *SdhRk.* (*ca.* fifteenth century), pp. 61, 212, 266, 298, 531; *Psbp.* (date uncertain), pp. 11, 50; *SdhSS.* (1726 A.D.), pp. 42, 352, 353, 442, 469; *ŚSdhAv.* (1773 A.D.), pp. 2, 143, 468.

[14] See, for example, *SdhRv.*, pp. 34, 520; *SdhAl.*, pp. 19, 93, 106, 229, 418, 780; *SdhRk.*, pp. 61, 212, 266, 298, 531; *SdhSS.*, pp. 352, 353, 442; *ŚSdhAv.*, pp. 2, 468.

CHAPTER V

DHAMMA IN SINHALESE BUDDHIST LITERATURE PRIOR TO THE NINETEENTH CENTURY

Sinhalese men and women have been Buddhist for many centuries. They have chosen so to live, have decided that it has been worthwhile to participate in the Buddhist tradition and to pass from one generation to another the notion that life lived Buddhistically, lived according to *dhamma*, has been eminently worth living. It appears that there has been conviction that posterity would be betrayed if *dhamma* were not transmitted.

Apart from an occasional flash back to the canon or the commentaries, the following discussion will be based on a few Pāli texts and a majority of the most popular Sinhalese Buddhist classics, written in a period spanning approximately seven centuries—from the eleventh to the eighteenth.

Definitions of Dhamma

The *Dharmapradīpikā*, a Sinhalese text dating from about 1200 A.D., written as a commentary on the Pāli *Mahābodhivaṃsa*, dating from approximately the tenth century, generally follows the standard definitions previously noted. There are a few variations that are of interest. Whereas the *Papañcasūdanī* (*MA.* I. 17) interpreted "*diṭṭhadhammo viditadhammo*" as having to do with "truths,"[1] the *Dharmapradīpikā* understands *dhamma* in "*diṭṭhadhammo pattadhammo*" as *dhamma* that is the paths, fruits, and *nirvāṇa*.[2] There is no con-

[1] *MA.* I. 17: "'Diṭṭhadhammo, viditadhammo' ti ādisu saccesu."

[2] *Dhpr.*, p. 236 (on *Mhbv.*, p. 36): "Adhigato kho myāyaṃ dhammo yana tanhi 'dhamma' śabdaya 'diṭṭhadhammo pattadhammo' yanādi tanhi seyin mārgaphala nirvāṇayehi väṭeyi."

tradiction here; the commentarial tradition has maintained the position that realization of the four truths is synonymous with entering the stream. The *Dharmapradīpikā* is consistent but more comprehensive.

In the *Dīgha-nikāya* (*D.*II.8, 54) a passage speaks of the *Bhagavans* as being characterized by "such morals [*evaṃ-sīlā*], such *dhammas* [*evaṃ-dhammā*], such wisdom [*evaṃ-paññā*]." Whereas the Pāli commentarial tradition interprets *dhammā* in this context, in the plural form, as having to do with *samādhi*, keeping a continuity of the very old triad of *sīla*, *samādhi*, and *paññā*,[3] the *Dharmapradīpikā* interprets *dhamma* in this usage as referring to the natures of the *Bhagavans*.[4] One definition not thus far explicitly noted in this study is provided by the *Dharmapradīpikā; dhamma* also carries the meaning *vyavahāraya*, "that which is customary, proper."[5]

The *Abhidhānappadīpikā*, a Pāli dictionary that probably preceded the *Dharmapradīpikā* by a few years, provides a concise list of definitions,[6] which I will note in the following summary of findings at this stage of the study.[7]

guṇa (*DA. DhsA. DhpA.* *Abhidhp. Dhpr.*)
"quality, in the sense of virtuous, moral quality"

---

[3] See above, Chapter II, in the discussion developed in the section, "Commentarial Definitions of *Dhamma*".

[4] *Dhpr.*, p. 236: "'evaṃ dhammā te buddhā bhagavanto ahesum' yana tanhi svabhāvayehi väṭeyi."

[5] *Ibid.*

[6] I have consulted two editions of this work. The definitions of *dhamma* are found in Subhūti's edition at paragraph 784, p. 220, and in Moragallē Ñāṇobhāsatissa's edition at paragraph 757, p. 156. The former edition provides English and Sinhalese translations but is now rare. The latter edition is readily available in Sri Lanka.

[7] I place in parentheses the sources in which the terms are listed and note here the particular references. *DA.*I.99; *DhsA.*, p. 38; *DhpA.*I.18; *MA.*I.17; *BuA.*, p. 13; *Abhidhp.*, p. 220 (Subhūti's edition), p. 156 (Ñāṇobhāsatissa's edition); *Dhpr.*, pp. 236–237. I have noted these sources and definitions in Carter, "Traditional definitions of the term *dhamma*," *op. cit.*, pp. 333–334.

desanā (*DA. DhpA. Dhpr.*)
"teaching"

pariyatti (*DA. DhsA. DhpA. MA. BuA. Abhidhp. Dhpr.*)
"authoritative teaching, texts"

nissatta (*DA. DhpA. Abhidhp. Dhpr.*)
"that without a living being"

nissatta-nijjīvatā (*DhsA.*)
"that without a living being—lifelessness"

suññatā (*MA. BuA.*)
"emptiness, voidness"

hetu (*DhsA.*)
"cause"

saccāni (*MA. Abhidhp.* ?)
"truths"

sacca (*Abhidhp.* ?)
"truth"

catusaccadhamma (*BuA.*)
"*dhamma* that pertains to [the] four [noble] truths"

samādhi (*MA. BuA. Abhidhp.*)
"rapt concentration"

paññā (*MA. BuA. Abhidhp. Dhpr.*)
"wisdom"

pakati (*MA. BuA. Abhidhp. Dhpr.*)
"natural condition"

sabhāva (*MA. BuA. Abhidhp. Dhpr.*)
"inherent nature"

puñña (*MA. BuA. Abhidhp.*)
"merit"

āpatti (*MA. BuA. Abhidhp. Dhpr.*)
"an offense committed within the *saṅgha*"

ñeyya (*MA. BuA. Abhidhp. Dhpr.*)
"that to be known"

(*ādi*) (*DA. DhsA. MA. BuA. Abhidhp.*)

"etcetera [that is, the scope of meaning of the term is not exhausted by the definitions listed]"

ñaya (*Abhidhp.*)

"proper manner, propriety"

ācāra (*Abhidhp.*)

"[proper] conduct"

kāraṇa (*Abhidhp.*)

"reason, cause"

maggaphalanibbāna (*Dhpr.*)

"paths, fruits, and *nibbāna*"

vyavahāra (*Dhpr.*)

"that which is customary"

kusaladhamma (*Dhpr.*)

"*dhamma* that pertains to what is wholesome"

The Noble Quest

Where does one begin a study of *dhamma*? With the life of the Buddha? Which account of that life? These are weighty questions, ones that will repay reflection. In the previous consideration of the noble quest, we focused attention on the *Ariyapariyesanā Sutta*, on Siddhattha Gotama, a man of vision and immense commitment, who went forth in quest of *dhamma*, attained it, and shared his penetrating knowledge of that-now-become-known so that others might be enabled to complete their quest.

Now we turn to a perspective on that impressive life, a view long endorsed by Sinhalese Buddhists that sees in the accomplishment of the Buddha, not only a beginning of a movement with enormous ramifications in the history of Asia, in the process of one's own living, but also a culmination of many lives of the *Bodhisattva* continually and consistently in pursuit of salvific Truth. These former lives, fading into a distant past that borders on mystery, are held in focus by the objective of the *Bodhisattva's* quest, and are remembered because of the straightforward moral implications for men and women who seek to become religiously engaged with that for which the *Bodhisattva* sought, with that which the Buddha taught about that which he rediscovered—*dhamma*. The quest was for *dhamma* and to *dhamma*, *NOW*, one can go for refuge.

> "Of what sort is *dhamma* as refuge?" One should go to *dhamma* as refuge [thinking], "I go to *dhamma* as refuge, [to *dhamma*] that was realized by our *Guru* of the three worlds, Fully Enlightened One, noble Lord, who had toiled in search throughout four innumerable *laks* of aeons until the moment, while seated on the diamond seat at the base of the *bodhi* tree, everything to be known was understood."[8]

The *Bodhisattva's* attitude toward *dharma* (the more frequent Sinhalese form for the Pāli *dhamma*) as mentioned throughout the *Daham Sāraṇa* and other Sinhalese Buddhist texts reflects the attitude of the authors of those texts and, it is likely, represents the manner in which a considerable number of Sinhalese viewed *dharma*. The *Bodhisattva* aspired to the realization of *dharma*,[9] to *dharma* that was realized by former Buddhas,[10] and his aspiration is to be instrumental in shaping the attitude of one who goes to *dharma* as refuge.[11]

The *Bodhisattva* is represented as one having fondness (*sineha*)

---

[8] Carter, "*Dhamma* as a Religious Concept . . .," *op. cit.*, p. 671. *DahamS.*, p. 1: "Kebanduvū daham saraṇa da yat:—Apa tilōguru sammāsambudu rajānanvahansē sārāsaṅkhya kalpa lakṣayak muḷullehi soyā vehesī antayehi bō mädä vajrāsanayehi väḍahiňdä sav nē gevā dat keṇehi pasak kaḷā vū daham saraṇa yemi yi daham saraṇa yā yutu."

[9] *Ibid.*, pp. 45, 56, 58, 64, 77.

[10] *Ibid.*, p. 48. Occasionally, the author writes that *dharma* is "the unique refuge"—"asādhāraṇa vū saraṇayekä yi," (p. 163) or "there is no other refuge for beings but *dharma* alone"—"sattvayāṭa dharmaya ma mut anik saraṇayek nätä yi" (p. 223). It appears that the author is so writing in order to stress the topic of his present concern. In *Butsaraṇa*, a work written by Vidyacakravartin, who perhaps was the author of *Daham Saraṇa*, it is written, "'I go to the Buddha as refuge,' [the Buddha] who is the *dharmacakravartin*, who is the one refuge for the three worlds"—"Tun lovaṭa ekasaraṇa vū dharmacakravarti vū 'budun saraṇa yemi.'" (p. 274).

[11] See Carter, "*Dhamma* as a Religious Concept . . .," *op. cit.*, p. 671.

for *dharma*,[12] who causes those liking *dharma* to run to him.[13] He is viewed as having produced an earnest wish (*abhilāsa*) for *dharma*,[14] and in the person of Dahamsoñda is seen as one having affection for *dharma* (*dhammakāma*),[15] seeking *dharma*,[16] having an intense desire for *dharma* (*dam lobaya*).[17]

Dharmalobhaya, intense desire for *dharma*, was the motivating force that sustained the *Bodhisattva* through many lives.[18] In his case this intense desire was primarily directed toward *dharma* that he sought to realize. In the person of Dahamsoñda, moreover, this intense desire was also for the purpose of hearing *dharma*[19] and, in most cases, where *dharmalobhaya* is used to describe an intense desire on the part of gods and men it means an intense desire to hear *dharma*.[20]

The *Bodhisattva* while living in the animal realm in former lives gave his life for others and in so doing he is considered as having

---

[12] *Butsaraṇa*, p. 16. [13] *Ibid.*, p. 281. [14] *DahamS.*, p. 87.
[15] *RasaV.*, p. 3. [16] *Ibid.*, p. 4.
[17] *Dahamsoñda Kava*, vs. 105. See also vs. 110 where the *Bodhisattva* is described as having an intense longing for *dharma* (*dam doḷaya*). M. Piyaratana Thera writes in his glossary of the *Dahamsoñda Kava*, p. 126, "The word *doḷa* comes from the Pāli term *dohaḷa*. It means the two hearts. This word, which is used for the desire [āśāva] that comes by the uniting of the mother's heart and the heart of a child lying in her womb, is now used for all desires"—"Damdoḷa: 'doḷa' yanu (pā) dohaḷa śabdayeni, hṛdaya deka yana artha yi. Mavugē hṛdaya ya gäbehi vasana daruvāgē hṛdaya ya yana deka sambandhavīmen ätivana āśāvaṭa vyavahṛta meya dän siyalu āśāvanaṭa vyavahāra karanu läbē."

Having an intense longing for the welfare of others is an admirable characteristic. "Moreover, the manner in which the desire for *dharma* [*dharma lobhaya*] is protected should be known for certain . . . by good persons who delight in *dharma*, who are engrossed in self welfare and who have taken an intense longing for the welfare of others"—"Tava da dharmapriya vū ātmahita tatpara vū parahitayehi doḷagattā vū satpuruṣayan visin . . . dharma lobhaya rakṣā karaṇa paridi niścaya koṭä data yutu." *DahamS.*, p. 249.

[18] *DahamS.*, pp. 50, 86, 120, 126, 170; *SdhAl.*, p. 101.
[19] *SdhAl.*, p. 102; *ŚSdhAv.*, p. 16.
[20] *PūjāV.*, p. 652; *ŚSdhAv.*, pp. 14, 17, 18; *SdhSS.*, p. 369. See also *DahamS.*, p. 135, where the *Bodhisattva* as Śakradevendra caused a king to abandon *lobhaya* by the preaching of *dharma*. The king's *lobhaya* was for sense pleasures.

given his life for *dharma*.[21]

The author of *Daham Saraṇa* communicated afresh to his readers a notion that had enabled men and women centuries before his time to gain hope, to live in the world in a manner that was not limited to the mundane, a notion that continued in the minds of Sinhalese long after the author's demise, when he wrote the following:

> Going to *dharma* as refuge should be done by good persons [thinking], "This very *dharma* that was protected in many births by this noble *Cakravartin* King of *dharma*, who is my Lord, will protect us from this birth up to the birth when we will see *nirvāṇa*."[22]

A verse in the *Theragāthā* reads as follows:

> *Dhamma*, indeed, protects one who lives *dhamma*,
> *Dhamma* well lived brings ease.
> This is the blessing when *dhamma* is well lived,
> One who lives *dhamma* goes not to a poor end.[23]

This verse occurs also in the *Jātaka*[24] and the commentarial tradition interprets *dhamma* in this context to mean the ten modes of wholesome conduct[25] or, somewhat more comprehensively viewed, *dhamma* that is well lived (*sucaritadhamma*).[26] "This *dhamma* that is protected [*rakkhita*] preserves [*paṭirakkhati*] the one protecting it."[27]

The commentary on the *Theragāthā* considers *dhamma* that is

---

[21] *DahamS.*, pp. 89, 135.

[22] *Ibid.*, p. 111: "Mesē māgē svāmidaru vū dharmacakravartīn vahansē visin aneka jātiyehi rakṣā kaḷā vū dharmaya ma me jātiyehi paṭan geṇä nivan daknā jāti dakvā apa rakṣa karannē yä yi satpuruṣayan visin daham saraṇa yā yutu."

[23] *Thag.*, vs. 303: "Dhammo have rakkhati dhammacāriṃ, dhammo suciṇṇo sukham āvahāti: es 'ānisaṃso dhamme suciṇṇe, na duggatiṃ gacchati dhammacārī."

[24] *Jā.*IV.54, 496. See also *JāA.*I.31.

[25] *JāA.*IV.54 (on *Jā.*IV.53). The comment is not on this verse but on *dhamma* appearing at *Jā.*IV.53, line 6. The context does not vary in the usage of *dhamma* there nor at *Jā.*IV.54. Regarding the ten modes of wholesome conduct, *dasakusalakammapatha*, see above, note 71, Chapter II.

[26] *JāA.*IV.499 (on *Jā.*IV.496).

[27] *JāA.*IV.55 (on *Jā.*IV.54).

well lived as being ordinary and extraordinary (*lokiyalokuttara*), common and uncommon, pertaining to mores and having to do with that in terms of which mores are structured, as limited to the world and as transcending the world. A parallel is apparent in the manner in which these two modes of *dhamma*, so understood, provide protection: "'It [*dhamma*] protects' means it protects one from the *dukkha* of hells [*apāya* (The implication is that ordinary good behavior can also accomplish this end.)] and, having become the support for one's freedom from the whirl, it protects one from the *dukkha* of *saṃsāra* [This observation suggests a form of good behavior that, of course, includes what is commonly expected and transcends it.]."[28]

The verse, noted above from the *Theragāthā*, for centuries continued to express how Buddhists found confidence and hope in living *dhamma*.[29] Consider the manner in which this verse is introduced in the *Rasavāhinī*, a work of the fourteenth century:

> Oh the majestic power of *dhamma*! For one living *dhamma* there is neither fear nor panic in this world and also the next. Having departed [from this world] he attains heaven and *nibbāna*. Therefore it was said, "*Dhamma* indeed protects. . . ."[30]

Shortly thereafter, the *Saddharmālaṅkāra*, following the *Rasavāhinī* introduced the same verse:

> The majestic power of *dharma* is indeed very wonderful. It is indeed unthinkable. For those living *dharma* there is neither fear nor panic in either this world or the next. It also makes one reach the attainment of heaven and release in the next world. Therefore, this was said, "*Dhamma* indeed protects. . . ."[31]

---

[28] *ThagA.*II.128 (on *Thag.*, vs. 303): "Tattha dhammo ti, lokiya-lokuttaro sucarita-dhammo. Rakkhatī ti, apāya-dukkhato rakkhati, saṃsāra-dukkhato ca vivaṭṭūpanissayabhūto rakkhati yeva."

[29] The verse is quoted at *SnA.*I.315 (on *Sn.*, vs. 288); *DhpA.*I.(i).82, IV.105 (compare *SdhRv.*, p. 1056); *BuA.*, p. 144.

[30] *RasaV.*, p. 288: "Aho dhammānubhāvo nām'eso idha loke pi paraloke pi dhammacārino bhayaṃ vā chambhitattaṃ vā na hoti. Pecca saggaṃ ca nibbāṇaṃ ca pāpuṇāti. Tena vuttaṃ 'Dhammo have rakkhati. . . .'"

[31] *SdhAl.*, p. 743: "Dharmānubhāvaya itā āścarya mäyi. No sitiya häkke mäyi. Dharmaya häsireṇavunṭa melova paralova dekhi ma bhayek tätigän-

It is obvious that for the author of the *Rasavāhinī* and the author of the *Saddharmālaṅkāra*, living *dharma* was the way to salvation. There is a sense of confidence born of experience, a sense of hope for that yet to come, that seems to have led these men to speak of the majestic power of *dharma*. Their awareness seems to have involved a perception, through *saṃsāra*, of that which enables one to balance one's life in a world that is awry. And *dhamma* also provides a sense of security:

> One should go to *dharma* as refuge thinking, "I go to the *dharma*-gem as refuge, [the *dharma*-gem] that was established by the *Guru* of the three worlds, Noble Fully Enlightened One, [who] having said, 'There is nothing other than this one *dharma* that is a protection for these people, a refuge for these people, a father for these people, a mother for these people, a bannister for these people,' he said, '*Dhamma* indeed protects. . . .'"[32]

In the *Butsaraṇa*, a text written in the thirteenth century, Ālavaka is recorded as having asked the Buddha, "What well lived brings ease?" To this the Buddha replied:

> "*Dhamma*, indeed, protects the one living *dhamma*. . . ." As these are the words of all Buddhas including myself, if *dukkha* in hell [*niraya*] were to recede, it would recede before *dharma* alone. If *dukkha* of the animal realm were to perish, it would perish through this *dharma* alone. If the pain of hunger in the belly of *pretas* were to be extinguished, it would become extinguished because of this *dharma* alone. If one were to escape from the *dukkha* of the realm of *asuras*, there would be no other expedient than this *dharma*. O Ālavaka, if the Buddhas were to accomplish the attainment of heaven and the attainment of *nirvāṇa* for the

---

mek no vannēya. Paralova svargamokṣa sampattiyaṭat pamuṇuvannē mäyi. Esē heyin kiyana ladī: 'Dhammo have rakkhati. . . .'"

[32] *DahamS.*, pp. 187–188: "Movunṭa rakṣāva nam, movunṭa saraṇa nam, movunṭa piyō nam, movunṭa mavu nam, movunṭa atalombu nam eka ma dharmaya mut an däyek nätä yi vadāra, 'Dhammo have rakkhati . . .' tilōguru samyak sambuddhayan vahansē visin siṭuvā vadāḷa dharmaratnaya saraṇa yemi yi daham saraṇa yā yutu." The Pāli verse under consideration is quoted at *DahamS.*, p. 251; *SdhRv.*, p. 1056; and *SdhSS.*, p. 111. The notion of one's being protected by *dharma* is frequently met in the *DahamS.* For examples, see pp. 108, 137, 156, 197, 216, 217, 219, 220, 243.

> beings of the world, they would do so through this *dharma* alone. *Dharma* is something that brings about well-being thusly. This *dharma* alone is what remains competent to accomplish Buddhahood. Therefore, Buddhahood is accomplished through this *dharma* alone; Pratyeka-buddhahood is accomplished by this *dharma* alone. Arahantship is accomplished by this *dharma* alone. For all well-being this alone is the root cause. For all prosperity this alone is a noble family. All *dukkha* is abandoned by this *dharma* alone. For all Buddhas, this *dharma* is a treasure ever held in their hands. For crossing over *saṃsāra*, there is no other expedient than this *dharma*. Therefore, Ālavaka, when one has lived in *dharma*, it brings ease.[33]

The *Bodhisattva*'s quest was for *dharma* and he realized it at the foot of the *bodhi* tree. Throughout the quest the *Bodhisattva* endured *dukkha* in order to make a protection for the world.[34] Having aspired after *dharma* he attained it through great effort.[35] A sense of gratitude was present in the mind of the author of the *Daham Saraṇa* when he wrote, "I received without effort this *saddharma* that was accomplished by many efforts by this my noble Lord."[36] Elsewhere in the same work the author referred to this *saddharma* as "the *saddharma* that was aspired after with such great effort by the Great One and has been met by us without effort."[37]

---

[33] *Butsaraṇa*, p. 154: "'Dhammo have rakkhati dhammacārim'....Me mā ätuḷu vū siyalu budunge mä bas heyin nirā duk pasubasut dahamaṭa mä pasubassi, tirisan duk nasut me dahamin mä nassi, pretayange kusa sāduk nivet me mä dharmaya hetu koṭa genä nivenne yä, asurakāyehi dukin väḷähetat me mä daham härä anek upāyek näta; āḷavakaya, buduhu loväs-sanaṭa divasäpat nīvansäpat sādā det nam, me mä dahamin mä sādhā dennāhä; dharmaya nam me se suva eḷavana deyeka, buddhatvaya sādhā dennaṭa nisi vä siṭiye me mä daham mä yä, eheyin budu bava me dahamin mä sǟdet, pasēbudu bava me mä dahamin mä sǟdet, rahat bava da me mä dahamin mä sǟdet, siyalu säpataṭa me mä nidāna vat, siyalu śrīyaṭa me mä kulage vat, siyalu duk me mä dahamin mä pahavat, siyalu budunaṭa me mä daham hastasāra vat, sasarin eteravannaṭa me mǟ [*sic*, read mä] daham härä anek upāyek näta. Eheyin āḷavakaya, dahamhi hasaḷa kalä suva eḷavayi vadārā." [34] *DahamS.*, p. 187. [35] *Ibid.*, pp. 62, 64.

[36] *Ibid.*, p. 60: "Esē māgē svāmidaruvan visin aneka yatnayen sādhāgat saddharmaya mama ayatnayen ladimi."

[37] *Ibid.*, p. 43: "'Mahatun visin mē sā mahat yatnayakin patanalada saddharmaya apa visin ayatnayen päminẹna lada....'" I have mentioned these observations and have shared these quotations in "*Dhamma* as a Religious Concept," *loc. cit.*

Hearing Dhamma

The Buddha "gave birth to *dharma* through *dharma* alone."[38]

I will hear only *dhamma*;
In *dhamma* my mind delights.
There is nothing higher than *dhamma*;
The three prosperities have *dhamma* as base.[39]

In the commentary on the *Dhammapada* it is mentioned that people who go about amusing themselves singing and dancing, in drinking liquor and gambling are unable to hear *dhamma*. They do such because of their passion, hatred, delusion and craving.[40] The author of the *Saddharmaratnāvaliya*, a Sinhalese text written in the thirteenth century, following the account in the *Dhammapada* commentary, notes that people did not listen to *dharma* because they spent their days in play and frolic and, he adds, they were accustomed to passing their time listening to stories about Rāma and Sītā.[41]

Disrespect for *dharma* that is preached is discerned when one chooses not to take the time or trouble to journey to the place where *dharma* is to be preached, when one is not content while listening, when one does not pay attention while *dharma* is being preached.[42]

One should draw near to hear *dharma* because the Buddha honored it,[43] because he also listened to it,[44] as did *arahants*, worthy ones,[45] and because of the special endeavors by the Buddha "for a very long

---

[38] *DahamS.*, pp. 88, 91: "Dharmayen ma dharmaya prasava kaḷaha."

[39] *RasaV.*, p. 2. At *SdhAl.*, p. 94, the three prosperities are noted with the foremost example of each: human prosperity, such as a *cakravartin's* etc.; heavenly prosperity, such as Śakra's etc.; the prosperity of *nirvāṇa*, that is, the attainment of *samyak sambodhi* etc.

[40] *DhpA.* III. 362.

[41] *SdhRv.*, p. 915.

[42] *Purāṇasiṃhalabaṇapota*, p. 33. See, also, p. 16. The date of this work is uncertain.

[43] *SdhRk.*, p. 212. See, also, *PSBP.*, p. 15.

[44] *SdhRk.*, p. 74. See, also, *ŚSdhAv.*, p. 511.

[45] *DhpAg.*, p. 149 (on *DhpA.* II. 176). *Saddhammopayana*, vs. 536.

time on our behalf for the sake of *dharma*."[46] Hearing *dharma* is preferable to grasping for kingship of the gods[47] and while listening one should do so like one athirst for drink, like one destitute gaining wealth.[48] (So ardent in listening to *dharma* was one person, it seems, that though bitten by a snake he made no disturbance in the assembly and by the power of his attentiveness the venom did not spread in his body.)[49]

Without the hearing of *dharma*, *dharma* cannot be established. Hearing *dharma*, learning it, sharing it has been a means of preserving it and has enabled people to enter into the practice; and the practice, if thoroughly pursued would lead one to full penetration, realization, *nirvāṇa*[50] and cessation of *dukkha*.[51] *Dharma* should not only be heard but also put into practice.[52] The fact that one might not have a suitable offering for the *saṅgha* should in no way inhibit one from listening to *dharma* and striving to live accordingly.[53]

> Let beings hear the ambrosia, stirred by the Conqueror.
> Let them be attached to it;[54] let them worship, revere it.
> And in their standing, going, reclining, and sitting,
> Let them remember it. It is forever a support.[55]

---

[46] *ŚSdhAv.*, p. 511: "Dharmaya nisā apa venuven mahat dīrghakālayak karaṇa lada vīrya viśeṣaya. . . ."

[47] *Sdhup.*, vs. 538. [48] *MhvT.*I.4.

[49] *RasaV.*, p. 108. See also *SdhAl.*, p. 420. A frog by listening only to the sound of *dharma* preached by the Buddha attained prosperity in heavenly realms; *Lōvädasaṅgarāva* (*ca.* fifteenth century), vs. 130. See also *SdhAl.*, p. 16. Much the same happened to a deer, *RasaV.*, p. 106; and a rat snake, *SdhAl.*, p. 653.

[50] *ŚSdhAv.*, p. 511; *PūjāV.*, p. 44; *DahamS.*, p. 1.

[51] *Lōvädasaṅgarāva*, vs. 26.

[52] *Ibid.*, vss. 7, 12, 30, 36. *SdhRv.*, p. 551 (on *DhpA.*II.160).

[53] *SdhAl.*, pp. 105–106.

[54] *Bhajantu* from √*bhaj*, from which root is derived the Pāli *bhatti* and the Sanskrit *bhakti*, "fervent devotion."

[55] *Saddhammasaṃgaho*, vs. 64, p. 89:
"Suṇantu santo amataṃ jineritaṃ
Bhajantu pūjentu upāsayantu taṃ
Thāne ca gamane sayanāsane ca
Sarantu taṃ hoti sadā parāyanaṃ."

But how are people to know *dharma* unless they are told and how can they be told without others to tell them? There have been preachers of *dharma* and hearers of *dharma* in Sri Lanka for centuries.

A little more than six centuries ago, perhaps, the author of the *Saddharmālaṅkāra* reminded his readers of the value of giving *dharma*:

> The gift of *dharma* given, in the form of preaching to others engaged with the intention of crossing over, without expectation of gain and service [from others] is more noble than all gifts.[56]

This man stood in a tradition already over sixteen centuries old and, by writing as he did, made his contribution to that tradition and to posterity. What is it that provides the continuity of that tradition? It is, of course, persons—persons engaged in living *dhamma* by giving *dhamma*, by tasting *dhamma* and by delighting in *dhamma*.

> The gift of *dhamma* excells all gifts.
> The flavor of *dhamma* excells all flavors.
> Delight in *dhamma* excels all delights.
> The destruction of craving excels all *dukkha*.[57]

This gift of *dhamma*, even just one verse of it, is of far greater value than material gifts given to Buddhas, *paccekabuddhas*, and *arahants* comprising an assembly spreading from as high as one can conceive to the ends of the world.[58] Without hearing *dhamma* people would not know what acts were wholesome or meritorious, would not know how to live well and hence, this gift excels all gifts.[59] The flavor of *dhamma* is comprised of the thirty-seven *dhammas*

---

[56] *SdhAl.*, p. 19: "Siyalu dānayaṭa vaḍā lābha satkārayehi nirapekṣava niśaranāddhyāśayen yedī anunṭa baṇa kīm vaśayen dennā vū dharma dānaya ma utum vannēya."

[57] *Dhp.*, vs. 354. This verse is quoted at *SA.*I.84 (on *S.*I.32); *Dhpr.*, p. 109; *Sdhs.*, p. 75; *Sdhup.*, vs. 522; *PūjāV.*, p. 599; *SdhAl.*, p. 13; *SdhSS.*, p. 494. The point that the gift of *dhamma* excels all gifts is made at *Dhpr.*, p. 106; *RasaV.*, p. 231; *SdhAl.*, pp. 15–16; *Paricchedasatara*, c. II. 5.

[58] *DhpA.*IV.74 (on *Dhp.* vs. 354). *Dhpr.*, p. 108, provides a Sinhalese translation.

[59] *DhpA.*IV.75. *Dhpr.*, p. 108.

that have to do with enlightenment and the nine *dhammas* that transcend the world.[60] Delight in *dhamma* is that delight which "arises within one relating or hearing *dhamma*, produces a state of joy and exaltation, causes tears to flow, produces wonder and, having put an end to the whirl of *saṃsāra*, has as its end the state of arahantship."[61]

Describing Dhamma

Sinhalese writers of the past developed to a high degree the technique of using metaphor and simile. The books that they wrote were not too readily available to a large reading audience and hence were probably, until recent times, heard more than read. The stylistic procedure of developing verbal images or word pictures was largely due to the authors' desire to strike the imagination of one who listened—to inspire the hearer through imagery rather than argument, through affective poetry rather than cogent prose.

One of the most frequent metaphors in Theravāda literature represents *dhamma* as the ambrosia, *amata*.[62] Whoever might have been the person who chose first to use this metaphor, chose adroitly for the word *amata*, meaning ambrosia, is also a standard epithet for *nibbāna*, "that without death," *amata*.

In the *Amāvatura*, the title itself meaning "The Ambrosial Water," *dharma* that transcends the world is depicted as ambrosial milk

[60] *DhpA.*IV.75. See also *Paricchedasatara*, c. II. 2, and *ThagA.*I.221 (on *Thag.* vs. 103).

[61] *DhpA.*IV.75–76: "Esā dhammaṃ kathentassa vā suṇantassa vā anto uppajjamānā pītiudaggabhāvaṃ janeti assūni pavatteti lamahaṃsaṃ janeti sāyam saṃsāravaṭṭassa antaṃ katvā arahattapariyosānā hoti."

[62] *Miln.*, pp. 22, 167, 346. See also *UdA.*, p. 324 (on *Ud.*, p. 62): "The one who, having heard the preaching of *dhamma* of the *Bhagavan*, penetrates *dhamma*, drinks the drink of ambrosia"—"Yo Bhagavato dhamma-desanaṃ sutvā dhammaṃ paṭivijjhati: amātapānaṃ pibati. . . ." See also *AA.*I.100–101, 239. The metaphor occurs in the *Mahābodhivaṃsa* (*ca.* tenth century), pp. 51, 58, 114.

(*lovuturādham amākiri*)[63] The ambrosia of *dharma* when one is immersed in it quenches the heat of the *dukkha* of *saṃsāra*.[64] This ambrosia falls like rain,[65] and using it the Buddha annointed young princes.[66] It is poured in the ear of those hearing[67] and on one's heart.[68] To taste the flavor (*rasa*) of this ambrosia of *dharma* is noted as a characteristic of wise men[69] and a characteristic of an *arahant*.[70]

Metaphors and similes when utilized require an added dimension of involvement on the part of writer, hearer, and reader to determine the relevance or adequacy of the metaphor and simile by drawing on personal experience. Explaining the meaning of trust (*viśvāsaya*)[71] in the three gems the author of the *Purāṇasiṃhalabaṇapota* wrote regarding the *dharma*-gem:

> and [trust is] faith activated toward the *dharma*-gem through such considerations as, "*Dharma* is characterized as leading on. It is like an obstacle to hell [*apāya*], like a highway to *nirvāṇa*, like a great ship in the ocean of *saṃsāra*, like a great flight of steps to heaven, like a light to destroy the darkness called defilements, and it is like an ambrosia to destroy all *dukkha*."[72]

---

[63] *AmāV.*, p. 173. The late learned *bhikkhu* Sorata explains *lovuturādham amākiri* as the four paths, four fruits and *nirvāṇa; AmāVgpv.*, p. 108.

[64] *PūjāV.*, p. 216. See also *DahamS.*, pp. 72, 194.

[65] *PūjāV.*, p. 225. See also *AmāV.*, p. 33; *SdhSS.*, p. 393.

[66] *PūjāV.*, p. 289.

[67] *DahamS.*, p. 44.

[68] *Ibid.*, p. 204.

[69] *SdhRv.*, p. 459.

[70] *SdhSS.*, p. 350. See also *Dhātuvaṃsaya*, p. 4.

[71] Compare *DahamS.*, p. 109, where it is said, "Trust should not be put in *saṃsāra* which is not to be trusted by those who have knowledge"—"Nuvaṇättavun visin aviśvāsanīya vū saṃsāraya hā viśvāsa nokaṭa yutuyä yi."

[72] *PSBP.*, p. 5. The date of this work is uncertain. It appears likely that it was written not much more than two centuries or so ago. The Sinhalese for the quotation above is as follows: "Dharma nairyānikaya apāyaṭa maha akulak vänna nivāṇaṭa mahamagak vänna sasara sayuraṭa maha näväk vänna devulovaṭa mahahiṇak vänna siyalu kelesun namäti an̆duru nasannaṭa ālokayak vänna siyalu duk nasannaṭa amāvak vännä yi yanādīn dharmaratnayehi karaṇa ädihili da."

Dharma for centuries has been viewed as being like medicine for one ill with defilements, sickness and old age;[73] like rain that cools the heat of *saṃsāra*,[74] like a drum that can be sounded.[75] The drum metaphor was given added force by the author of *Daham Saraṇa* when he described the *Bodhisattva's* praising Dīpaṅkara as one who had sent forth the "*abhayabheri* that is called *dharma*."[76] *Abhaya* means the absence of fear and when a king had this drum (*bheri*) sounded it announced the setting free of those under the sentence of capital punishment.[77]

Dharma is also considered a heavenly *mantra* that provides security by destroying the poison of passions,[78] that assures the desired objective,[79] a wish-granting tree,[80] and a wish-granting gem.[81]

Through metaphors and similes Sinhalese authors of old sought to adorn a message singularly straightforward—that *dharma* enables one to move beyond the fears of *saṃsāra*[82] and effects heaven and *nirvāṇa*.[83]

Readers of this study who are familiar with the custom of sending

---

[73] *Miln.*, pp. 110, 335 (*dhammosadha*); *Miln.*, p. 335 (*dhammāgada*); *DhpA.*, p. 21 (*bhesajja*); *Mhbv.*, p. 84 (*dhammosadha*); *RasaV.*, p. 297 (*mahāgada*); *Butsaraṇa*, p. 297 (*behet*); *SdhRv.*, p. 141 (*behet*). See *SdhRv.*, p. 959.

[74] *Bu.*, c. XI. 6 (*dhammavuṭṭhi*); *Mhbv.*, p. 50 (*dhammaratanavassa*); *Dhpr.*, p. 206 (*dharmavarsā*); *PūjāV.*, p. 41 (*dahamväsi*); *SdhRv.*, pp. 152, 959; *SdhRk.*, p. 65; *SdhSS*, p. 533.

[75] *Miln.*, p. 21 (*dhammabheri*); *SdhRv.*, p. 91 (*sadaham namäti aṇabera*); *SdhRk.*, p. 188 (*dharmabheri*).

[76] *DahamS.*, p. 16.

[77] This observation was first shared with me by Dr. G. D. Wijayawardhana, Senior Lecturer in the Department of Sinhalese in the University of Sri Lanka.

[78] *SdhRk.*, p. 65, and *DahamS.*, p. 317. See *DahamS.*, p. 204, where "*svakkhato bhagavatā dhammo*" appears to have been viewed as a charm.

[79] *DahamS.*, p. 160.

[80] *RasaV.*, p. 109, and *DahamS.*, p. 72.

[81] *RasaV.*, p. 109, and *DahamS.*, p. 181.

[82] *DahamS.*, pp. 189, 194, 196, 229, 244, 256, 264, 285; *RasaV.*, p. 237.

[83] *DahamS.*, pp. 68, 235, 238, 277, 278, 299, 313; *SdhAl.*, pp. 114, 147; *SdhRk.*, pp. 61, 62; *SdhRv.*, p. 961. This is mentioned in Carter, "*Dhamma* as a Religious Concept." *op. cit.*, p. 672.

during the Christmas season cards bearing greetings relevant to the occasion will remember having seen cards on which were printed pictures depicting scenes of animals, which by nature are mutually hostile, being with each other in apparent harmony and peace. These pictures seem to express a notion that somehow lower nature has been transcended and a higher order has been attained.[84] Approximately five hundred years ago a Sinhalese author wrote in the same vein in praise of *dharma* and described it as the *dharma*

> that makes dear mutual friends of antagonists who bear animosity from birth and are greatly angered by the mere sight of each other; such as men and demons, gods [*suras*] and evil spirits [*asuras*], *garuḍhas* and serpents, cobras and frogs, elephants and lions, leopards and deer, crows and owls, cats and mice.[85]

This study of *dharma* in Sinhalese literature written in Sri Lanka from about the eleventh to the eighteenth centuries—with occasional reference to much older Pāli sources—demonstrates the manner in which several Buddhist authors understood *dharma*. The sources that defined the term listed the definitions briefly. But in discussing the lives of the Buddha and others—how he, as the *Bodhisattva*, sought *dharma*, attained it at the *bodhi* tree and, as the Buddha, chose to verbalize it that others might attain it, chose to share it with men and women who in turn chose to live it and share it with others—the Sinhalese sources consulted herein provided their readers and hearers with what amounts to well over six thousand printed pages.

For these authors salvation was possible because there was *dharma* and was contingent on hearing, practicing, and realizing *dharma*. And they found that in this process of salvation life was enriched,

---

[84] Compare the prophetic utterance at *Isaiah* 11:6–9 in the Hebrew Scriptures.

[85] *SdhRk.*, p. 62: "Tava da jātivaira bända unun duṭu kalhi krǟratararoṣayen no satuṭu vana nara rākṣasasurāsura garudhoraganāgamaṇdhukagajasiṃhadivi—muva kākolūka mārjāra mūsikādi vū pratimallayan ovunovun hā priyamitra karavannā vū dharmaya."

made more meaningful, was ennobled, and, also, that this world, ideally, could become less awry. In what appears to have been a masterful understatement, a sixteenth century Sinhalese poet wrote of the world without *dharma*:

> Like a lake having no lotus,
> Like a necklace having no central gem,
> Like a face without a nose,
> The world without *dharma* is not attractive.[86]

[86] *Dahamsoňda Kava*, vs. 75:
"kamala näti vila mena
taraḷa miṇa näti hara mena
gahana sun vata mena
daham näti lova novē sasobana."
Compare *RasaV.*, p. 2.

CHAPTER VI

DHAMMA IN THE CONTINUING TRADITION

Today there are Buddhists in Sri Lanka. This fact is, of course, patent and, of course, significant. Since there are Sinhalese Buddhists in Sri Lanka, in the world, it would be instructive to learn from them what their thoughts about *dhamma* are and have been in recent years.

Sinhalese Buddhists have continued providing definitions of the term *dhamma* and we will note their observations. More important than these definitions, both in the history of the Theravāda tradition and in the Sinhalese Buddhist community today, is the notion of *dhamma* as one of the three gems; and our task would be incomplete without drawing attention to the continuity and contemporaneity of this notion.

Definitions of Dhamma

In previous chapters the definitions of the term *dhamma/dharma* have been listed along with the sources providing those definitions.[1] In keeping with that procedure two more Sinhalese sources may be noted and their definitions given in order to bring the survey of the definitions up to relatively recent times. One source, the *Abhidhānappadīpikāsūci*, was written by W. Subhūti nearly ninety years ago. It is a work explaining more fully the definitions given in the *Abhidhānappadīpikā*. The second source is the admirable Sinhalese dictionary, *Śrī Sumaṅgala Śabdakoṣa*, compiled by the learned Wälivitiyē Sorata approximately twenty years ago.

[1]See Carter, "Traditional definitions of the term *dhamma*," *op. cit.*, pp. 329–337 and especially pp. 333–334 where a summation of the definitions provided in this study are also listed.

The *Abhidhānappadīpikā* gives the compound *saccappakati* as a definition of *dhamma* and Subhūti takes *sacca*, in the compound, as "truth."[2] In his *Abhidhānappadīpikāsūci*, Subhūti defines *dhamma* in terms of "truth" in the singular: "[*dhamma* occurs] in the sense of 'truth' in such passages as 'one having seen *dhamma*, having attained *dhamma*'."[3] The commentary on the *Majjhima-nikāya* speaks of "truths" in its listed definitions and the commentary on the *Buddhavaṃsa* speaks of "*dhamma* that is the four truths."[4] Some Sinhalese sources had incorporated *nirvāṇa* into their translation of the phrase.[5]

Subhūti adds several synonyms to our expanding list of definitions of *dhamma*: "constitution, quality" (*vikāra*), "condition" (*paccaya*), "that which has arisen conditionally" (*paccayuppanna*), "object" (*visaya*), and "custom" (*yutti*), and as a separate term, *nibbāna*. These additions to the list of meanings, Subhūti mentions, fall into the category of *ādi*, "etcetera," noted in the *Abhidhānappadīpikā*.[6]

Sorata, in his Sinhalese dictionary, gives additional terms in his list of definitions: "the noble path" (*āryamārga*), "the texts that are the three *piṭakas*" (*tripiṭakapāliya*), "good conduct" (*sucaritaya*), and "that which was spoken by the Buddha" (*buddhabhāṣitaya*).[7]

The definitions of the term *dhamma* given in the Pāli and Sinhalese sources mentioned thus far can be summarized as follows:

DA.	*DhsA.*	*DhpA.*	*MA.*	*BuA.*	*Abhidhp.*	*Dhpr.*	*AbhidhpS.*	*Śssk.*
(1)	(2)	(3)	(4)	(5)	(6)	(7)	(8)	(9)

---

[2] *Abhidhp.* (Subhūti's edition), paragraph 784, p. 220. Subhūti provides the English translation "truth" and the Sinhalese term *satya*.

[3] *AbhidhpS.*, p. 184: "'diṭṭhadhammo pattadhammo' ti ādīsu sacce."

[4] *MA.* I. 17; *BuA.* 13.

[5] See above, Chapter II, in the section "Hearing and Penetrating *Dhamma*." See also above, Chapter V, in the discussion under "Definitions of *Dhamma*," where the phrase is defined in terms of the paths, fruits, and *nirvāṇa*.

[6] *AbhidhpS.*, p. 184. It should be noted that Subhūti, having provided additional synonyms for the definition of *dhamma* in the *Abhidhp.*, ends his list with *ādi*, "etcetera."

[7] *Śssk.*, *s.v. dhamma*, I. 481b; *dharma*, I. 482a.

guṇa “quality, in the sense of virtuous, moral quality”	(1)	(2)	(3)			(6)	(7)	(8)	(9)
desanā “teaching”	(1)		(3)				(7)		
pariyatti “authoritative teaching, texts”	(1)	(2)	(3)	(4)	(5)	(6)	(7)	(8)	
nissatta “that without a living being”	(1)		(3)			(6)	(7)	(8)	
nissatta-nijjīvatā “that without a living being—lifelessness”		(2)						(8)	(9)
suññatā “emptiness, voidness”				(4)	(5)				(9)
hetu “cause”		(2)							(9)
saccāni “truths”				(4)		(6?)			
catusaccadhamma “*dhamma* that pertains to [the] four [noble] truths”					(5)				
sacca “truth”						(6?)		(8)	(9)
samādhi “rapt concentration”				(4)	(5)	(6)		(8)	(9)
paññā “wisdom”				(4)	(5)	(6)	(7)	(8)	(9)
pakati “natural condition”				(4)	(5)	(6)	(7)	(8)	(9)
sabhāva “inherent nature”				(4)	(5)	(6)	(7)	(8)	(9)
puñña “merit”				(4)	(5)	(6)	(7)	(8)	(9)
āpatti “an offense committed within the *saṅgha*”				(4)	(5)	(6)		(8)	(9)
ñeyya				(4)	(5)	(6)	(7)	(8)	(9)

"that to be known"									
(*ādi*)	(1)	(2)		(4)	(5)	(6)		(8)	
"etcetera [that is, the scope of meaning of the term is not exhausted by the definitions listed]"									
ñāya						(6)		(8)	(9)
"proper manner, propriety"									
ācāra						(6)		(8)	(9)
"[proper] conduct"									
kāraṇa						(6)		(8)	(9)
"reason, cause"									
maggaphalanibbāna							(7)		
"paths, fruits, and *nibbāna*"									
ariyamagga (*āryamārga*)									(9)
"noble path"									
vyavahāra							(7)		
"that which is customary"									
kusaladhamma							(7)		(9)
"*dhamma* that pertains to what is wholesome"									
vikāra								(8)	
"constitution, quality"									
paccaya								(8)	
"condition"									
paccayasamuppanna								(8)	
"that which has arisen conditionally"									
visaya								(8)	
"object"									
yutti								(8)	(9)
"custom, fitness"									
nibbāna									(9)
tripiṭakapāli									(9)
"the texts that are the three *piṭakas*"									
sucarita									(9)
"good behavior, good conduct"									

buddhabhāṣita (9)
"that which was spoken by the Buddha"

The nine sources consulted[8] give thirty-three definitions for the one term *dhamma*/*dharma*. One should note well the use of *ādi*, technically meaning "beginning with" as a lead term in an incomplete listing, and hence carrying the force of "such as" or "etcetera," "and so forth," in the list of terms.

Dhamma in the Tisaraṇa

> What refuge is there for you from *dharma*? *Dharma* means books written on *ola* leaves. How can those books be support for you? Is it not that those books exist by your "refuge" [*saraṇa*]?[9]

These words, representing a gross misunderstanding, were spoken by F. S. Sirimanne, a Wesleyan catechist, on August 28, 1873, in the debate between representatives from the Wesleyan clergy and Buddhist *bhikkhus* held in Pānadura, Sri Lanka. In a response to Mr. Sirimanne, Guṇānanda, a leading orator among the *bhikkhus* at that time, said:

> What is said by going for refuge in *dharma* is not going for refuge in *baṇa* books. The noble gem of the ninefold *saddharma* that transcends the world preached by the Buddha is called *dharma*. That *dharma* is the teacher even of the Buddha. If a person were to believe in [*viśvāsa karaṇavā*][10] that *dharma* and practice accord-

---

[8](1) *DA*.I.99; (2) *DhsA*., p. 38; (3) *DhpA*.I.(i).18; (4) *MA*.I.17; (5) *BuA*., p. 13; (6) *Abhidhp*., p. 220 (Subhūti's edition), p. 156 (Ñāṇobhāsatissa's edition); (7) *Dhpr*., pp. 236–237; (8) *AbhidhpS*., pp. 183–184; (9) *Śssk*., I.481b, 482a.

[9]*Pānadurē Vādaya*, edited by P. A. Peiris and James Dias (Colombo: Lanka Free Press, n.d.), p. 43: "Dharmayen nuṁbalāṭa saraṇa tibenavā da? Dharmaya kiyannē puskolavala liyā tibena pot ya. Ē pot nuṁbalāgē saraṇin pavatinavā misa ē potē nuṁbalāṭa pihiṭa vennē kohoma da?" See also *Buddhism and Christianity: Being an Oral Debate at Panadura between the Rev. Migettuvatte Guṇānanda & the Rev. David de Silva;* Introduction and Annotations by J. M. Peebles (Colombo: Mahabodhi Press, n.d.).

[10]*Viśvāsa karaṇavā* is a verbal construction that could mean either "trust

ing to it, he would obtain deliverance in the next world. The idea of going for refuge in *dharma* should be understood in this way.[11]

In the rapid movement of that public debate Guṇānanda failed to make a distinction between *ola* leaf books (that in which the teaching of the Buddha is recorded) and *pariyatti* (the teaching itself that is to be thoroughly learned, the authoritative teaching). Nevertheless, this orator was consistent with a tradition that was at least fifteen hundred years old[12] when he spoke of the ninefold *dharma* that transcends the world as *dharma* to which one goes for refuge.

Several authors have written on *dharma* as one of the three refuges and have interpreted it in terms of the authoritative teaching and the ninefold *dharma* that transcends the world.[13] In such cases *dharma* is explained in the manner adopted by Buddhaghosa in his

---

in, rely on" or "believe in." The context of the passage and Guṇānanda's considerable experience in debates with Christian missionaries and exposure to their terminology might suggest the rendering given above. I am indebted to Professor M. Palihawadana of the University of Sri Lanka for this observation.

[11] *Pānadurē Vādaya*, p. 76: "Dharmayē saraṇa yanavā ya kiyannē baṇa potvala saraṇa yāma novē. Dharmaya kiyannē budun vadāḷa navalōkottara śrī saddharmaratnayaṭa ya. Ē dharmaya buduṇṭat guru vē—ē dharmaya yamek viśvāsa karanavā nam elesa piḷipadinavā nam eyin paralova gälavīma läbē. Dharmayē saraṇa yāmē adahasa meyin tērum gaṇitvā."

[12] See above, note 196, Chapter II, for Pāli commentarial references and note 14, Chapter IV for Sinhalese references.

[13] Māpalagama Siri Somissara, *Bauddha Dharma Mārgaya* (Colombo: Vijayasēna saha Sahōharayo, Second impression, 1967 [first edition 1965?]), pp. 185–186. Rērukānē Candavimala, *Pohoya Dinaya* (Colombo: A.D.P. Sugatadāsa, Anula Mudraṇālaya, 1966), pp. 30, 32. Rērukānē Candavimala, *Bauddhayāgē At Pota* (Colombo: A.D.P. Sugatadāsa, Anula Mudraṇālaya, 1966 [fifth impression of the work first published in 1949]), p. 22. Rērukānē Candavimala, *Sūvisi Maha Guṇaya* (Colombo: A.D.P. Sugatadāsa, Anula Mudraṇālaya, 1969 [first impression 1964]), pp. 429 *passim*. Kiriällē Ñāṇavimala, *Bauddha Ädahilla* (Colombo: M. D. Guṇasēna, 1957), p. 66. See also the article, "Dhammam Saraṇam Gacchāmi," signed Buddhaputra, in *Budusaraṇa*, śrī bu. varṣa 2514 vū navam masa ava aṭavak pohōda (Wednesday, February 17, 1971), Vol. 7, No. 7, p. 6. See further *Siṃhala Upāsaka Janālaṅkāraya*, edited by D.P.R. Samaranāyaka (Colombo: M. D. Guṇasēna, 1961), p. 51. This work is readily available to Sinhalese readers in Sri Lanka.

Visuddhimagga,,[14] either in the form of brief paraphrases[15] or in a somewhat extended discussion as in the work *Sūvisi Maha Guṇaya*,[16] on the "Twenty-four Great Qualities" of the Buddha, *dhamma* and *saṅgha*, by the learned *bhikkhu* Rērukānē Candavimala.

R. Candavimala is a prolific writer on the contemporary Sinhalese scene who has recently retired from his position as a professor of Buddhist Studies at the Vidyālaṅkara University of Ceylon, now designated The University of Sri Lanka, Vidyālaṅkara Campus. His books tend to be recommended by academics and non-academics, laymen and *bhikkhus*, as the work of a learned *bhikkhu* who was well versed in the Sinhalese Buddhist tradition.

I will let the ideas of Candavimala provide a structure for this portion of the study drawing the reader's attention to the points wherein he provides information not already noted in this study. Candavimala mentions *dharma* as the authoritative teaching, *paryāpti*, and analyzes this aspect of *dharma* as applying to the words of the Buddha during the forty-five years of his preaching ministry. *Dharma* in this sense is twofold: the words of the Buddha in the *Vinaya-piṭaka* are understood as *vinaya* and all the rest are called *dharma*.[17] *Dharma* in the sense of the words of the Buddha is threefold: his first utterance after Enlightenment, his last utterance before his *parinirvāṇa* and those utterances throughout the intervening years. The words of the Buddha, Candavimala notes, can be alternatively considered as threefold: *Vinaya-piṭaka*, *Sūtrapiṭaka* and *Abhidharma-piṭaka*. Candavimala continues his discussion by listing the canonical books in the three *piṭakas* and notes that they also comprise the five

[14] *Vism.* VII. 68 ff. See above, Chapter III. See *Abhinava Katikāvata Saha Baṇadaham Pota,* edited by Maḍugallē Siddhārtha (Colombo: M. D. Guṇasēna, second impression, 1968, p. 15.

[15] As is done by Kiriällē Ñāṇavimala, *loc. cit.*, and R. Saraṇasēkara, *Daham Guṇaya* (Colombo: M. D. Guṇasēna, second impression, 1967 [first impression, 1958], pp. 1–2.

[16] Candavimala, *Sūvisi Maha Guṇaya*, pp. 429–503.

[17] Candavimala, *Sūvisi Maha Guṇaya*, p. 429.

nikāyas.[18] These five portions (*nikāyas*) can be further divided into the 84,000 *dharmaskandhas*, divisions of *dharma*.[19] The three major sections (*piṭakas*), *vinaya*, *sūtra*, and *abhidharma*, represent the words of the Buddha.[20]

In his treatment of *dharma* as *svākkhāta*, well proclaimed, Candavimala differs little from the interpretation recorded in the *Visuddhimagga*. However, in considering *dharma* as *akālika*, timeless, Candavimala elaborates that the Buddha preached the way to heaven that is characterized by time (*kālika*) because it was better for ordinary persons to do meritorious acts and attain subsequently a good bourne than to do bad acts and fall into bad states (*apāya*). The ninefold *dharma* that transcends the world is, as was noted in the *Visuddhimagga*, timeless in that it yields its fruit instantaneously.[21]

Candavimala concludes his discussion on *dharma* as timeless by contributing an interpretation not previously noted in this study. He refers to one passage in the *Saṃyutta-nikāya*[22] where the terms "visible," "timeless," and so forth, refer to the *dharma* taught by the Buddha and the *dharma* that pertains to *śramaṇas*. Candavimala concludes that the authoritative teaching (*paryāpti*) and practice (*pratipatti*) are timeless.[23]

Dharma is visible, actual (*sandiṭṭhika*) for Candavimala and it is this on two levels: the ninefold *dharma* that transcends the world is visible, present, actual, in that it can be realized personally[24] and

---

[18] *Ibid.*, p. 431.

[19] *Ibid.*, pp. 431–432. Compare the discussion given to this concept of *dharmaskandhas* by É. Lamotte, *Histoire du bouddhisme indien*, p. 162. Lamotte notes one reference, *Thag.*, vs. 1024, where this concept occurs in the canon. However, this *gāthā* occurs with another *gāthā*, spelling out more fully what is meant, at *Sdhs.*, p. 30. This text mentions these *gāthās* were said by the ancients, *porāṇas*.

[20] Compare É. Lamotte, *Histoire du bouddhisme indien*, pp. 200–201.

[21] Candavimala, *Sūvisi Maha Guṇaya*, p. 466.

[22] The passage will be found at *S.*I.117.

[23] Candavimala, *Sūvisi*, p. 467. He does not explain in what sense he understands *paryāpti* and *pratipatti* to be "timeless."

[24] *Ibid.*, p. 451.

the authoritative teaching is visible, present, in that it has bearing on this life itself. Candavimala focuses on *pirit* as an example of the words of the Buddha, the authoritative teaching, having the quality of being actual, pertaining to this life.[25]

Pirit, the Sinhalese form of the Pāli term *paritta*, means protection or safeguard and has come to designate a ceremony in which *bhikkhus* chant in sustained and melodious fashion several canonical *suttas*.[26] This practice, it seems reasonable to suggest, is at least 1,500 years old[27] and continues to flourish today in Sri Lanka.

In 1925, Wilhelm Geiger and his wife attended a *pirit* ceremony in Sri Lanka. Geiger wrote of their observations:

> I do not hesitate to confess that the little ceremony made a deep impression on us both. The demeanour of the priests was so serious and dignified, the quiet devotion of my friend was so sincere, that we told ourselves: here is yet true and genuine piety; the Buddha-teaching has here yet spiritual force.[28]

There are, of course, many levels in terms of which the *pirit* ceremony might be viewed. Professor Geiger's familiarity with the Pāli language enabled him to understand what he heard and for such a person, Sinhalese as well as foreigners, the *pirit* ceremony conveys an added depth of meaning.[29]

---

[25] *Ibid*., p. 455.

[26] These *suttas* have been collected and published by several writers with a Sinhalese translation provided. I note two: *Piruvānā Potvahansē nohot Purātana Sanna sahita Maha Pirit Pota*, edited with a Sinhalese *sanna* by Watuvattē Pemānanda (Colombo: Ratnākara Pot Veḷaňda Śālāva, 1957); *Piruvānā Potvahansē nam yut Mahapiritpota*, edited with a Sinhalese *sanna* by Devundara Śrī Vācissara (Colombo: M. D. Guṇasēna, third impression, 1969).

[27] See *DA*. III. 898 (on *D*. III. 114); *DA*. III. 969–970 (on *D*. III. 204–205); *MA*. III. 340 (on *M*. II. 104); *KhpA*. I. 161–169 (on the *Ratana sutta*); *DhpA*. II. 236–238 (on *Dhp*., vs. 109); *DhpA*. III. 436–449.

[28] Wilhelm Geiger, "Memories of Ceylon," *JPTS*. (1924–27), pp. 228–29.

[29] But there are many who do not understand the Pāli being chanted although the majority of Sinhalese Buddhists who arrange a *pirit* ceremony, I should think, have a general knowledge of the content of each *sutta*. Through the centuries the *pirit* ceremony in Sri Lanka functioned not entirely without what one might call magical aspects. Geiger, aware of this, noted, "In a purified form magic art was also admitted into the official religion."

On another level, Candavimala mentions, "Even today, for many people, disease and the like are dispelled by that *sutta* [*Ratana Sutta*]."[30] This is interpreted as an example of how the authoritative teaching is actual, present. R. Saraṇasēkara likewise notes this dimension of *pirit* when he writes, "By merely listening to that preaching an untimely calamity of some people is avoided."[31] It was, no doubt, in this spirit that *Set Pirit* was chanted, in 1969, for the safety of the Apollo 11 astronauts.[32]

The characteristic, "Come! Look!" as it pertains to *dharma* as the authoritative teaching and as the four paths, four fruits and *nirvāṇa*, is placed squarely in the context of sharing a message. It demonstrates a missionary motivation. *Dharma* in this sense is suitable for telling, beckoning, urging others to listen and live accordingly.[33]

Nothing new is added by Candavimala in his discussion of the ninefold *dharma* that transcends the world in terms of its being characterized as leading on (*opanayika*). However, he expands the treatment of this characteristic presented in the *Visuddhimagga* to include the authoritative teaching (*paryāpti*). The authoritative

Culture of Ceylon in Mediaeval Times, p. 173. Geiger's qualification," purified," possibly reflects his awareness that "magic" as a description of the function of the ceremony was somehow not entirely adequate. A non-German-speaking anthropologist might do well to tred lightly in stressing a magical dimension in the *pirit* ceremony should he, at the same time, find composure in listening to a Bach choral during a crisis period.

[30] Candavimala, *Sūvisi*, p. 455: "Adat ē suturen bohō denāṭa rōgādiya duru vē."

[31] Saraṇasēkara, *op. cit.*, p. 87: "E desum äsum matin mä peḷakagē akal piripatudu paha vannē yä."

[32] Held under the auspices of the Mahā Bōdhi Samāgama at the Agraśrāvaka Mahā Vihāra in Colombo and led by the visiting Sāñchi Vihārādhipati, Häḍigalle Paññātissa. Beneath the *samādhi* Buddha statue was placed a picture of the three astronauts.

[33] Candavimala, *Sūvisi*, pp. 468–475. Consider the observation by Bhikṣu Sumedha, "Of the truth that He taught, the Teacher spoke only two words by way of propaganda, only two words of great dignity and import—'Ehi Passiko [*sic*],' Come and see!" *The Ceylon Daily News*, Friday, July 17, 1970, (Esala Supplement), p. 11.

teaching is capable of leading the mind onwards.[34]

And, Candavimala concludes, *dharma* is to be known personally by the wise.[35]

The ninefold *dharma* that transcends the world was fully realized by the Buddha and preached by him.[36] More classically expressed, it was by that *dharma* that the Buddha received his consecration (*abhiṣeka läbū*).[37]

Dhamma at Present and in Future

The phrase "*dhamma* at present and in future" does not occur in the Pāli or Sinhalese literature consulted for this study. These sources speak rather of a disappearance of the *saddhamma* or of the *sāsana*.

In a sense—indeed, in the highest sense—*dhamma* is timeless. It is depicted in the Pāli canon as holding sway over the phenomenal world, as being present whether or not *Tathāgatas* arise. It is truth in the highest sense that was sought and found by the Buddha. *Dhamma* as *nibbāna* is outside time. Yet, *dhamma* as the ninefold *dhamma* that transcends the world maintains a delicate position of being in time even while, at the instant of its first realization, it is not only timeless (*akālika*) in yielding irrevocable fructification but also it lifts a person into a level of reality that is not primarily interpreted in terms of time. *Dhamma* is also in time and of time and restricted by time.

Dhamma that is in time is *dhamma* in the form of the Buddha's teachings (*āgama*, *pariyatti*), which have come down through the centuries to the present day. *Dhamma* in the form of practice (*paṭipatti*) is also in time in the sense that it is a way of life, a prescribed mode of behavior from day to day. *Dhamma* that is attainment, penetration (*adhigama*, *paṭivedha*) represents in the first

---

[34] Candavimala, *Sūvisi*, pp. 482–483. [35] *Ibid.*, pp. 486–491.
[36] *Ibid.*, p. 468. [37] Somissara, *op. cit.*, p. 24.

case the attainment of the paths and fruits at which time one is in the world but not limited by the world, in time, but a master of time because time has become relative and *saṃsāra* limited. When *nibbāna* is attained, penetrated, time has been transcended.

Before we turn again to the writing of Candavimala for an interpretation of *dhamma* at present and in future, some comment on two terms and a brief glance at Pāli sources might enable us more easily to catch the thrust of his observations. Firstly, *saddhamma* is understood as "true [*sat*] *dhamma*" and "*dhamma* of the good ones [*sat*]," that is, the Buddha, *paccekabuddhas* and *sāvakas*.[38] *Saddhamma* as a term is very old, being present throughout the canon. It is difficult to discern when this term began to circulate in the early Buddhist community. Possibly it was used at the very early days or months or years. Perhaps the *dhamma*, which the early Buddhists had in mind as needing to be qualified by the adjective "true" or the descriptive phrase "of the good ones," was somehow in need of differentiation. Possibly *saddhamma* first referred to the teaching of the Buddha, which is the true teaching, as opposed to other teachings or to the teaching of a good one, as opposed to other teachers and, in the course of time, might have extended its scope of reference to include all aspects of the Buddhist way of life in so far as those aspects could be traced to the Buddha, to what he said and demonstrated.

Secondly, the term *sāsana*, "message, instruction, order," has had a long and varied, engaging, provocative history. It, too, occurs throughout the canon. *Sāsana* means what the Buddha instructed his disciples to do. The *suttas* never speak of the Buddha's attaining, penetrating *sāsana*—this would be absurd. Nevertheless, the Buddha did instruct and in terms of what Buddhists understood by that instruction an institution was formed. A detailed study of the term *sāsana* would demonstrate a gradual development in meaning that

[38] See for example *DhpAg.*, p. 2; *Śssk.*, p. 987a: "Saddharma—buddhādisatpuruṣayangē dharmaya."

would reflect a doctrinal and sociological movement from "instruction" to "institution," from "the Buddha's order" to "the Buddhist Order."[39]

A notion that the *saddhamma* might not last forever is noted in the Pāli *suttas*[40] but it appears that *sāsana* as a term designating that which will disappear is of later usage. In any case, the Sinhalese Buddhist tradition has had something to say about the condition of the *saddhamma* or *sāsana* in time during the course of roughly the past 2,500 years.

The Buddhist tradition remained fluid in the attempts to come to grips with the notion of the disappearance of the *saddhamma*. In the *Milindapañha* a threefold classification, attainment, realization (*adhigama*), practice (*paṭipatti*), and externals (*liṅga*), was used to describe stages of the disappearance of the *saddhamma*.[41]

The commentarial tradition that developed in Sri Lanka reached a consensus that the authoritative teaching (*pariyatti*) was the basis of the *saddhamma* or *sāsana* and that generally the time span from the *parinibbāna* of the Buddha to the final disappearance of the *saddhamma* would be five thousand years.[42] The commentary on the *Saṃyutta-nikāya* varies in its discussion in noting that there would be a period in which a counterfeit (*paṭirūpaka*) *saddhamma* would come on the scene.[43] The commentary on the *Theragāthā* is unique

---

[39] For a further consideration of the term *sāsana* see John Ross Carter, "A History of *Early Buddhism*," *Religious Studies*, Vol. 13, No. 3 (September, 1977), pp. 263–287, especially pp. 266–270.

[40] See *PD.*, p. 54, for *sutta* references.

[41] *Miln.*, pp. 133–134. Incidentally, this text mentions that practice is the basis of the *sāsana* at p. 133: "Paṭipattimūlakaṃ mahārāja Satthusāsanaṃ paṭipattisārakaṃ." See *AA.* I. 92–93, regarding a decision on the part of the elders to resolve this divergence between practice as the basis or *pariyatti* as the basis.

[42] The comments regarding the 5,000 years are to be found at *VA.* I. 30; *DA.* III. 898 (on *D.* III. 114); and *DhsA.*, p. 27. However, *VA.* breaks this period into five segments of 1,000 years each and structures those segments into a decreasing grade of the four paths and four fruits. *DA.* breaks its five segments in relation to other categories.

[43] *SA.* II. 201, commenting on *S.* II. 224, where the notion of a "counterfeit" *saddhamma* occurs.

in speaking of the *sāsana* as having five *yugas* or "ages, stages."[44]

To provide a background in order to catch the thrust of Candavimala's comments does not require delving further into these notions about a disappearance of the *saddhamma* although this would, perhaps, yield interesting conclusions.[45]

When a Sinhalese *bhikkhu* considers the duration of the *saddhamma* it is informative that he first ponders what his tradition has said that might be relevant—he, of course, could have chosen to do otherwise. Candavimala draws his readers' attention to the commentaries on the *Aṅguttara-nikāya* and the *Dīgha-nikāya* and by noting their breakdown of five thousand years into five units of one thousand —each being a period in which certain spiritual attainments are possible—draws the following conclusions:

> Now is present the third thousand year period of the Buddha-*sāsana*. According to the *Manorathapūraṇī*, this is the period in which "non-returners" [*anāgāmins*] can exist. According to the *Dīgha-nikāyaṭṭhakathā*, it is the time when *arahants* having the three knowledges[46] can exist.[47]

One observes that Candavimala, in dealing with the present situation, finds the old tradition relevant. Yet, he believes that the statements in the two commentaries which he consulted are not quite adequate. "*Paryāpti* [the authoritative teaching] is the basis of the *saddharma*,"[48] he reminds his readers and he draws attention to the

[44] *ThagA.* III. 89 (on *Thag.*, vs. 977).

[45] See *Miln.*, pp. 133–134; *DA.* III. 898 (on *D.* III. 114); *SA.* II. 201–202 (on *S.* II. 224); *AA.* I. 87 ff.; *VbhA.*, pp. 431–432; *ThagA.* II. 89 (on *Thag.*, vs. 977). See, further, *PūjāV.*, pp. 195, 721–722, 735, 788; *SdhRk.*, pp. 230–237.

[46] These three knowledges are: (1) knowledge that is recollection of former abodes (*pubbe nivāsānussatiñāṇa*), (2) knowledge of the moving from one state in one life and reappearance into another in another life (*cuti-upapattiñāṇa*), and (3) knowledge that one's defilements are destroyed (*āsavānaṃ khayañāṇa*).

[47] Candavimala, *Sūvisi*, p. 501: "Dänaṭa pavatnē budusasnē tun vana varṣa dahasa ya. Mē kālaya manōratha-pūraṇiyehi kiyana andamaṭa anāgāmin siṭiya häki kālaya yi. *Dīghanikāyaṭṭha kathāvehi* däkvena andamaṭa trividyā äti rahatun siṭiya häki kālaya yi."

[48] *Ibid.*

presence of *paryāpti* in many countries today. With regard to the future he says,

> It [*paryāpti*] will persist for a long time even though from time to time the extent to which it is present might be more or less. Leaving aside five thousand years, it cannot be imagined that it will perish even in ten thousand years.[49]

Concluding his observations regarding the *saddharma* at present and in future. Candavimala notes the presence of scripture (*daham pot*), persons who remember *dharma*, the frequent preaching of *dharma*, and makes the point that one has no reason to doubt the presence of the authoritative teaching (*paryāpti*). He goes on to note that there are many who are engaged in the practice (*pratipatti*) and likewise one has no reason to doubt the presence of this practice. When these two aspects of *saddharma* are present, one is not able to say that the third, realization, penetration (*prativedha*), is not present.[50]

> Since penetration is something that cannot be seen [by an observer] it is difficult to grasp its being or not being at anytime whatsoever.[51]

The penetration of which Candavimala speaks is comprised of the ninefold *dhamma* that transcends the world.[52] An observer cannot see this penetration but one who realizes it truly sees.

Candavimala's comments are highly instructive. Whether the *sāsana* as an institution or system of thought continues to exist on a mundane, social level is contingent upon what men choose to do. *Dhamma* as religious texts (*āgama*) or authoritative teaching (*pariyatti*) is in the hands of men. It exists like other things exist and,

---

[49] *Ibid.*: "Eya kalin kalaṭa pätira pavatnā pradēśa aḍu väḍi vemin, dīrgha kālayak pavatinu äta. Varṣa pandahasakin tabā dasadahasakinudu eya näti vetäyi no siṭiya häki ya."

[50] *Ibid.*, p. 503.

[51] *Ibid.*; "Prativedhaya no penena deyak bävin ehi äti näti bava kavadāvat tērum gänīma apahasu ya."

[52] *Ibid.*, p. 439. See also Saraṇasēkara, *op. cit.*, p. 98.

should men choose, it too can cease to exist. The manner in which a person lives in accordance with the authoritative teaching will determine his success or failure in his search for penetration: the practice (*paṭipatti*) is contingent upon what men choose to do. It too can cease to exist.

The ninefold *dhamma* that transcends the world, that is, the four paths, four fruits and *nibbāna*, is not limited by the world. *Dhamma* in its aspect of the four paths and four fruits, is in the world, is in time in so far as there are men who are capable of attaining it. Its arising in the lives of men is contingent upon what men choose to do. Although the four paths and the four fruits are considered compounded, that is to say briefly, not *nibbāna*, they merge with *dhamma* that is *nibbāna*. *Dhamma* in its aspect of *nibbāna* is beyond time, ever there: was, is, and will be.

CONCLUSION

Dhamma has had a place in the Western academic tradition for over a century and a quarter. Scholars working in this tradition have sought to understand the term and, drawing on the labors of men and women who preceded them, they have made their contribution to the increase of Western man's knowledge about it. With the accumulation of Pāli *ola* leaf manuscripts, the magnificent work of the Pali Text Society that enabled Western scholars to have at their finger tips the Pāli sources, the increase of learned articles on *dhamma*, Western scholars significantly enlarged their knowledge about *dhamma* relatively quickly.

We have seen that scholars in the West, upon meeting the term *dhamma*, soon became restless in trying to find a suitable equivalent in Western languages. The first chapter of this study traced a facet of that history of restlessness in the West.

Most of the Western scholars who investigated *dhamma* were primarily concerned with what it "originally" meant when the Buddha spoke it. To some extent this orientation toward the "original" was due to current views of historiography at the time. Percolating throughout the works of the early scholars of the Theravāda Buddhist movement was what one might call a reverse chronological correspondence theory of truth. The operative assumption seems to have been that the further *back* into time one could peg an event or an idea, the nearer to the original one moved and correspondingly the nearer to the truth of the matter one came.

Some Western academics might have first met *dhamma* in *ola* leaf manuscripts, others in a printed book. Through historical sensitivity they sought to reconstruct on one side of a spectrum what the term *dhamma* meant for the Buddha and on the other side, what it meant in the Pāli sources at the time they were written. Occasionally, in a brilliant probe into the past through the context of Pāli sources, some scholars saw something more than a problematic term; they saw a concept that was solemn and intriguing. Some had the learned patience to sort through the Pāli sources to classify the many notions that were connoted by the one term *dhamma*.

E. Burnouf, about the middle of the nineteenth century, translated *dharma/dhamma* as "la Loi," and Professor Rhys Davids, sometime later thought *dhamma* was somehow in back of "law," was that which the concept "law" represents. For Beckh, writing about 1916, *dharma/dhamma* seemed to hold in one notion that which the West has tended to bifurcate into moral and natural law.

It was Mrs. Rhys Davids, writing early in this century, who first set about to interpret the Theravāda movement in terms of *dhamma* and she continued to probe for its meaning during the many years of her study. *Dhamma* could have meant the message of "the good way of life,"[1] she thought, and in one sense, as we have seen, she was in agreement with Buddhists. She discerned a moral imperative in *dhamma* that seemed to her not adequately communicated through "law," "truth," and the like. She moved away from her earlier translation, "Norm," and preferred for a time "conscience," but not without some restlessness, sensing also that *dhamma* meant "will" or "the force of the Ought." In one of her last writings, she suggested that perhaps *dhamma* represents "the ideal of ever becoming a more in the long way towards the Most."[2]

Mrs. Rhys Davids appears to have been pressing behind the notion of *dhamma* as teaching (*desanā*), trying to discern *dhamma's* depth of meaning, seeking a normative quality in *dhamma* that was in some way personal. The many English equivalents for *dhamma* that were suggested by Mrs. Rhys Davids do not represent so much slip-

[1] C. A. F. Rhys Davids, *JRAS* (Oct. 1924), p. 675.

[2] Mrs. Rhys Davids, "Editor's Introduction," *The Minor Anthologies of the Pali Canon*, Part IV, p. xii.

shod tampering with Buddhist thought as an inchoate awareness that the concept "truth" in the West in her milieu did not seem to be integrally related to persons, that truth was somehow out there, so to speak, apart from persons.[3] And so, it seems, she turned to "conscience" or "the force of the Ought" as interpretations for *dhamma*, having abandoned concepts like "truth," "law," and "Norm." She caught a glimpse of the intimate relation between that truth and persons.

It is difficult to state succinctly what position Mrs. Rhys Davids finally took on the matter of *dhamma*. It is clear that she recognized that *dhamma* had a deeply profound meaning for the Buddha however she might have chosen, now here, now there, to translate the term. She sensed a moral aspect in *dhamma* that seemed to her to be at the basis of religious life. In making these two points, she moved very near to the attitude of Sinhalese Buddhists.

Professor and Mrs. Geiger published, in 1920, a work that represented a landmark in the history of *dhamma* in Western academia. Their work was a monumental attempt to understand the meaning of the term as it appeared throughout the Pāli canon. Among its many meanings, *dhamma*, these authors noted, was an expression for the Absolute. It was venerated by the Buddha and is the central concept in Buddhist thought.

We have noted above an important verse in the *Theragāthā* (vs. 303).[4] Professor and Mrs. Geiger thought that in this verse *dhamma* was conceived as a personal deity. Professor Geiger, a leading scholar

[3] Wilfred Cantwell Smith in his article, "A Human View of Truth," *Studies in Religion*, Vol. 1, No. 1 (1971), pp. 6–24, draws attention to a tendency developing for some time in the West to make truth amoral. He makes the point that a personalist view of truth sees it as integral to moral living. Apparently, Mrs. Rhys Davids sensed that "truth" was conceived impersonally at the time of her writing and such impersonal notion, she seems to have thought, could not have generated and sustained moral living for centuries.

[4] *Dhammo have rakkhati dhammacāriṃ*, "*dhamma* indeed protects the one living *dhamma*." See *PD.*, p. 76.

of the Sinhalese language, was, no doubt, aware that *rakinavā*, the Sinhalese verb meaning "to protect," (Pāli *rakkhati*), was regularly used in the sense of a female canine, hen or the like protecting her offspring. This verb used in its Pāli form in the *gāthā* does provide a forceful, graphic metaphorical statement that, perhaps, led the Geigers to their conclusion. Furthermore, it is understandable that Westerners writing fifty years ago would have interpreted such sense of protection in terms of major concepts in the religious traditions in the West.

The Pāli commentarial tradition and the Sinhalese Buddhist writers have consistently interpreted this protection as not involving the activity of a deity.

Mrs. Rhys Davids also commenting on this verse said that *dhamma* is not guarded by men, rather, it guards man.[5] As we have now seen, some Buddhists, however, have discerned a relationship reciprocally dynamic.[6]

Some Western scholars, particularly the Geigers and Mrs. Rhys Davids, spoke of the relation of *dhamma* with *brahman* and, through their observations, Western scholars began to see *dhamma* as more central in Buddhist thought than they had previously. If the relationship between *dhamma* and *brahman* is considered homologously, the example is illustrative. The Pāli commentarial tradition provides little illumination on this point except that it is consistent in glossing *brahma*-(occurring as first member of a compound and when so used in Pāli its gender is uncertain) as "the highest," "the best," (*seṭṭha*).

The integral relation between the Buddha and *dhamma* was seen by some Western academics when they considered the passage wherein the Buddha said, "He who sees *dhamma* sees me." The Pāli commentarial tradition, although varying in its explanations of *dhamma* and *kāya* (body), are consistent at least in stressing the

---

[5] Mrs. Rhys Davids, *A Manual*, p. 168.

[6] See the discussion above, Chapter V, in the section "The Noble Quest."

continuity of that which the Buddha rediscovered and that which he said about it.

Mrs. Rhys Davids was brilliantly penetrative when she said, over sixty years ago, that "the function and hall-mark of a Buddha was not to devise, or create a new Dhamma, but to rediscover, recreate and revive that ancient norm."[7] During the course of the remaining years of her work she thought the Buddhists had subsequently made *dhamma* external, formulating it into a body of doctrine. She was convinced that *dhamma*, when the Buddha first spoke of it, did not mean "an external code of doctrines."

Mrs. Rhys Davids noted in two of her works that when she had asked a man of Ceylon or pupils of Ceylon, "What is dhamma?" or "What for you is dhamma?" the reply was "The Sutta-Piṭaka."[8] We have seen in our survey of the Pāli canon and commentaries that *dhamma* had levels of meaning and in Chapter III this became clearer when we discussed the summary provided by Buddhaghosa in his *Visuddhimagga*. These levels, we noted, were maintained throughout the Sinhalese Buddhist tradition. The person(s) who gave "The Sutta-Piṭaka" in answer to Mrs. Rhys Davids's question about the meaning of *dhamma* left much unsaid.

Mrs. Rhys Davids was not off the track. Her discernment that *dhamma* rediscovered by the Buddha was not a body of doctrines was very close to the historical Theravāda Buddhist position, we have here found. Her rigorous opposition to the interpretation of *dhamma* as "doctrine" and the like did not allow the observation that religious men and women do not honor, revere in the final analysis doctrines but, rather, that which doctrines represent.

The Western scholars whose works we have studied did not stress *dhamma's* meaning the four paths, four fruits, and *nibbāna*. Mrs. Rhys Davids and I. B. Horner were aware of this aspect of Buddhist

---

[7] Mrs. Rhys Davids, *Buddhism*, p. 33.

[8] See Mrs. Rhys Davids, "Introduction," in *Gradual Sayings*, Vol. I, viii, and *What Was the Original Gospel in "Buddhism"?*, p. 49.

thought and discussed it—the later in considerable detail—but did not mention how the paths, fruits, and *nibbāna* were held in the concept *dhamma* as the *navavidhalokuttaradhamma*, "the ninefold *dhamma* that transcends the world." Professor and Mrs. Geiger noted a few passages where *dhamma* in the *suttas* was glossed in the commentaries by the ninefold *dhamma* that transcends the world,[9] but, disappointingly, Professor Geiger, with his remarkable ability, did not pursue the matter further.

Professor and Mrs. Geiger, I. B. Horner, and Edward Conze were aware of a close relationship between *dhamma* and *nibbāna*, but they let the matter rest. R. L. Slater wrote about *nibbāna* as an example of the manner in which paradox plays a significant role in religious language. In the course of his study he spoke of a relationship between *dhamma* and *nibbāna* and noted that whether or not *nibbāna* was taken as "the consummating, central term of Buddhism" depends on the suggestive significance one assigns to *dhamma*.[10] We have seen some of the connotations that Theravāda Buddhists in Sri Lanka have given to *dhamma*; and *nibbāna* is included.

Slater spoke of *nibbāna* as the *gospel* of Buddhism and mentioned that the greatest assurance a devout Buddhist could have was the assurance that he had attained the stream (*sotāpanna*) and that he would certainly attain *nibbāna*.

We have seen that the injunctions *ehi*, *passa*, "Come! Look!" were used to describe *dhamma* and such imperatives are usually reserved for that which has been seen and the sight of which is considered worthy to be shared—a rainbow, a sunset, the true manner of living, Truth. This *ehi-passa* characteristic that was ascribed to *dhamma* seems to represent an attitude that led Buddhists to begin and sustain a vast, impressive missionary movement. *Dhamma* appears to have been the "Good News."

In differing slightly with Slater, I do not wish to leave the reader

[9] See *PD.*, p. 102.

[10] See R. L. Slater, *Paradox and Nirvana*, n. 76, p. 63.

with the notion that *nibbāna* is a term buried in a maze of intricate classifications. Not in the least. Slater was near the mark when he said *nibbāna* was the "consummating" term. My point is that Sinhalese Buddhists have said that the relationship between the concept *dhamma* and the notion *nibbāna* is integral.

Let me give an example. In June 1970, my wife and I made a journey to Anurādhapura and Mihintalē in Sri Lanka. We were a part of a mass movement of Sinhalese men, women, and children from most parts of the island. Among the impressive ancient ruins at Anurādhapura, in the presence of the *bodhi* tree, people walked slowly, sat quietly and listened to *baṇa* at specified times during the day and night. At dusk we heard a *baṇa* sermon during which several in the audience of three hundred or so would periodically say softly but noticeably, "*sādhu, sādhu, sādhu*"—an expression suggesting that what was said was well said,[11] that what was said was evocative of praise. When events in the life of the Buddha and when the term *nirvāṇa* were mentioned in the sermon, "*sādhu*" was often heard from someone with us in the audience. "*Sādhu*" was not said when the word *dharma* occurred in the sermon. Now this might lead one to conclude that only the Buddha and *nirvāṇa* were of significance for Sinhalese Buddhists.

Let me continue the story. The holiday period in which this mass movement to Anurādhapura and Mihintalē took place occurs during a two or three day period around the full moon *poya* (*uposatha*) day in the month of *Poson*. Sinhalese Buddhists have another holiday on the full moon *poya* in the month of *Vesak* at which time the birth, enlightenment and *parinibbāna* of the Buddha are commemorated. *Poson poya* has a different but not dissimilar significance. *Poson poya* commemorates the coming of Mahinda to Sri Lanka to preach *dhamma* and he preached it first at Mihintalē a few miles from Anurādhapura. What I mentioned earlier as a mass movement was more like a pilgrimage. Along the route *dan salas* (or *dāna śālāvas*) were on the

[11] See *AA*.IV.167.

roadside at which a traveler is given refreshments while on his way to commemorate the coming of *dhamma* to Sri Lanka. There was a sense of cheerful piety.

While at Anurādhapura Sinhalese Buddhists read *dhamma*, heard *dhamma* and at Mihintalē they climbed a peak to honor the point at which *dhamma* was preached by Mahinda.

The men and women whom we saw were where they were because *dhamma* had come; were there because *dhamma* was in their lives.

In the course of this study we have seen that *dhamma* has been viewed as religious texts (*āgama*) and attainment (*adhigama*). The former can be an object for study; the latter is pre-eminently the objective in life. The word "attainment" is, in Pāli, formed from √*gam* and the prefix *adhi* and, apparently, was not arbitrarily selected. We have seen *adhi* + √*gam* before when it was used to refer to the attainment of *dhamma* by the Buddha.

Long ago, *dhamma* was interpreted as threefold: the authoritative teaching (*pariyatti*), practice (*paṭipatti*), and penetration (*paṭivedha*). Remarkable in this threefold interpretation is what it assumes—the relation of *dhamma* with persons. If one were to erase the assumption that persons are to become involved with *dhamma*, the threefold classification would loose its coherence. *Dhamma* is to be mastered, pondered, followed, lived, attained, and realized.

We have seen that *dhamma*, which is a refuge for men and women, is understood as the authoritative teaching and the ninefold *dhamma* that transcends the world. The ninefold *dhamma* falls into the category of attainment (*adhigama*) or penetration (*paṭivedha*). When one goes to *dhamma* as refuge, one becomes aware that the *dhamma* taught by the Buddha without distortion is worthy to become an authoritative norm for living life. One also becomes aware that *dhamma* that the Buddha realized, about which he taught, is worthy to be the objective.

Men and women in the Theravāda Buddhist tradition have discussed the one word *dhamma* in terms of three notions. They have discovered that these notions are not separate, unrelated concepts but, rather, that they are united with, integral to, inseparable from *dhamma*, salvific Truth. They have found that Truth is not remote from persons; that a man's proper relation with himself, with society, with the world, with Reality is in terms of that salvific Truth.

Dhamma, salvific Truth, is available to men because of a momentous event in history when the Buddha rediscovered it and spoke to men about it. This Truth is available to men today because it abides and because what the Buddha said about it has been passed down by men for centuries. It is available and men can participate in it by living truly, by living according to that Truth about which the authoritative teaching speaks. And in so living, Truth is lived. Salvific Truth is available and men can perceive it. They can by living it penetrate more deeply into it and at a fructifying instant it is totally realized.

One term, *dhamma*, has been used by men and women in the Theravāda Buddhist tradition for centuries because they have discovered that it has adequately represented the salvific Truth in the teachings of the Buddha, the authoritative teaching (*dhamma* that is *pariyatti*), salvific Truth in the way of living (*dhamma* that is *paṭipatti*), and salvific Truth, Reality, rediscovered by the Buddha and the objective for mankind (*dhamma* that is *adhigama*, *paṭivedha*: *nibbāna*).

The Buddha has been remembered by Buddhists because he rediscovered salvific Truth and through preaching it enabled men and women to hold it in mind, in heart, and through their living it to be held by it in the process of transcending, of salvation. "*Dhamma*: because it holds, supports"—"*dhāretī ti dhammo.*"

ABBREVIATIONS

A. *The Aṅguttara-nikāya* (PTS edition)
AA. *Manorathapūraṇī:* the commentary on the *Aṅguttara-nikāya* (PTS edition)
Abhidhp. *Abhidhānappadīpikā*
AbhidhpS. *Abhidhānappadīpikāsūci*
AK. *L'Abhidharmakośa de Vasubandhu*
AmāV. *Amāvatura*
AmāVgpv. *Amāvaturu Gätapada Vivaraṇaya* by Wälīviṭiyē Sorata
Ap. *The Apadāna* (PTS edition)
ApA. *Visuddhajanavilāsinī nāma Apadānaṭṭhakathā* (PTS edition)
BD. *The Book of the Discipline*
BHSD. Franklin Edgerton, *Buddhist Hybrid Sanskrit Dictionary*
BJTS. Buddha Jayanti Tripitaka Series
Bu. *The Buddhavaṃsa* (PTS edition)
BuA. *Madhuratthavilāsinī nāma Buddhavaṃsaṭṭhakathā* (PTS edition)
Cp. *The Cariyā-Piṭaka* (PTS edition)
CpA. *Acariya Dhammapāla's Paramatthadīpanī;* Being the Commentary on the *Cariya-Piṭaka* (PTS edition)
D. *The Dīgha-nikāya* (PTS edition)
DA. *The Sumaṅgala-vilāsinī:* the commentary on the *Dīgha-nikāya* (PTS edition)
DAG. or *DhpAg.* *Dahampiyā Aṭuvā Gäṭapadaya*
DahamS. *Daham Saraṇa*
DhA. or *DhpA.* *The Commentary on the Dhammapada: Dhammapadaṭṭhakathā* (PTS edition)
Dhp. *The Dhammapada* (PTS edition)
DhpA. or *DhA.* *The Commentary on the Dhammapada: Dhammapadaṭṭhakathā* (PTS edition)
DhpAg. or *DAG.* *Dahampiyā Aṭuvā Gäṭapadaya*
Dhpr. *Dharmapradīpikā*
Dhs. *The Dhammasaṅgaṇī* (PTS edition)
DhsA. *The Atthasālinī:* the commentary on the *Dhammasaṅgaṇī* (PTS edition)
DPL. R. C. Childers, *A Dictionary of the Pali Language*
EBTMP. I. B. Horner, *The Early Buddhist Theory of Man Perfected*
HOS. The Harvard Oriental Series
Itv. *Iti-vuttaka* (PTS edition)
ItvA. *Paramattha-Dīpanī; Iti-Vuttakaṭṭhakathā:* the commentary on the

Iti-vuttaka (PTS edition)

Jā. *The Jātaka; Together with Its Commentary* (PTS edition)

JāA. *The Jātaka; Together with Its Commentary* (PTS edition)

JāAg. *Jātaka Aṭuvā Gäṭapadaya*

JPTS. *Journal of the Pali Text Society*

JRAS *Journal of the Royal Asiatic Society*

Khp. *The Khuddaka-Pāṭha; Together with Its Commentary Paramatthajotikā I* (PTS edition)

KhpA. *The Khuddaka-Pāṭha; Together with Its Commentary Paramatthajotikā I* (PTS edition)

LUAB. H. Oldenberg, *Die Lehre der Upanishaden und die Anfänge des Buddhismus*

M. *Majjhima-nikāya* (PTS edition)

MA. *Papañcasūdanī Majjhimanikāyaṭṭhakathā:* the commentary on the *Majjhima-nikāya* (PTS edition)

Mbv. *Mahā-Bodhi-Vaṁsa* (PTS edition)

Mhv. *The Mahāvaṃsa* (PTS edition)

MhvT. *Vaṃsatthappakāsinī:* the commentary on the *Mahāvaṃsa* (PTS edition)

Miln. *The Milindapañho* (PTS edition)

Nd. 1. *Niddesa I: Mahāniddesa,* (PTS edition)

Nd. 2. *Niddesa II: Cullaniddesa* (PTS edition)

Netti. *The Netti-pakaraṇa* (PTS edition)

PD. Magdalene und Wilhelm Geiger, *Pāli Dhamma: vornehmlich in der kanonischen Literatur*

Pm. *Paramatthamañjūsā:* the commentary on the *Visuddhimagga*

Psbp. or *PSBP.* *Purāṇasiṃhalabaṇapota*

PTS. The Pali Text Society

Pṭs. *Paṭisambhidāmagga* (PTS edition)

PṭsA. *The Saddhammappakāsinī:* the commentary on the *Paṭisambhidāmagga* (PTS edition)

PTSD. *The Pali Text Society's Pali-English Dictionary*

Pug. *The Puggala-paññatti* (PTS edition)

PugA. *Puggala-paññatti-aṭṭhakathā:* the commentary on the *Puggala-paññatti* (PTS edition)

PūjāV. *Pūjāvaliya*

Pv. *Petavatthu* (PTS edition)

PvA. *Dhammapāla's Paramattha-Dīpanī,* Part III, Being the Commentary on the *Peta-Vatthu* (PTS edition)

RasaV. *Rasavāhinī*

S. *The Saṃyutta-nikāya* (PTS edition)

SA. *Sārattha-ppakāsinī:* the commentary on the *Saṃyutta-nikāya* (PTS edition)

SdhAl. *Saddharmālaṅkāraya*

SdhRk. *Saddharmaratnākaraya*

SdhRv. *Saddharmaratnāvaliya*
Sdhs. *Saddhammasaṃgaha*
SdhSS. *Saddharma Sārārtha Sangrahaya*
Sdhup. *Saddhammopāyana*
Sdpj. *Saddhamma-Pajjotikā:* the commentary on the *Mahāniddesa*
SED. B. Clough, *A Siṇhalese-English Dictionary*
Sn. *Sutta-Nipāta* (PTS edition)
SnA. *Sutta-Nipāta Commentary; Being Paramatthajotikā* II (PTS edition)
ŚsdhAv. *Śrī Saddharmāvavāda Saṃgrahaya*
Śssk. *Śrī Sumaṅgala Śabdakoṣa*
Thag. *The Thera- and Therī-gāthā:* Part I, *Theragāthā* (PTS edition)
Thig. *The Thera- and Therī-gāthā:* Part II, *Therīgāthā* (PTS edition)
ThagA. *Paramattha-Dīpanī Theragāthā-Aṭṭhakathā:* the commentary on the *Theragāthā* (PTS edition)
ThigA. *Paramattha-Dīpanī Therīgāthā-Aṭṭhakathā:* the commentary on the *Therīgāthā*
UCR. *University of Ceylon Review*
Ud. *Udāna* (PTS edition)
UdA. *Paramattha-Dīpanī Udānaṭṭhakathā:* the commentary on the *Udāna*
UJ. *Upāsakajanālaṅkāra* (PTS edition)
VA. or *VinA.* *Samantapāsādikā:* the commentary on the *Vinaya Piṭaka* (PTS edition)
VbhA. *Sammoha-vinodanī Abhidhamma-Piṭake Vibhangaṭṭhakathā* (PTS edition)
Vin. *The Vinaya Piṭakam* (PTS edition)
VinA. or *VA.* *Samantapāsādikā:* the commentary on the *Vinaya Piṭaka* (PTS edition)
Vism. *Visuddhimagga*
Vv. *The Vimāna-Vatthu* (PTS edition)
VvA. *Dhammapāla's Paramattha-Dīpanī*, Part IV, Being the Commentary on the *Vimāna-Vatthu* (PTS edition)
WZKM. *Wiener Zeitschrift für die Kunde des Morgenlandes*
ZDMG. *Zeitschrift der deutschen morgenländischen Gesellschaft*

BIBLIOGRAPHY

Books, Articles, and Translations in Western Languages

L'Abhidharmakośa de Vasubandhu, traduit et annoté par Louis de La Vallée Poussin, quatrième chapitre, Paris: Paul Geuthner, 1924.

Adikaram, E. W. *Early History of Buddhism in Ceylon.* Colombo: M. D. Gunasena & Co., Ltd., 1953.

Anesaki, M. "Tathāgata," *Encyclopaedia of Religion and Ethics.* Edited by James Hastings, Vol. XII, Edinburgh: T. & T. Clark, 1954, pp. 202b–204b.

Basham, A. L. *History and Doctrines of the Ajīvikas: A Vanished Indian Religion.* London: Luzac & Co., Ltd., 1951.

Bechert, Heinz. "Über Singhalesisches im Pālikanon," *Wiener Zeitschrift für die Kunde Süd und Ostasiens*, Band I (1957), pp. 71–75.

Beckh, Hermann. *Buddhismus.* 2 Vols., 2nd eds., Berlin: G. Göschen'sche Verlagshandlung, 1919 (Vol. I), 1920 (Vol. II).

The Book of the Discipline (*Vinaya-Piṭaka*). Vol. IV, translated by I. B. Horner, "Sacred Books of the Buddhists," Vol. XIV, London: Luzac & Co., Ltd., 1962.

Buddhadatta, A. P. "The Second Great Commentator, Ācariya-Dhammapāla," *University of Ceylon Review*, Vol. III, No. 2 (November, 1945), pp. 49–57.

———. "Who Was Buddhaghosa?" *University of Ceylon Review*, Vol. II, Nos. 1 and 2 (October, 1944), pp. 77–85.

Buddhism and Christianity: Being an Oral Debate at Panadura Between the Rev. Migettuvatte Gunananda & the Rev. David de Silva. Introduction and Annotations by J. M. Peebles, Colombo: Mahabodhi Press, n.d.

A Buddhist Manual of Psychological Ethics: of the Fourth Century B. C. A translation of the *Dhammasaṅgaṇī* by Caroline A. F. Rhys Davids, Vol. XII of "The Oriental Translation Fund, new series," London: The Royal Asiatic Society, 1900.

Burnouf, E. *Introduction à l'histoire du buddhisme indien.* Paris: Imprimerie Royale, 1844.

Carter, John Ross. "*Dhamma* as a Religious Concept: A Brief Investigation of Its History in the Western Academic Tradition and Its Centrality within the Sinhalese Theravāda Tradition," *Journal of the American Academy of Religion*, Vol. 44, No. 4 (December, 1976), pp. 661–674.

———. "A History of *Early Buddhism*," *Religious Studies*, Vol. 13, No. 3 (September, 1977), pp. 263–287.

_______. "Traditional definitions of the term *dhamma*," *Philosophy East and West: A Quarterly of Asian and Comparative Thought*, Vol. XXVI, No. 3 (July, 1976), pp. 329–337.

Chalmers, Robert. "Tathāgata," *Journal of the Royal Asiatic Society* (January, 1898), pp. 103–115.

Childers, Robert Caesar. *A Dictionary of the Pali Language*. London: Trübner & Co., 1875.

Clough, B. *A Sinhalese-English Dictionary*. New and enlarged edition, Colombo: Wesleyan Mission Press, 1892.

Conze, Edward. *Buddhism: Its Essence and Development*. New York: Harper & Brothers, 1959.

_______. *Buddhist Thought in India: Three Phases of Buddhist Philosophy*. London: George Allen & Unwin Ltd., 1962.

Cūlavaṃsa: Being the More Recent Part of the Mahāvaṃsa. Part II, translated by Wilhelm Geiger, Colombo: Ceylon Government Information Department, 1953.

Davids, Mrs. C. A. F. Rhys. *The Birth of Indian Psychology and Its Development in Buddhism*. London: Luzac & Co., 1936.

_______. *Buddhism: A Study of the Buddhist Norm*. "Home University Library," London: Williams and Norgate, n.d. [1912].

_______. *Buddhism: Its Birth and Dispersal*. "The Home University Library of Modern Knowledge," London: Thornton Butterworth Ltd., 1934.

_______. *Buddhist Psychology: Supplementary Chapters*. London: Luzac & Co., 1924.

_______. "Editor's Introduction," *The Minor Anthologies of the Pali Canon*. Part IV, Vimana Vatthu: Stories of the Mansions and Peta Vatthu: Stories of the Departed, translated by Jean Kennedy and Henry S. Gehman respectively; edited with Introduction by Mrs. Rhys Davids, "Sacred Books of the Buddhists," Vol. XII, London: Luzac & Co., Ltd., 1942.

_______. *Gotama The Man*. London: Luzac & Co., 1928.

_______. *Indian Religion and Survival: A Study*. London: George Allen and Unwin Ltd., 1934.

_______. "Introduction," *The Book of the Gradual Sayings*. Vol. I, translated by F. L. Woodward, London: Luzac & Co., Ltd., 1960, pp. v-xviii.

_______. *Kindred Sayings on Buddhism*. Calcutta: The University of Calcutta, 1930.

_______. *A Manual of Buddhism: For Advanced Students*. London: The Sheldon Press, 1932.

_______. "Notices of Books," a review of *Pāli Dhamma: vornehmlich in der kanonischen Literatur* von Magdalene und Wilhelm Geiger, *Journal of the Royal Asiatic Society* (October, 1924), pp. 673–675.

_______. *Outlines of Buddhism: A Historical Sketch*. London: Methuen & Co., Ltd., 1934.

———. "Preface to the Second Edition," *Dialogues of the Buddha*. Part II, translated by T. W. and C. A. F. Rhys Davids, "Sacred Books of the Buddhists," Vol. III, 4th ed., London: Luzac & Co., Ltd., 1959, pp. ix-xiv.

———. *Sakya or Buddhist Origins.* London: Kegan Paul, Trench, Trübner & Co., Ltd., 1931.

———. *What was the Original Gospel in "Buddhism"?* London: The Epworth Press, 1938.

———. *The Will to Peace.* London: T. Fisher Unwin Ltd., 1923.

Davids, T. W. Rhys. *Buddhism: Being a Sketch of the Life and Teachings of Gautama, the Buddha.* A new and revised edition, London: Society for Promoting Christian Knowledge, 1903.

———. *Buddhism: Its History and Literature.* "American Lectures on the History of Religions, First Series, 1894–1895," New York: G. P. Putnam's Sons, 1896.

———. *Buddhist India.* London: T. Fisher Unwin, 1903.

———. "Cosmic Law in Ancient Thought," *Proceedings of the British Academy*, Vol. VIII, pp. 1–11.

———. *Early Buddhism.* "Religions: Ancient and Modern," London: Archibald Constable and Co., Ltd., 1908.

———. *Lectures on the Origin and Growth of Religion As Illustrated by Some Points in the History of Indian Buddhism.* "The Hibbert Lectures, 1881," London: Williams and Norgate, 1881.

de Harlez, C. "Tathāgata," in "Correspondence," *Journal of the Royal Asiatic Society* (January, 1889), p. 131.

Dīghanikāya: Das Buch der langen Texte des buddhistischen Kanons. In auswahl übersetzt von R. Otto Franke, Göttingen: Vandenhoeck & Ruprecht, 1913.

Edgerton, Franklin. *Buddhist Hybrid Sanskrit Grammar and Dictionary.* Vol. II: Dictionary, New Haven: Yale University Press, 1953.

Foucher, A. *The Life of the Buddha: According to the Ancient Texts and Monuments of India.* Abridged translation by Simone Brangier Boas, Middletown, Connecticut: Wesleyan University Press, 1963.

Frauwallner, E. *The Earliest Vinaya and the Beginnings of Buddhist Literature.* "Serie Orientale Roma," Roma: Instituto Italiano per il medio ed estremo Oriente, 1956.

Geiger, Magdalene und Wilhelm. *Pāli Dhamma: vornehmlich in der kanonischen Literatur.* "Abhandlungen der Bayerischen Akademie der Wissenschaften; Philosophisch-philologische und historiche Klasse," Band XXXI, 1. Abhandlung (vorgelegt am 1, Mai, 1920). München: Verlag der Bayerischen Akademie der Wissenschaften, 1920.

Geiger, Wilhelm. *Culture of Ceylon in Mediaeval Times.* Edited by Heinz Bechert, Wiesbaden: Otto Harrassowitz, 1960.

———. "Dhamma und Brahman," *Zeitschrift für Buddhismus*, 3. Jahrg., 2. Heft (März, 1921), pp. 73–83.

———. "Memories of Ceylon," *Journal of the Pali Text Society* (1924–27), pp. 227–233.

———. *Pāli Literature and Language*. Translated by Batakrishna Ghosh, Delhi: Oriental Books Reprint Corporation, 1968.

Glasenapp, Helmuth von. "Der Ursprung der buddhistischen Dharma-Theorie," *Wiener Zeitschrift für die Kunde des Morgenlandes*, Band XLVI, 1. und 2. Heft (1939) pp. 242–266.

———. "Zur Geschichte der buddhistischen Dharma-Theorie," *Zeitschrift der deutschen morgenländischen Gesellschaft*, Neue Folge Band XVII (1938), pp. 383–420.

Hardy, R. Spence. *Eastern Monachism: An Account of the Origin, Laws, Discipline, Sacred Writings, Mysterious Rites, Religious Ceremonies, and Present Circumstances af the Order of Mendicants founded by Gótama Budha*. London: Partridge and Oakey, 1850.

Horner, I. B. "Abhidhamma Abhivinaya," *The Indian Historical Quarterly*, Vol. XVII, No. 3 (September, 1941), pp. 291–310.

———. "An Aspect of Becoming in Early Buddhism," *The Indian Historical Quarterly*, Vol. XII, No. 2 (June, 1936), pp. 282–286.

———. "Early Buddhist Dhamma," *Artibus Asiae*, Vol. XI, 1/2 (1948), pp. 115–123.

———. *The Early Buddhist Theory of Man Perfected: A Study of the Arahan*. London: Williams & Norgate Ltd., 1936.

———. "Some Aspects of Movement in Early Buddhism," *Artibus Asiae*, Vol. X/2 (1947), pp. 138–141.

———. "Translator's Introduction," *The Book of the Discipline*. Vol. I, translated by I. B. Horner, "Sacred Books of the Buddhists," Vol. X, London: Luzac & Co., Ltd., 1949, pp. v-lx.

———. "Translator's Introduction," *The Collection of The Middle Length Sayings*. Vol. I, translated by I. B. Horner, London: Luzac & Co., Ltd., 1954, pp. ix-xxvi.

Jayatilleke, K. N. *Early Buddhist Theory of Knowledge*. London: George Allen & Unwin Ltd., 1963.

Jayawickrama, N. A. "The Sutta Nipāta: Its Title and Form," *University of Ceylon Review*, Vol. VI, No. 2 (April, 1948), pp. 78–86.

Keith, A. Berriedale. *Buddhist Philosophy in India and Ceylon*. Oxford: The Clarendon Press, 1923.

———. "The Doctrine of the Buddha," *Bulletin of the School of Oriental Studies*, Vol. VI, Part 2 (1931), pp. 393–404.

———. "Pre-Canonical Buddhism," "*The Indian Historical Quarterly*, Vol. XII, No. 1 (1936), pp. 1–20.

King, Winston L. *Buddhism and Christianity: Some Bridges of Understanding*. London: George Allen and Unwin Ltd., 1963.

_______. *A Thousand Lives Away: Buddhism in Contemporary Burma.* Oxford: Bruno Cassirer, 1964.

Lamotte, Étienne. *Histoire du bouddhisme indien: des origenes à l'èra Śaka.* Louvain: Institut Orientaliste, 1958.

_______. *The Spirit of Ancient Buddhism.* Translated by Rachel Toulmin, Venezia-Roma: Instituto per la Collaborazione Culturale, 1961.

La Vallée Poussin, Louis de. "Nirvāṇa," *Encyclopaedia of Religion and Ethics.* Edited by James Hastings, Vol. IX, Edinburgh: T. & T. Clark, 1917, pp. 376a–379b.

_______. *Nirvāna: Études sur l'histoire des religions.* Paris: Gabriel Beauchesne, 1925.

_______. *The Way to Nirvāṇa: Six Lectures on Ancient Buddhism as a Discipline of Salvation.* "Hibbert Lectures, February—April, 1916," Cambridge: The University Press, 1917.

Law, Bimala Churn. "Buddhist Conception of Dharma," *Journal of the Department of Letters,* Calcutta University Press, Vol. XXVIII (1935), pp. 1–19.

_______. *Concepts of Buddhism.* Leiden: H. J. Paris, 1937.

_______. *A History of Pāli Literature.* Vol. I, London: Kegan Paul, Trench, Trübner & Co., Ltd., 1933.

Lewis, H. D., and Slater, Robert Lawson. *The Study of Religions: Meeting Points and Major Issues.* Harmondsworth, England: Penguin Books Ltd., 1969.

Ling, T. O. "Dhamma," in *a dictionary of Comparative Religion.* S. G. F. Brandon General Editor, London: Weidenfeld & Nicolson, 1970, p. 235.

Malalasekera, G. P. *Dictionary of Pāli Proper Names.* 2 Vol., London: Luzac & Co., Ltd., 1960.

_______. *The Pāli Literature of Ceylon.* Colombo: M. D. Gunasena & Co., Ltd., 1958.

Masson-Oursel, P. "Note sur l'acception, à travers la civilisation indienne, du mot dharma," *Journal Asiatique,* Tome XIX, No. 2 (Avril-Juin, 1922), pp. 269–275.

Mees, Gaultherus H. *Dharma and Society.* The Hague: N. V. Servire, 1935.

The Minor Readings and the Illustrator of Ultimate Meaning. Translated by Bhikkhu Ñāṇamoli, London: Luzac & Co., Ltd., 1960.

Nakamura, Hajime. "The Indian and Buddhist Concept of Law," *Religious Pluralism and World Community: Interfaith and Intercultural Communication.* Edited by Edward J. Jurji, Leiden: E. J. Brill, 1969, pp. 131–174.

Nyāṇaponika Thera. *The Threefold Refuge.* "The Wheel Series," No. 76, Kandy, Ceylon: Buddhist Publication Society, 1965.

Oldenberg, Hermann. *Buddha: His Life, his Doctrine, His Order.* Translated by William Hoey, London: Williams and Norgate, 1882.

_______. *Buddha: sein Leben, seine Lehre, seine Gemeinde.* Berlin: Verlag von Wilhelm Hertz, 1881.

———. *Die Lehre der Upanishaden und die Anfänge des Buddhismus.* Göttingen, Vandenhoeck & Ruprecht, 1915.

Oltramare, Paul. *L'histoire des idées théosophiques dans l'Inde*, Tome II, *La théosophie bouddhique.* "Annales du Musée Guimet: bibliothèque bouddhique d'études," Paris: Librairie orientaliste Paul Geuthner, 1923.

The Pali Text Society's Pali-English Dictionary. Edited by T. W. Rhys Davids and William Stede, London: Luzac & Co., Ltd., 1966.

Pande, Govind Chandra. *Studies in the Origins of Buddhism.* "Ancient History Research Series," Vol. I, Allahabad: Department of Ancient History, Culture and Archaeology at The University of Allahabad, 1957.

The Path of Purification (Visuddhimagga) by Bhadantācariya Buddhaghosa. Translated by Bhikkhu Ñyāṇamoli, Colombo: M. D. Gunasena & Co., Ltd., 1964.

Pettazzoni, Raffael. *Essays on the History of Religions.* Translated by H. J. Rose, Leiden: E. J. Brill, 1954.

Pratt, James Bissett. *The Pilgrimage of Buddhism and a Buddhist Pilgrimage.* London: Macmillan & Co., Ltd., 1928.

Przyluski, Jean. "Origin and Development of Buddhism," *The Journal of Theological Studies*, (October, 1934), pp. 337–351.

Raju, P. T. "The Buddhistic Conception of Dharma," *Annals of the Bhandarkar Oriental Research Institute*, Vol. XXI (1939–1940), Poona, 1941, pp. 192–302.

———. *Idealistic Thought of India.* Cambridge, Massachusetts: Harvard University Press, 1953.

Rosenberg, Otto. *Die Probleme der buddhistischen Philosophie.* Aus dem Russischen übersetzt von Frau E. Rosenberg, "Materialien zur Kunde des Buddhismus," herausgegeben von M. Walleser, Heft 7/8, Heidelberg, Leipzig: in Kommission bei O. Harrassowitz, 1924.

Schayer, Stanislav. "Precanonical Buddhism," *Archiv Orientální*, Journal of the Czechoslovak Oriental Institute, Prague, Vol. VII (1935), pp. 121–132.

Senart, Émile. "Tathāgata," in "Correspondence," *Journal of the Royal Asiatic Society* (October, 1898), pp. 865–868.

Shawe, F. B. "Tathāgata," in "Correspondence," *Journal of the Royal Asiatic Society* (April, 1898), pp. 385–386.

Slater, Robert Lawson. *Paradox and Nirvana: a study of religious ultimates with special reference to Burmese Buddhism.* Chicago, Illinois: The University of Chicago Press, 1951.

Smith, Wilfred Cantwell. "A Human View of Truth," *Studies in Religion*, Vol. I, No. 1 (1971), pp. 6–24.

———. "Religious Atheism? Early Buddhist and Recent American," *Milla wa-Milla*, No. 6 (December, 1966), pp. 5–30.

Stcherbatsky, Th. *The Central Conception of Buddhism and the Meaning of the Word 'Dharma'.* London: The Royal Asiatic Society, 1923.

———. *The Conception of Buddhist Nirvāṇa.* Leningrad: Academy of Sciences of the USSR., 1927.

———. "The 'Dharmas' of the Buddhists and the 'Guṇas' of the Sāṃkhyas," *The Indian Historical Quarterly,* Vol. X, No. 4 (December, 1934), pp. 737–760.

———. "The Doctrine of the Buddha," *Bulletin of the School of Oriental Studies,* Vol. VI, Part 4 (1932), pp. 867–896.

Thapar, Romila. *Aśoka and the Decline of the Mauryas.* Oxford: Oxford University Press, 1963.

Thomas, Edward J. *The History of Buddhist Thought.* London: Routledge & Kegan Paul Ltd., 1959.

———. *The Life of Buddha as Legend and History.* London: Routledge & Kegan Paul Ltd., 1960.

Tibet's Great Yogī Milarepa: A Biography from the Tibetan being the Jetsün-Kahbum or Biographical History of Jetsün-Milarepa, according to the late Lama Kazi Dawa-Samdup's English Rendering. Edited with Introduction and annotations by W. Y. Evans-Wentz, London: Oxford University Press, 1928.

Warren, Henry Clarke. *Buddhism in Translations.* "Harvard Oriental Series," Vol. III, Cambridge, Massachusetts: Harvard University Press, 1922.

Welbon, Guy Richard. *The Buddhist Nirvāna and Its Western Interpreters.* Chicago: The University of Chicago Press, 1968.

Wijesekera, O. H. de A. "Discoid Weapons in Ancient India: A Study of Vedic *Cakra, Pavi* and *Kṣurapavi,*" *The Adyar Library Bulletin,* Vol. XXV, Parts 1–4, pp. 250–267.

———. "The Symbolism of the Wheel," *S. K. Belvalkar Felicitation Volume,* Banaras: Motilal Banarasi Dass, 1957.

Willman-Grabowska, Helena. "Évolution sémantique du mot 'dharma'," *Rocznik Orjentalistycany,* Lwów, Tom X (1934), pp. 38–50.

Pāli and Sinhalese Sources

Abhidhānappadīpikā nam Pālinighaṇḍuva. Edited by Moragallē Siri Ñāṇobhasatissa Thera, Colombo: M. D. Guṇasēna, 1960.

Abhidhānappadīpikā: or Dictionary of the Pali Language. Edited by Waskaḍuwe Subhūti, 2nd. ed., Colombo: Frank Luker, Acting Government Printer, 1883.

Abhinava Katikāvata Saha Baṇadaham Pota. Edited by Maḍugallē Siddhārtha, Colombo: M. D. Guṇasēna, 1968.

Achariya Dhammapāla's Paramatthadīpanī: Being the Commentary on the Cariya-Piṭaka. Edited by D. L. Barua, London: Published for the Pali Text Society by Humphrey Milford, Oxford University Press, 1939.

Amāvatura. Edited by Wälīviṭiyē Sorata Nāyaka Thera, Mt. Lavinia, Ceylon: Abhaya Prakāśakayō, 1960.

The Aṅguttara-nikāya. Part I, edited by the Rev. Richard Morris, 2nd. ed., revised by A. K. Warder, London: Published for the Pali Text Society by Luzac & Co., Ltd., 1961.

The Aṅguttara-nikāya. Part II, edited by the Rev. Richard Morris, London: Published for the Pali Text Society by Luzac & Co., Ltd., 1955.

The Aṅguttara-nikāya. Parts III-V, edited by E. Hardy, London: Published for the Pali Text Society by Luzac & Co., Ltd., 1958.

Aṅguttaranikāya: The Thirteenth Book in the Suttantapiṭaka. Part II, with the Sinhala Translation by the *Aṅguttaranikāya* Editorial Board of the Tripiṭaka Translation Committee, "Buddha Jayanti Tripiṭaka Series," Volume XIX, Colombo: Published under the Patronage of the Government of Ceylon, 1963.

The Apadāna of the Khuddaka Nikāya. Parts I-II, edited by Mary E. Lilley, London: Published for the Pali Text Society by the Oxford University Press, 1925 (Part I), 1927 (Part II).

The Atthasālinī: Buddhaghosa's Commentary on the Dhammasaṅgaṇī. Edited by Edward Müller, London: Published for the Pali Text Society by Henry Frowde, Oxford University Press, 1897.

The Buddhavaṃsa and the Cariyā-Piṭaka. Edited by the Rev. Richard Morris, London: Published for the Pali Text Society by Henry Frowde, Oxford University Press, 1882.

Butsaraṇa. Edited by Labugama Laṅkānanda Thera, 3rd. ed., Colombo: M. D. Guṇasēna, 1968.

Candavimala, Rērukānē. *Bauddhayāgē At Pota.* Colombo: A. D. P. Sugatadāsa, Anula Mudraṇālaya, 1966.

———. *Pohoya Dinaya.* Colombo: A. D. P. Sugatadāsa, Anula Mudraṇālaya, 1966.

———. *Sūvisi Maha Guṇaya.* Colombo: A. D. P. Sugatadāsa, Anula Mudraṇālaya, 1969.

The Chronicle of the Island of Ceylon or the Dīpavaṃsa: A Historical Poem of the Fourth Century A.D. Edited by Bimala Churn Law, *The Ceylon Historical Journal,* Vol. VII (July 1957 to April 1958), published as a monograph in 1959.

The Commentary on the Dhammapada. New edition, Vol. I, Part I, edited by Helmer Smith, London: Published for the Pali Text Society by the Oxford University Press, 1925.

The Commentary on the Dhammapada. Vol. I, Part II, edited by H. C. Norman, London: Published for the Pali Text Society by Henry Frowde, 1909.

The Commentary on the Dhammapada. Vols. II-IV, edited by H .C. Norman, London: Published for the Pali Text Society by Henry Frowde, Oxford University Press, 1911 (Vol. II), 1912 (Vol. III), 1914 (Vol. IV).

Dahampiyā Aṭuvā Gäṭapadaya. Edited by Mäda-Uyangoḍa Vimalakīrti Thera and Nāhinnē Sominda Thera, Colombo: M. D. Guṇasēna, 1967.
Daham Saraṇa. Edited by Kiriällē Ñāṇavimala Thera, Colombo: M. D. Guṇasēna, 1965.
Dahamsoňda Kava. Edited by Makuluduve Piyaratana, Colombo: M. D. Guṇasēna, 1963.
The Dhammapada. New edition by Sūriyagoḍa Sumaṅgala Thera, London: Published for the Pali Text Society by Humphrey Milford, 1914.
Dhammapāla's Paramattha-Dīpanī. Part III, Being the Commentary on the *Peta-Vatthu*, edited by E. Hardy, London: Published for the Pali Text Society by Henry Frowde, Oxford University Press, 1894.
Dhammapāla's Paramattha-Dīpanī. Part IV, Being the Commentary on the *Vimāna-Vatthu*, edited by E. Hardy, London: Published for the Pali Text Society by Henry Frowde, Oxford University Press, 1901.
The Dhammasaṅgaṇi. Edited by Edward Müller, London: Published for the Pali Text Society by Henry Frowde, Oxford University Press, 1885.
Dharmapradīpikā. Edited by Baddēgama Vimalavaṃsa Thera, 2nd. ed., Colombo: M. D. Guṇasēna & Co., 1967.
Dhātu Vaṃsaya. Edited by Munidāsa Kumāratuṃga, Colombo: M. D. Guṇasēna & Co., n.d.
The Dīgha Nikāya. Vol. I, edited by T. W. Rhys Davids and J. Estlin Carpenter, London: Published for the Pali Text Society, Luzac & Co., Ltd., 1949.
The Dīgha Nikāya. Vol. II, edited by T. W. Rhys Davids and J. Estlin Carpenter, The Pali Text Society, London: Geoffrey Cumberlege, Oxford University Press, 1947.
The Dīgha Nikāya. Vol. III, edited by J. Estlin Carpenter, London: Published for the Pali Text Society by Messrs. Luzac & Co., Ltd., 1960.
Iti-vuttaka. Edited by Ernst Windisch, London: Published for the Pali Text Society by Geoffrey Cumberlege, Oxford University Press, 1948.
Jātaka Aṭuvā Gäṭapadaya. Edited by Mäda-Uyangoḍa Vimalakīrti Thera and Nāhinnē Sominda Thera, Colombo: M. D. Guṇasēna & Co., 1961.
The Jātaka: Together with Its Commentary. Vols. I-VI, edited by V. Fausbøll, London: Published for the Pali Text Society by Messrs. Luzac & Co., Ltd., 1962 (Vol. I), 1963 (Vols. II-V), 1964 (Vol. V).
The Khuddaka-Pāṭha: Together with Its Commentary Paramatthajotikā I. Edited by Helmer Smith from a collation by Mabel Hunt, London: Published for the Pali Text Society by Luzac & Co., Ltd., 1959.
Lōväḍasaṅgarāva. Edited by V. D. de Länarōl, Colombo: Ratnākara Pot Veḷaňda Śālāva, 1967.
Madhuratthavilāsinī nāma Buddhavaṃsaṭṭhakathā of Bhadantācariya Buddhadatta Mahāthera. Edited by I. B. Horner, London: Published for the Pali Text Society by Humphrey Milford, Oxford University Press, 1946.
The Mahā-Bodhi-Vaṁsa. Edited by S. Arthur Strong, London: Published for the Pali Text Society by Henry Frowde, Oxford University Press, 1891.

The Mahāvaṃsa. Edited by Wilhelm Geiger, London: Published for the Pali Text Society by Henry Frowde, Oxford University Press, 1908.

Majjhima-nikāya. Vol. I, edited by V. Trenckner, London: Published for the Pali Text Society by Luzac and Co., Ltd., 1964.

Majjhima-nikāya. Vols. II-III, edited by Robert Chalmers, London: Published for the Pali Text Society by Luzac & Co., Ltd., 1960.

Monorathapūraṇī: Buddhaghosa's Commentary on the Aṅguttaranikāya. Vol. I, edited by Max Walleser, London: Published for the Pali Text Society by the Oxford University Press, 1924.

Manorathapūraṇī: Buddhaghosa's Commentary on the Aṅguttaranikāya. Vol. II, edited by Max Walleser and Hermann Kopp, London: Published for the Pali Text Society by the Oxford University Press, 1930.

Manorathapūraṇī: Commentary on the Aṅguttara Nikāya. Vol. III, edited by Hermann Kopp, London: Published for the Pali Text Society by the Oxford University Press, 1936.

Manorathapūraṇī: Commentary on the Aṅguttara Nikāya. Vol. IV, edited by Hermann Kopp, London: Published for the Pali Text Society by Humphrey Milford, Oxford University Press, 1940.

Manorathapūraṇī: Commentary on the Aṅguttara Nikāya. Vol. V, with Indexes to Vols. I-V, edited by Hermann Kopp, London: Published for the Pali Text Society by Luzac & Co., Ltd., 1956.

The Milindapañho: Being Dialogues Between King Milinda and the Buddhist Sage Nāgasena. Edited by V. Trenckner, London: Published for the Pali Text Society by Luzac & Co., Ltd., 1962.

Ñāṇavimala, Kiriällē. *Bauddha Ädahilla.* Colombo: M. D. Guṇasēna, 1957.

The Netti-pakaraṇa: With Extracts from Dhammapāla's Commentary. Edited by E. Hardy, London: Published for the Pali Text Society by Messrs. Luzac & Co., Ltd., 1961.

Niddesa I: Mahāniddesa. Edited by L. de La Vallée Poussin and E. J. Thomas, London: Published for the Pali Text Society by Humphrey Milford, Oxford University Press, Vol. I, 1916, Vol. II, 1917.

Niddesa II: Cullaniddesa. Edited by W. Stede, London: Published for the Pali Text Society by Humphrey Milford, Oxford University Press, 1918.

Pānadurē Vādaya. Edited by P. A. Peiris and James Dias, Colombo: Laṅka Free Press, n.d.

Papañcasūdanī Majjhimanikāyaṭṭhakathā of Buddhaghosācariya. Parts I-II, edited by J. H. Woods and D. Kosambi, London: Published for the Pali Text Society by the Oxford University Press, 1922 (Part I), 1923 (Part II).

Papañcasūdanī Majjhimanikāyaṭṭhakathā of Buddhaghosācariya. Parts III-IV, edited by I. B. Horner, London: Published for the Pali Text Society by the Oxford University Press, 1933 (Part III), 1937 (Part IV).

Paramatthadīpanī: Dhammapāla's Commentary on the Therigāthā. Edited by E. Müller, London: Published for the Pali Text Society by Henry Frowde, Oxford University Press, 1893.

Paramattha-Dīpanī: Iti-Vuttakaṭṭhakathā (Iti-Vuttaka Commentary) of Dhammapālācariya. Vols. I-II, edited by M. M. Bose, London: Published for the Pali Text Society by Humphrey Milford, Oxford University Press, 1934 (Vol. I), 1936 (Vol. II).

Paramattha-Dīpanī Theragāthā-Aṭṭhakathā: The Commentary of Dhammapālācariya. Vol. I, edited by F. L. Woodward, London: Published for the Pali Text Society by Humphrey Milford, Oxford University Press, 1940.

Paramattha-Dīpanī Theragāthā-Aṭṭhakathā: The Commentary of Dhammapālācariya. Vols. II-III, edited by F. L. Woodward, London: Published for the Pali Text Society by Messrs. Luzac & Co., Ltd., 1952 (Vol. II), 1959 (Vol. III).

Paramattha-Dīpanī Udānaṭṭhakathā (Udāna Commentary) of Dhammapālācariya. Edited by F. L. Woodward, London: Published for the Pali Text Society by the Oxford University Press, 1926.

Paramatthamañjūsā of Bhadantācariya Dhammapāla Thera: Or The Commentary of the Visuddhimagga. Vols. I-III, edited by Morontuḍuwē Dhammānanda Thera, Colombo: Mahabodhi Press, 1928 (Vol. I), 1930 (Vol. II), 1949 (Vol. III).

Pariccheda Satara. Edited by Vaṃśanātha Deśabandhu, Maradāna, Colombo: Karuṇādhāra Mudraṇalaya, 1964.

Paṭisambhidāmagga. Vols. I-II, edited by Arnold C. Taylor, London: Published for the Pali Text Society by Henry Frowde, Oxford University Press, 1905 (Vol. I), 1907 (Vol. II).

Petavatthu. Edited by [J.] Minayeff, London: Published for the Pali Text Society by Henry Frowde, Oxford University Press, 1888.

Piruvānā Potvahansē num yut Mahapiritpota. Edited with a Sinhalese *sanna* by Devundara Śrī Vācissara, Colombo: M. D. Guṇasēna, 1969.

Piruvānā Potvahansē nohot Purātana Sanna sahita Maha Pirit Pota. Edited with a Sinhalese *sanna* by Watuvattē Pemānanda, Colombo: Ratnākara Pot Veḷan̆da Śālāva, 1957.

Piyaratana, Valbōlānē, and Dhammakitti, Alavaturē. *Pūjāvali gāṭapada vivaraṇaya.* Part I, Colombo: Laṅkabhinava Viśrāta Yantrālaya, 1941.

The Puggala-paññatti. Part I.—Text, edited by Richard Morris, London: Published for the Pali Text Society by Henry Frowde, Oxford University Press, 1883.

Puggala-paññatti-aṭṭhakathā: From the Pañcappakaraṇaṭṭhakathā (Ascribed to Buddhaghosa). Edited by Georg Landsberg and Mrs. [C. A. F.] Rhys Davids, *Journal of the Pali Text Society* (1914), pp. 170–254.

Pūjāvaliya. Edited by Kiriällē Ñāṇavimala Thera, Colombo: M. D. Guṇasēna & Co., 1965.

Purāṇasiṃhalabaṇapota. Edited with a glossary by Jinavara Dharmakīrti Śrī Ratanapāl Thera, Colombo: Mahabodhi Press, 1929.

Rasavāhinī. Edited by Kiriällē Ñāṇavimala Thera, Colombo: M. D. Guṇasēna & Co., 1961.

Saddhamma-pajjotikā: The Commentary on the Mahā-Niddesa. Vols. I-II, edited by A. P. Buddhadatta, London: Published for the Pali Text Society by Humphrey Milford, Oxford University Press, 1931 (Vol. I), 1939 (Vol. II).

Saddhammappakāsinī: Commentary on the Paṭisambhidāmagga. Vols. I-II, edited by C. V. Joshi, London: Published for the Pali Text Society by Humphrey Milford, Oxford University Press, 1933 (Vol. I), 1940 (Vol. II).

Saddhammappakāsinī: Commentary on the Paṭisambhidāmagga. Vol. III, edited by C. V. Joshi, London: Published for the Pali Text Society by Geoffrey Cumberlege, Oxford University Press, 1947.

Saddhamma Saṃgaho. Edited by Nedimāle Saddhānanda, *Journal of the Pali Text Society* (1890), pp. 21–90.

Saddhammopāyana. Edited by Richard Morris, *Journal of the Pali Text Society* (1887), pp. 35–98.

Saddharmālaṅkāraya. Edited by Kiriällē Ñāṇavimala Thera, Colombo: M. D. Guṇasēna, 1954.

Saddharmaratnākaraya. Edited by Kalupaluvāvē Devānanda Thera, Colombo: Ratnākara Pot Veḷaňda Śālāva, 1955.

Saddharmaratnāvaliya. Edited by Kiriällē Ñāṇavimala Thera, Colombo: M. D. Guṇasēna, 1961.

Saddharma Sārārtha Sangrahaya. Edited by Kiriällē Ñāṇavimala Thera, Colombo: M. D. Guṇasēna, 1957.

Samantapāsādikā: Buddhaghosa's Commentary on the Vinaya Piṭaka. Vols. I-V, edited by J. Takakusu and M. Nagai, London: Published for the Pali Text Society by Humphrey Milford, the Oxford University Press, 1924, (Vol. I), 1927 (Vol. II), 1930 (Vol. III), 1934 (Vol. IV), 1938 (Vol. V).

Sammoha-vinodanī Abhidhamma-Piṭake Vibhangaṭṭhakathā. Edited by A. P. Buddhadatta, London: Published for the Pali Text Society by the Oxford University Press, 1923.

Saṃyutta-nikāya. Parts I-V, edited by M. Léon Feer, London: Published for the Pali Text Society by Messrs. Luzac & Co., Ltd., 1960.

Saṃyuttanikāya: The Seventh Book in the Suttantapiṭaka. Part I, with the Sinhala Translation by the *Saṃyuttanikāya* Editorial Board of the Tripiṭaka Translation Committee, "Buddha Jayanti Tripiṭaka Series," Volume XIII, Colombo: Published under the Patronage of the Government of Ceylon, 1960.

Saraṇasēkara, R. *Daham Guṇaya.* Colombo: M. D. Guṇasēna, 1967.

Sārattha-ppakāsinī: Buddhaghosa's Commentary on the Saṃyutta-nikāya. Vols. I-III, edited by the F. L. Woodward, London: Published for the Pali Text Society by Humphrey Milford, Oxford University Press, 1929 (Vol. I), 1932 (Vol. II), 1937 (Vol. III).

Siṃhala Upāsaka Janālaṅkāraya. Edited by D. P. R. Samaranāyaka, Colombo: M. D. Guṇasēna, 1961.

Somissara, Māpalagama Siri. *Bauddha Dharma Mārgaya.* Colombo: Vijayasēna saha Sahōdarayo, 1967.

Sorata, Wälīviṭiyē. *Amāvaturu Gäṭapada Vivaraṇaya.* Maradana, Colombo: Chandrasēna Press, 1949.

________. *Śrī Sumañgala Sabdakoṣa.* Part II, Colombo: Anula Press, 1956, Part I, 2nd edition, 1963.

Śrī Saddharmāvavāda Saṃgrahaya. Edited by Vēragoḍa Amaramoli Thera, Colombo: Ratnākara Mudraṇālayaya, 1956.

Subhūti, W. *Abhidhānappadīpikāsūci: A Complete Index to the Abhidhānappadīpikā.* Colombo, H. C. Cottle, Acting Government Printer, 1893.

Sumaṅgala-vilāsinī: Buddhaghosa's Commentary on the Dīgha-Nikāya. Part I, edited by T. W. Rhys Davids and J. Estlin Carpenter, London: Published for the Pali Text Society by Henry Frowde, Oxford University Press, 1886.

Sumaṅgala-vilāsinī: Buddhaghosa's Commentary on the Dīgha-Nikāya. Parts II-III, edited by W. Stede, London: Published for the Pali Text Society by Humphrey Milford, the Oxford University Press, 1931 (Part II), 1932 (Part III).

Sutta-Nipāta. New edition by Dines Andersen and Helmer Smith, London: Published for the Pali Text Society by Geoffrey Cumberlege, Oxford University Press, 1948.

Sutta-Nipāta Commentary: Being Paramatthajotikā II. Vols. I-II, edited by Helmer Smith, London: Published for the Pali Text Society by Humphrey Milford, Oxford University Press, 1916 (Vol. I), 1917 (Vol. II).

The Thera- and Therī-gathā: (Stanzas Ascribed to Elders of the Buddhist Order of Recluses). Edited by Hermann Oldenberg and Richard Pischel, 2nd ed., with Appendices by K. R. Norman and L. Alsdorf, London: Published for the Pali Text Society, Luzac & Co., Ltd., 1966.

Udāna. Edited by Paul Steinthal, London: Published for the Pali Text Society by Geoffrey Cumberlege, Oxford University Press, 1948.

Upāsakajanālaṅkāra. Edited by H. Saddhatissa, London: Published for the Pali Text Society, Luzac & Co., Ltd., 1965.

Vaṃsatthappakāsinī: Commentary on the Mahāvaṃsa. Vols. I-II, edited by G. P. Malalasekera for the Government of Ceylon, London: Published for the Pali Text Society by Humphrey Milford, Oxford University Press, 1935.

The Vimāna-Vatthu: of the Khuddaka Nikāya Sutta Piṭaka. Edited by Edmund Rowland Gooneratne, London: Published for the Pali Text Society by Henry Froude [*sic*], Oxford University Press, n.d. [1886?].

The Vinaya Piṭakam. Vols. I-V, edited by Hermann Oldenberg, London: Published for the Pali Text Society, Luzac & Co., Ltd., 1964.

Visuddhajanavilāsinī nāma Apadānaṭṭhakathā. Edited by C. E. Godakumbura, London: Published for the Pali Text Society, Luzac & Co., Ltd., 1954.

Visuddhimagga of Buddhaghosācariya. Edited by Henry Clarke Warren, revised by Dharmananda Kosambi, "Harvard Oriental Series," Vol. XLI, Cambridge, Massachusetts: Harvard University Press, 1950.

The Visuddhi-magga of Buddhaghosa. Vol. I, edited by C. A. F. Rhys Davids, London: Published for the Pali Text Society by Humphrey Milford, Oxford University Press, 1920.

Visuddhimārgaya with the Mahā Sanya of Parākramabāhu. Part II, edited by Bentara Śraddhātiṣya, Kaḷutara, Ceylon: Vidyātilaka Yantrālaya, 1950.

INDEX

DHAMMA 「ダンマ」

昭和53年9月20日　初版発行

©

著　者　J. R. CARTER

発行所　株式会社　北星堂書店

代表者　中　土　順　平

東京都千代田区神田錦町3ノ12

〒101　振替口座　東京 8-16024

電話　(03) 294－3301 (代表)

THE HOKUSEIDO PRESS

12, 3-Chome, Nishikicho, Kanda, Tokyo, Japan

落丁・乱丁本はお取替致します